Penguin Books

Only FOOLS and HEARSES

Dav grew up by the coast in Warrnambool, Victoria. He went to boarding school in Geelong and studied Agricultural Science at Melbourne University. After a few years in the workforce Dav felt life had become predictable so he headed overseas, hoping to stumble upon 'something' along the way. This book, which began as a weekly column in the British magazine *TNT*, became that 'something'. Dav is currently managing his boutique wine cellar in Warrnambool but plans to hit the road again for more hearse-touring adventures – after all, there's still a few more continents to conquer.

Only FOOLS and HEARSES

DAV ARDLIE

Penguin Books

PENGUIN BOOKS

Published by the Penguin Group
Penguin Group (Australia)
250 Camberwell Road, Camberwell, Victoria 3124, Australia
(a division of Pearson Australia Group Pty Ltd)
Penguin Group (USA) Inc.
375 Hudson Street, New York, New York 10014, USA
Penguin Group (Canada)
90 Eglinton Avenue East, Suite 700, Toronto, Canada ON M4P 2Y3
(a division of Pearson Penguin Canada Inc.)
Penguin Books Ltd
80 Strand, London WC2R 0RL, England
Penguin Ireland
25 St Stephen's Green, Dublin 2, Ireland
(a division of Penguin Books Ltd)
Penguin Books India Pvt Ltd
11 Community Centre, Panchsheel Park, New Delhi – 110 017, India
Penguin Group (NZ)
Cnr Airborne and Rosedale Roads, Albany, Auckland, New Zealand
(a division of Pearson New Zealand Ltd)
Penguin Books (South Africa) (Pty) Ltd
24 Sturdee Avenue, Rosebank, Johannesburg 2196, South Africa

Penguin Books Ltd, Registered Offices: 80 Strand, London, WC2R 0RL, England

First published by Penguin Group (Australia), a division of Pearson Australia Group Pty Ltd, 2005

10 9 8 7 6 5 4 3 2 1

Cover and text design by David Altheim © Penguin Group (Australia)
Map illustrated by Ian Faulkner
Cover photographs supplied by author
Typeset in 11/17 pt Minion by Post Pre-press Group, Brisbane, Queensland
Printed and bound in Australia by McPherson's Printing Group, Maryborough, Victoria

National Library of Australia
Cataloguing-in-Publication data:

   Ardlie, Davin.
   Only fools and hearses.

   ISBN 0 14 300293 7.

   1. Ardlie, Davin – Journeys – Europe. 2. Backpacking –
   Europe. 3. Europe – Description and travel. I. Title.

   914.0456

www.penguin.com.au

ACKNOWLEDGEMENTS

Not having written before, I assumed that writing a book would be a rather simple matter. A year and numerous cut lunches later I now realise that writing a book is a very complex matter, and one that cannot be achieved alone. Without the assistance, guidance, support and inspiration of the following people *Only Fools and Hearses* would have forever remained the world's longest unfinished Word document.

Thank you to: my Mum (Anne), Dad (John) and sister (Kate) for their support; Paul Wegner, Jason White, John Delbridge and Nathan Wilkinson – my partners in crime; Lynette Eyb, Editor of *TNT* magazine, for giving me the opportunity to discover I could write; Lucy Raymond for convincing and helping me to write this book; Cameron, Don and Cec Butts for reading my crude initial drafts; Angela Makiv and Joanna Gilbert for employing me through the lean times; Lucy Rowe and Richard Bright for publicity ideas and feedback; Rupert Stinson (1975–2004) and Finn Stinson (1973–2004) for pursuing what was important; the Big Girl for her inspiration and reliability; Penguin's Clare Forster for her vision and faith in publishing my first book; Kirsten Abbott for recommending it to Clare; and finally, Tricia Cortese for her continual enthusiasm, patience and editorial expertise.

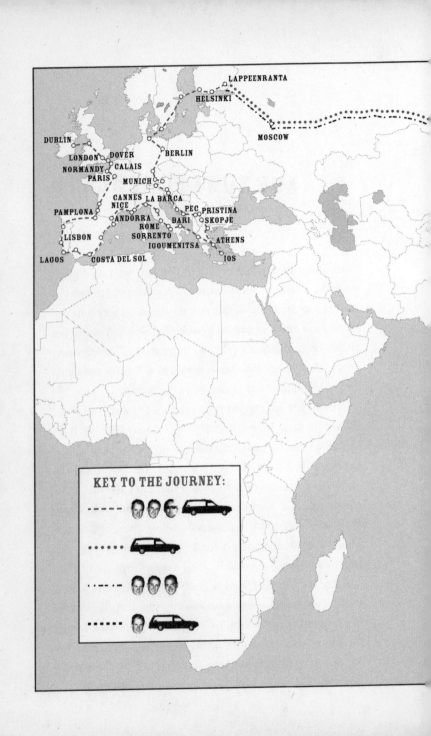

LAPPEENRANTA
HELSINKI
MOSCOW

DUBLIN
LONDON DOVER BERLIN
NORMANDY CALAIS
PARIS MUNICH
CANNES LA BARCA
NICE PEC PRISTINA
PAMPLONA ANDORRA BARI SKOPJE
ROME
LISBON SORRENTO
IGOUMENITSA ATHENS
LAGOS COSTA DEL SOL IOS

KEY TO THE JOURNEY:

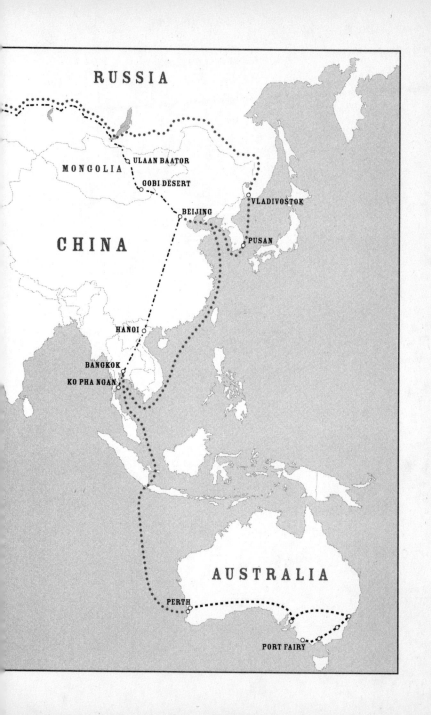

DAV WEGS WHITEY JD

CONTENTS

1	Sowing the seed	1
2	Light-fingered frogs	23
3	Cinq oeufs s'il vous plâit	34
4	A public display of affection	47
5	A deflating experience	67
6	Easy days	79
7	Guandong-style chicken with cashew nuts	84
8	Losing the Midas touch	100
9	A man down	124
10	Back on top	141
11	'Macedonian paperweight?'	149
12	Cannonball run	184
13	Fork in the road	200
14	Tomorrow	209
15	A girl down	223
16	The wool curtain	242
17	Something unexpected	256
18	Lost in translation	278
19	Time gentlemen, please	292
20	The end . . . or the beginning?	307
	Epilogue	321

DAV   WEGS   WHITEY

1: SOWING THE SEED

I made my way across the foyer of Bourke and Sons in my dirty labouring gear and approached the receptionist, who I assumed to be Mrs Bourke due to the family nature of the business and because of her name badge, which read Mrs Bourke.

Mrs Bourke looked up from her work and cupped a hand over the phone. Behind her narrow spectacles she raised both eyebrows in an invitation to speak. Her cool demeanour reminded me of my primary school headmistress, Miss Fotheringham, and suddenly I felt like a shy schoolboy again. It was foolish of me to feel so nervous. I was no longer a timid eight-year-old boy reporting for discipline, but an assured 27-year-old man enquiring about a car; however, this was my first visit to a funeral parlour.

'Excuse me, I was wondering if you could help me? I'm looking for a second-hand *horse*.'

Still Mrs Bourke remained silent. Her contorted eyebrow movements triggered another untimely primary-school flashback, this time from my grade-four poetry recital, when nerves had also put strange words into my mouth. Back then I had recovered strongly enough to complete *The Man from Snowy River* faultlessly, and earn an honourable mention for my efforts. I started to address Mrs Bourke again but anxiously farted, loudly, ensuring there would be no honourable mention this time around. I took a few deep breaths to compose myself.

'Sorry. Please excuse me. I was wondering if you could help me? I'm looking for a second-hand *hearse*.'

I spat it out. Finally. At least now we could have a meaningful discussion. Yet Mrs Bourke only repeated the astonished eyebrow movements that had accompanied my blundering first effort. It was clear that she thought I was stark raving mad.

Then Mrs Bourke did something that shocked me: she spoke. Her tone, in keeping with her controlled demeanour, was measured and polite.

'I'm terribly sorry, I *don't* think I will be able to help you.'

She then flicked her eyebrows towards the exit and smiled thinly before returning to her phone call. Without further ado I made my way to the door, promising myself this would be my first and last visit to a funeral parlour. I stepped back into the sleeting rain. It felt strangely warmer than the office. For a change, the continuous rain and gloom of Dublin didn't concern me in the slightest.

I plodded along past Trinity College and onto Dame Street like I did every day; except today I didn't stop for a quick pint in one of the lively establishments lining the cobblestone alleyways of Temple Bar, preferring to get home and have a hot shower. With head down and hands in pockets, I walked through

St James Gate and past the Guinness factory, bracing myself against the howling gale that blew across the exposed River Liffey at Victoria Quay, before heading to grimy old Smithfield.

The alcoholics and prostitutes of Benburb Street were nowhere to be seen, the fierce conditions having driven even these desperate souls indoors. As I entered our apartment foyer, finally out of the foul weather, I was encouraged by the thought that things could've been worse: it could've been winter.

* * *

I was sharing a small apartment in North Dublin with two mates from Australia, Paul Wegner (Wegs) and Jason White (Whitey). We'd chosen Dublin because Whitey disliked the size and anonymity of London and I couldn't get a permit to work in England again, after playing a season of cricket there some years earlier. Wegs had spent some time in England as well but didn't really care where he ended up, just so long as the nightlife was good. It had proven to be a simple decision, made even easier by the fact we were all quite partial to the occasional Guinness.

We had met a few years earlier, back when I had been working as a project manager for a large company responsible for the implementation of vast commercial blue-gum plantations all over Australia. As the ink was drying on my Bachelor of Agricultural Science qualification I accepted my first job in the real world – an eager and conscientious new graduate. I spent my first year learning the ropes in southern Victoria before being transferred to the other side of the country, and into the lush tree-growing environment around Albany in the south-west of

Western Australia. As a young, single bloke it was an exciting move.

I arrived in Albany on a Tuesday afternoon, tired from the three-day drive across the Nullarbor from Victoria. After checking into my hotel, I immediately did a single man's reconnaissance of Albany. I drove down the main drag, York Street, and noted the Albany and Premier hotels, and a nondescript nightclub down the bottom end of town. I had no doubt they'd all become more familiar in time. From town I followed Marine Drive around the harbour to Middleton Beach and found not only decent waves but also a great pub overlooking them. I could definitely see myself spending a lazy Sunday afternoon at the Esplanade Hotel. Albany was looking the goods.

Before I'd had time to locate the golf course my mobile phone rang. It was the coach of the Collingwood Park Cricket Club in Albany. He'd heard that a young bloke 'who could play a bit' was moving to town, and he wondered if I was interested in having a hit. I wasn't too surprised to receive the call. Having grown up in a regional town, I knew how sporting clubs in the country were always desperate for numbers to keep them afloat.

Two hours later I found myself batting in the practice nets, facing up to a wild-looking bloke with long hair who was tearing in off a long run. I didn't even see the first ball he bowled, but felt the displaced air whistling past my chin as I thrust my bat out hopefully. I picked the ball up from the back of the nets and turned to find him standing on the pitch in front of me, with an outstretched right hand. He plucked the ball away with his left hand and grabbed my gloved right hand, shaking it strongly.

His large man-hand was about the same size as mine – with a batting glove on.

'G'day. I'm Whitey,' said the big bloke, with a gentle and disarmingly genuine smile. It was not the sort of smile I expected from a fiery opening bowler. He wasn't as scary as he looked, thank God.

'G'day. Dav,' I replied. 'Well bowled.' I added the last bit hoping the next ball would not be at chin height. Somehow I felt it wouldn't be.

I can't recall the rest of that training session exactly, but I must've started to hit a couple fairly well because on the following Saturday night I found myself sitting at the front bar of the White Star Hotel with Whitey, celebrating our team victory. I don't mind a beer. Neither does Whitey.

'Do you know a bloke called Paul Wegner?' I asked Whitey. 'They call him Wegs I think.'

'The bloke with the big forehead that plays footy for Mt Barker?' Whitey queried between healthy mouthfuls.

'Yeah.'

'He's a fuckin' wanker.'

Whitey was right. Wegs does have a big forehead.

'I met him the other night. He's not a wanker, he's a pretty good bloke, actually,' I said. 'Anyway, he's coming for a beer.' Wegs and I had met through a work colleague during the week, and he'd suggested we catch up for a beer on the weekend. 'You'll need someone to show you Albany nightlife,' he'd said.

'What . . .' Whitey started to object but he was cut off by the bustling arrival of a broad-shouldered bloke in bright clothing. Wegs.

'G'day, mate,' Wegs greeted me, adorned in nightclub attire and with hair shining brightly from a healthy application of product designed to keep his short curls under control. It wasn't going to be an early night.

'G'day, mate,' I replied, and then turned to Whitey. 'Whitey. Wegs. Wegs. Whitey.' It seemed odd that I was introducing two blokes of the same age, blokes who had always lived in the same town and who *knew of* each other without *knowing* each other, yet, in their twenty-five years, had never met. I knew misconceptions are common in small towns and was keen to clear up this one. The boys exchanged reserved 'G'day, mates' and shallow smiles, and shook hands.

'Four pints and three tequilas thanks, mate,' Wegs yelled across to the barman.

'Four beers? There's only three of us,' I questioned.

'Yep. Got to catch up to you boys,' Wegs replied as he emptied the first of the two pints. He also liked a beer. The tequila, well, that was to break the ice, Wegner style.

We divided up the salt, the lemon and the shot glasses, clashed them together and then slammed down the tequilas as a team. As the evening progressed I noticed that Wegs and Whitey no longer needed to speak through me, and that the same smile that had greeted me on the cricket pitch had now returned to Whitey's face. My Nanna would have said they were smiling with their eyes.

Our love of a good time saw us spend the remainder of that

year playing sport, partying and generally revelling in that time in one's life that's renowned for its diminished moral responsibility: the life of the single male.

However, I was forced to depart Albany, for work reasons, at the end of that stellar year, leaving Wegs and Whitey behind. As soon as I took up my new job in South Australia my life began to turn towards the predictable and mundane, and for the first time it was, at best, ordinary. I needed to change my current circumstances and follow my mum's wise advice to 'not look back one day and regret the things I hadn't done'.

A year or so after leaving Albany I decided to resign from my job that promised long-term security and a gold pen upon retirement, but not long-term satisfaction. Not for me anyway. I could sense change was in the wind. I could hear Ireland calling.

At around the same time in Albany, Wegs and Whitey were hearing the same call.

To his credit, Wegs had earned his trainee position on the wharf, at the tender age of eighteen, without actually being related to a union member. After five years he'd become a gifted forklift driver and highly qualified crane operator in the busy shifts, and a brilliant squid fisherman and amateur snooker champion during the quiet shifts. But now Wegs wanted more. Ireland was calling Wegs, too.

As a small-town boy Whitey hadn't travelled much. In fact, he'd never been further afield than Perth. For Whitey, Ireland was screaming.

And so, we answered the call and found ourselves reunited

in Dublin, working hard and partying harder and, basically, deferring life's responsibilities. It seemed we were good at that.

❂ ❂ ❂

The night before my ill-fated visit to Bourke and Sons in Dublin, Wegs had interrupted the English Premier League highlights to read out an advertisement from the *Evening Standard* for a car he thought sounded suitable for a European road trip we'd been planning. It was the only listing in its category: *funeral vehicles*.

Living and working in Ireland we'd become keen followers of the Premier League, largely by default given that soccer is not our national game. This interest started by becoming familiar with a few of the key teams and players and the weekend's results. Then, largely because there was nothing else to talk about at the pub, nothing else to watch on TV, and nothing else to read about in the paper, our passing interest in soccer became a passionate and informed knowledge of *football*.

This new-found obsession explains why Whitey and I told Wegs to shut up when he read out the advertisement during the highlights. It was odd for Wegs to interrupt his favourite program, but there were no Manchester United highlights that evening, so he'd begun to read the paper. Besides, we often ignored him because this was not the first or the last time that Wegs would have a stupid idea. The completion of the highlights meant we could finally devote our full attention to Wegs' strange new idea.

'How many do you reckon it would seat?' I asked Wegs, as he was now the authority on hearses.

'Buggered if I know, probably only room for two up front, or three if she's got a bench seat. Should be plenty of room to stretch out in the back, though.'

This highly informed discussion continued long into the night, with the novel idea of owning a funeral vehicle growing more attractive, and more definite, with every can of Carlsberg we consumed. So, after drinking more than casual labourers should on a week night, we resolved to investigate the matter further the following morning, which normally guaranteed we would wake up and put it all down to drunken enthusiasm, or just completely forget the conversation ever happened.

The following morning we all left independently for work and didn't speak any further about the grand plans we had made the night before. Surprisingly, I recalled our conversation and, although my drunken enthusiasm had now become hung-over enthusiasm, I was still keen to investigate.

Returning home that wet afternoon, I pushed aside the empty cans from the previous night to find the *Evening Standard* and the advertisement Wegs had drawn our attention to.

FUNERAL VEHICLES
1984 Ford Granada Cardinal Hearse
Coleman Milne Converted.
One owner. Low miles. 2500 Euro.

I was thinking about calling the contact number when the boys came home from work in the same condition as me, soaking wet. After colourfully voicing their views on the unpredictable Irish weather, they headed straight for the kitchen to prepare an after-work and pre-dinner snack. For Whitey it was a cheese single in day-old bread. For Wegs it was a cold can of baked beans, eaten with a butter knife. I declined his offer to share, feeling full after my bowl of two-minute noodles. Besides, we had no clean knives left.

Our hearse discussion immediately resumed and it turned out I wasn't the only one who had been giving serious thought to this odd proposition. The lads had been chatting with their workmates and were convinced it was worth investigating. Whitey's boss had even given him the number of his second cousin (twice removed) down in Cork, who just happened to be a 'used-hearse salesman'.

'Does all right out of it too, apparently,' Whitey enlightened us.

'Yeah, reckon he'd make a killing!' I chipped in, laughing at my lame joke.

It's likely I would have gone through my entire life without knowing that anyone actually traded in second-hand funeral vehicles, but I had been in Ireland long enough not to be surprised by this revelation.

It was 4.45 p.m. on Thursday, which meant we still had time to catch the 'used-hearse salesman' before he knocked off for the day. But who would make the call? No one volunteered. Unfortunately, even after my dishonourable mention at Bourke and

Sons, it was decided that I would be the one to make the call. I like to think this was because I was the oldest of the group and therefore regarded as the wisest, but in reality it was because I chose paper and Wegs chose scissors.

I sat down next to the phone and Whitey handed me the bit of four-by-two he had scrawled the number down on. I could just read the numbers but not the name as it had smeared badly in the rain. Whitey, fighting back laughter, said his name was Donal O'Donnell. Surely this name was far too Irish and far too comical to be true. I consulted the lump of four-by-two once more and the shape of the words seemed to be near enough to Donal O'Donnell. I decided to go with it and bravely dialled the number. What could I lose?

'CAB Motors, hocanihelpya?' (Irish accent)

'Um, er, I was wondering if I could have a word with um, um, Donal O'Donnell?' I enquired, snorting quite loudly at the end. I wasn't confident that the name was genuine or that I could continue the phone call. Earlier in the day at Bourke and Sons I had fumbled over my words because I was struck with nerves. Now I fumbled over my words because I was desperately trying not to burst out laughing. I looked to my mates for support but none was forthcoming. They were pissing themselves, as good mates do. I had to look away and bite my tongue.

'He's on another call. Would you care to wait?'

I snorted a brief response and composed myself in time to be greeted warmly by a friendly male voice wrapped in a typically melodic Cork accent.

'CAB Motors. Donal O'Donnell.'

'Um. G'day, Donal, I'm looking for a second-hand hearse.'
I punched the air as I articulated correctly, finally overcoming
my demons.

From that point, like most of my conversations with the
Irish, I understood very little of what Donal said. I find talking to the Irish incredibly difficult, especially over the phone.
If I misunderstand just a few words early in the conversation,
my brain has a nasty tendency to get lost and turn the rest into
background noise. That's why I was sacked from my pub job
in Temple Bar. I simply couldn't understand the orders, and
guessing them was just not cutting the mustard. I will always
maintain that 'half a pint of lager and lime' are seven individual
words, but listen to any Irishman and it sounds like it's just one
really long one.

''Alfapintalageralime.' (Irish accent)

Not only could I not understand but I also couldn't remember much of what Donal and I discussed that particular day.
What I did know, however, was that it was a Thursday night and
at 9 a.m. on Saturday we had to be down in Cork to test drive
a hearse.

❂   ❂   ❂

Much to my surprise CAB Motors in Cork was a large and
reputable Ford dealership – nothing like the type of premises
I had envisaged a used-hearse salesman would operate from
(not that I had any idea of what that might actually be). We
wandered around the large yard, looking for a hearse to buy
and having a casual kick of the footy.

Seconds later Donal O'Donnell strode out of the head office and made his way over to us. I was a bit apprehensive about the reception we'd receive, given that Wegs had signalled our arrival by slamming a wayward drop punt into the window of his office. He was a tall man with shiny silver hair and a beaming smile – nothing like we had expected. He didn't wear a dark suit or flowing black robes, probably because it wasn't a weekday, but rather he sported a V-necked sweater, cords and boat shoes and looked like he had just stepped out of the Ralph Lauren Spring catalogue. Perhaps he was 'doing all right out of it' after all.

Despite the errant football Donal O'Donnell greeted us the way all Irish people greet strangers, as family. We introduced ourselves and received firm handshakes and a toothy smile in return.

(Irish accent)

'How are ya, lads? Grand. Grand. After a hearse, eh? I've got just the one for ya. She's a grand driver, this one. Now let's —' Without waiting for a response he loped across the yard, motioning for us to follow.

We continued the pleasantries on the run as he led us to his extensive range of used hearses. The reason we hadn't seen any in the yard was because Donal considered displaying funeral vehicles alongside new family wagons to be bad for business. Fair enough, too. We crossed the road and entered the Cork showgrounds through a gap in the wire fence.

Donal O'Donnell was talking and walking flat out and we struggled to keep up. We finally caught up with him as he unlocked a huge padlock on large double doors that led into horse stables. We moved five abreast down a dark cobblestoned corridor, our footsteps echoing loudly throughout the vacant building. I began to panic slightly. Had I asked Donal O'Donnell for a second-hand *horse*. I was sure I hadn't. Maybe Donal had misheard.

I was incredibly relieved to see a large black hearse emerge from one of the stables ahead of us. Donal O'Donnell had sent his young assistant, Olcan, over earlier in the day to start up a couple of the hearses and clear out some cobwebs (literally). They opened the doors of the nearest stables to reveal three Mercedes and two Ford hearses. Each had obviously been there for a considerable period of time.

Not surprisingly, none of us had ever been inside a hearse, or knew of anyone who had. I guess most people who have ridden in one tend to keep their opinions to themselves. We were like kids in a candy store as we jumped around inside the roomy vehicles playing with all of the non-standard features, such as the flower holders and coffin rollers.

We cast our inexperienced eyes over each model, weighing up the pros and cons of the various set-ups. Buying a hearse would depend on it satisfying two main criteria: price and seating configuration. We sat in each car and analysed its viability as a touring wagon. Whitey ran his tape over the interior timberwork to ascertain where and if we could install a car fridge. Wegs sat in the front and played with the wipers and indicators, and occasionally tooted the horn. I was put in charge of the engine inspections and was pleased to report that I found engines in all five models.

After a while we split up to look at the hearses independently. Wegs and Whitey were looking at the Ford Granada, capably assisted by the silver-tongued Donal, while I moved off to look at the Mercedes models and was accompanied, as opposed to being assisted, by Olcan. I guess he thought it would give him a good opportunity to practise his used-hearse salesman techniques.

'Low miles; one owner; smooth ride; well maintained; flower racks; velour curtains; big windows – great vision.' Then, with a delightfully Irish touch, he added, 'And she's a nice black one, too.'

As a result of my shallow materialistic tendencies, and not Olcan's impressively unimpressive sales pitch, I found myself attracted to the older Mercedes with the leather seats and aesthetically pleasing body shape. Sensibly though, Wegs and Whitey were interested in the cheaper Ford model, which had seating for six. Eventually I was talked around and we eagerly bundled into the 1985 Ford Granada for a test drive.

'Mmmmm. What is that smell?' Wegs asked, sniffing deeply, trying to place the odd aroma permeating the hearse.

'Cabbage?' Whitey offered, and clambered in.

'More like old-man, I reckon,' I said, chiming into the debate. The car had the musty odour of a poorly ventilated house, reminding me of the homes I had entered with Mum when I tagged along on her Meals-on-Wheels rounds as a child.

The novelty of purchasing a hearse had captivated us for days and had carried us all the way from Dublin to Cork. In reality though, we could not afford to lose sight of our ultimate objective – to buy a suitable touring vehicle for our European holiday. So it was important that we give the hearse a good solid test. We didn't want to end up with a lemon.

We turned cautiously out of the showground and onto a quiet suburban road, Wegs concentrating hard as he drove slowly down the road.

Donal was correct in saying that she ran well. We couldn't even hear the engine tick over at twenty miles an hour. Although it was a very fitting pace for a funeral car, we needed to know if this 'big girl' could get to the speed limit, eventually.

'Kick her in the guts, Wegs,' I bellowed from the back seat.

With that, Wegs stood on the gas and the big girl dropped a gear as she roared into life. Like a caged beast enjoying her freedom, the hearse sped off down the leafy residential street breaking sixty miles an hour a couple of minutes later. A large school group assembled on the side of the road watched with amusement as a black blur sped past them. I turned around expecting to see scared young faces, whose belief in the eternal peace of the dearly departed had been shattered. Instead they were all laughing – or maybe grimacing – it was difficult to tell at seventy miles per hour.

We pulled over on the outskirts of town to change drivers. Whitey took over the driving responsibilities and I moved into the front seat. I pulled the passenger's seat forward so that Wegs could climb through for his turn in the back. After he had taken his seat I stepped outside to take a look. From here you could only see the head of the rear passenger in the middle of a three-metre-long window, as if on display. No wonder we had attracted so much attention, people don't expect to see someone sitting, as opposed to lying down, in the back of a hearse – or someone alive for that matter.

In order to put in some miles cruising on the open road, we headed towards the small coastal town of Kinsale. Upon entering the town we got stuck in the slowest-moving traffic, which wasn't actually stationary, that any of us could recall. We assumed it must have been a parade of sorts as the streets were lined deep with people. Our presence was quickly noted and a lot of pointing and curious looks were directed our way. After being so popular in suburban Cork we weren't surprised at the attention and Wegs and I began waving and smiling, and occasionally pretending to spot an old friend in the crowd.

Even though I regularly missed Sunday chapel at boarding school, it was I who recognised this must be a religious parade – why else were the townsfolk making the sign of the cross when we passed by? It seemed only polite that we should return the gesture. Wegs, being Catholic and far better at it than me, was in the back seat in full and unimpeded view of the townsfolk, enthusiastically crossing himself.

Whitey then noticed another hearse five cars ahead. I began to feel sick. Unknowingly, we had slotted ourselves neatly into a funeral procession respectfully making its way to the cemetery. This revelation caused panic within our hearse as we most certainly did not wish to appear disrespectful and incur the wrath of the local community. It was a delicate situation that called for cool heads.

Wegs and I decided it would be best if we both slid down on our seats out of view. This action did not amuse Whitey because he now became the sole subject of attention from the roadside mourners. He became uncharacteristically animated, screaming at us repeatedly to sit up. This meant the Kinsale locals, who hadn't seen two Australian dickheads crossing themselves, were treated to the sight of a long-haired madman screaming at himself.

But there was no way Wegs and I were going to face the music, no matter how cowardly our actions appeared.

'Just kick her in the guts and get us out of here,' I suggested from my cramped position.

Whitey immediately pulled out from the procession and sunk the slipper in. The big girl roared into life for the second time that day as we took off down the outside of the slow-moving convoy. It would have been a short and relatively painless manoeuvre had we not encountered a large speed hump at the exact moment we passed the front of the procession. But Whitey was on a mission and did not back off. We hit the speed hump at full throttle, just as we came alongside the legitimate hearse. It was precision timing. The force of the impact threw Wegs and me up off our seats and crashing into the roof in clear view of the adjacent undertakers and pallbearers.

We chose not to assume the position of lead hearse in the funeral procession but, instead, sped out of town, not daring to look back. We deservedly hit two more speed humps as we departed our living nightmare at high speed. Shaken from the experience we headed directly back to Cork, praying that no more recently departed local residents were to be laid to rest that day.

Unfortunately, we had to return through the centre of Cork

to reach Donal's yard. We pulled up at a major intersection in the middle of Cork and looked cautiously around for reactions. And there were plenty to gauge. I had never experienced anything like the response we received as we made our way through town that afternoon. The Cork community was completely transfixed. I had never laughed so heartily or waved so much in all my life. Could we be on to something here? If this was what it's like to be famous, and funny, then we wanted more of it.

We arrived back at CAB Motors with only one word for Donal O'Donnell.

'Sold!'

❂   ❂   ❂

'You guys are feckin' mad,' Bertie said, shaking his head, as he applied the finishing touches to the first sunroof he had installed in a hearse. 'Feckin' mad!'

It was paradoxical that an Irishman who fits sunroofs in Ireland was actually calling *me* mad. I would love to have stayed and chatted to the affable Bertie for longer, but his relentless banter had already added an extra hour to the sunroof installation and I was eager to get going. I was running late to meet the boys. My parents are always punctual and it has rubbed off on me. I hate being late for anything. I reckon it's rude.

The venue for our meeting was one of the few Dublin watering holes we had never frequented, even though it was less than a block from our apartment. I parked the hearse in the car park of our building, taking up two spaces, and jogged down the street to the bar on the corner. It was dark and smoky as

I entered the Phat Joint and an amateur DJ was spinning some tunes. I saw Wegs and Whitey at the bar and noticed they had ordered three pints of Guinness.

'Sorry I'm late, boys. Like most things in Ireland, it took a bit longer than expected but it looks great. You'll be impressed.'

'Good work, mate,' Wegs said, distributing a Guinness to each of us.

After a short wait for the stout to settle we clashed the overflowing pints and the meeting was called to order.

'Well, where are we at then?' I asked, mopping up my Guinness moustache with the back of my hand. The meeting had been called to discuss the progress of our respective tasks prior to our European road trip. I was in charge of sunroof installation and vehicle insurance, Wegs was in charge of finding a car stereo and Whitey was charged with the responsibility of finding and installing a car fridge – possibly the most important item on the list.

'Sunroof is in and insurance is under control,' I continued.

'I've got the car fridge ordered —' Whitey began.

'Stereo's ordered too. I can pick it up on Saturday morning,' Wegs interrupted.

'Good. That works well because the fridge is due on Saturday too. We can fit them this weekend. I'll organise to borrow some tools from the worksite,' Whitey said, adding confidently, 'won't take too long. Should be done by mid-afternoon.'

'Good work, team,' Wegs and I echoed together. We often did that.

The logistics were running surprisingly efficiently. I was

reminded of my university days when I did my best work under pressure – just before exams. We had less than a week until the lease on our apartment expired, the same day the ferry from Ireland to England was booked. Everything had to be road-worthy and shipshape by then.

We glossed over the details of our itinerary as we knew it would all come together in good time. All we had planned was to leave for England next Wednesday and make a beeline to France and then into Spain to make the Running of the Bulls festival in Pamplona in two weeks time. After that we had three months to fill in cruising through Europe on our way to the Oktoberfest in Germany. That was all we needed, or cared to know, for the time being. For now it was time to enjoy the notion of a wharfie, a carpenter and an agricultural scientist opening new chapters in their lives, in a car normally used to close one's final chapter.

We sat back and chatted about sport, girls and whose shout it was. Although it seemed we were no longer in a shout as we had been passed a fresh round by the barman. He told me it had come from the friendly gentleman at the end of the bar. I raised my glass in thanks, a gesture he returned with a smile and, of all things, a wink. What a friendly place.

'Cheers, mate,' I said, politely winking back. I wondered to myself why we'd never had a pint here before.

Until this point we had been swept up in the excitement of our European road trip, and had not paid much attention to the interior of the Phat Joint. Not that the dark and smoky interior commanded a lot of attention. In fact, the only colour in the drab establishment was provided by a large rainbow flag, 'artfully' suspended from the ceiling.

It then dawned on me why we'd never drunk here before. I subtly drew the colourful flag to the attention of Wegs and Whitey with animated eyebrow movements Mrs Bourke would have been proud of. We looked at one another in wide-eyed unison. And to think we considered ourselves men of the world! We decided it best not to hang around to find out whether these friendly locals had plans to add to our worldly experiences.

I addressed the troops. 'Wegs. Whitey. I propose that the next order of business be to adjourn this meeting to another venue, effective immediately.'

'I'll second that,' Whitey added instantly.

DAV WEGS WHITEY

2: LIGHT-FINGERED FROGS

When we arrived at Dover we sat down to our second team meeting in as many weeks. I don't want you to think we were preoccupied with organisation, that was definitely not our style. I just refer to this moment as a meeting because we were all seated at a table together, organising our paperwork for our impending transit to France. In fact, the real reason we sat at a large table together was so we could indulge ourselves, for one final time, in the greatest English tradition we knew – the all-day breakfast.

Our early morning ferry from Dublin to Liverpool had arrived just before midday and from Liverpool we'd driven directly to Dover, taking the M25 around London to save time because we didn't want to risk missing our non-refundable Channel Tunnel train to Calais. It was a particularly inflexible ticket that Wegs had pre-booked online, but as it was only 20 per cent of the normal fare it appealed to our budget. In our haste to arrive on time we'd forgotten to eat and we were starving. A big fry-up would be just the ticket.

'Full English, thanks,' Whitey ordered from the elderly waitress, 'with coffee and orange juice.'

'Full English for me too, please – but can I get an extra serve of black pudding and beans?' Wegs loved his baked beans and black pudding. Black pudding was an acquired taste and one that I had yet to acquire.

'Um. Steak, egg and chips for me, please,' I ordered. 'Oh yeah, and some brown sauce,' I added, nearly forgetting the main ingredient.

'Passports?' I said to the boys, initiating a quick checklist.

'Yep.'

'Yep, and one train ticket.' Wegs dug into his pocket and procured the documents as proof. We nodded our acknowledgement and sat back in our chairs. Everything was in order.

'Man, I hate this photo!' I said as I browsed the inside cover of my passport. The photo had been taken on the morning of a bad-hair day about eight years ago. I had braces on my teeth, and a bad outbreak of pimples. I'm not a vain person but I like to look presentable in a photo. But in this one, I looked ridiculous.

Whitey and Wegs had both seen the photo before but, as mates like to do, they both looked at it again and laughed heartily.

'Ha ha, you look like a smashed crab!' they both agreed, again.

'Yeah, piss off,' I laughed, and returned the hideous photo to the confines of my pocket.

The table service was slow so Whitey and I took the opportunity to unpack the video cameras we'd bought before leaving Dublin. Neither of us were particularly tech-savvy, but we had chosen some high-quality, expensive video cameras to document our journey. If the scenes we had witnessed whilst driving in Ireland over the last month were any indication, we would at least have some good entries for *Funniest Home Videos*.

Murphy's Law ensued and the food arrived shortly after we opened the camera cases. Silence descended as we eagerly tucked into the greasy offerings. As usual Wegs finished his meal first, despite it being roughly double the volume of ours. He stood up, wiped his mouth with the back of his hand and walked to an adjacent table, returning with a well-read copy of his favourite newspaper, *The Sun*. His Bible. Whitey and I continued to eat our breakfast in silence. We knew what was coming.

'Shit. Man U went down to Arsenal 2–1,' Wegs read aloud, more to himself than to us. He supported Manchester United as fiercely as if he had followed them since birth. In fact, his passion for the game, and for Manchester United, was becoming something of a liability as he was always at pains to share his unsolicited wisdom and opinions. Wisdom and opinions delivered with the assurance of a man who *knows* the tactics, the players and the politics of the game as well as anyone. If not better. As far as Whitey and I were concerned, *The Sun* had a lot to answer for.

'Apparently Solskjaer had a prick of a game. He always plays too deep, he's no bloody good. I don't know what Ferguson's thinking – he should trade him while he's still worth something,' reported Wegs, the oracle of all-things football. Whitey and I rolled our eyes as we had done so many times before.

'You finished, mate?' I asked Whitey, keen to change the subject.

'Yep. All done,' Whitey replied, pushing his knife and fork together on his unfinished plate.

'You ready, Wegs?' I asked, as Whitey and I pushed our chairs back.

'Uh huh,' he said, and hurriedly flicked towards the front of the paper. I stood up and stole a glance over Wegs' shoulder, surprised to find *The Sun* actually contained some useful information – I noticed it was Wednesday, 19 June.

'She'd breathe well,' I commented to Wegs.

'Gawd, ya not wrong!' Wegs said, admiring the page-three girl.

It was an unusually bright, warm day, and as we stepped out of the cafe we lowered our shades in unison. Whitey carried one black camera case. I had the other. Wegs was in the middle. It was a Blues Brothers' moment as we strode three abreast in sync towards our waiting chariot. I imagined the Lynyrd Skynyrd classic 'Sweet Home Alabama' playing over our slow-motion approach to the hearse.

We loaded the cases into the rear and clambered into our seats. Wegs was at the wheel, Whitey rode alongside him and I was in the rear. As they turned to face me I pulled my shades to the tip of my nose, looked over them and said, 'Kick her in the guts, boys.'

We drove to Folkestone to the Eurotunnel Terminal, and sat in a large waiting yard until our ticket number was called over the public-address system. When our boarding number was announced Wegs manoeuvred the hearse to the end of a long queue. The worm of cars slithered forward rapidly and soon we were driving in through the rear of the modern double-decker train.

The hearse dragged her exhaust noisily along the ground as she headed up the steep ramp onto the top level of the enclosed train. We followed the cars ahead of us, along the train through large double doors that separated each carriage and came to a stop about a dozen cars from the front of the train. The conductor closed the doors behind us. Each carriage appeared to hold around four normal-size cars. In our case there were two normal cars and one hearse. The cartoon instructions on the wall showed that the cars drive in through the rear of the train in England and then drive out the front of the train upon arrival in France. I was impressed by the efficiency of this system.

Moments later the train moved off jerkily towards France and the commencement of our European adventure. Back in the car we opened the fridge and grabbed a cold beer each. Depending on how you looked at it, this was to be our last beer in England, or our first beer in France. Either way, it tasted great.

❂   ❂   ❂

Moments after cracking our beers there was a knock on the back window of the hearse. We turned around to see two short conductors with their noses pressed to the glass. I jumped out to greet them.

'What's all this then?' chuckled the rounder of the two. At ·

least that's what I think he said. He had one of those heavy Northern English accents that Australians never, under any circumstance, fully understand.

'John,' he said, pointing to his ample stomach. 'I'm a Geordie and this 'ere is Thierry. He's a Frenchy.'

''Allo,' offered Thierry with a beaming grin. He was thinner than John the Geordie but sported the same goatee beard and crackling two-way radio.

'Dav. Pleased to meet you.' I shook their hands firmly.

'Ah. Bloody Aussies. Got some snags on the barbie?' John said. 'You've been all the talk over the radio you 'ave.'

'Why's that?' I enquired.

''Cos our job is so bloody boring,' he laughed, 'and because you are the first hearse we have ever loaded on, without a body!' I laughed along as if it was the first time I'd heard a lame 'dead' joke.

I outlined the details of our holiday to John and Thierry as they walked around the vehicle. Thierry was softly spoken with a heavy French accent, which made answering his relentless questions quite a hit-and-miss affair.

We returned to the rear of the vehicle and John asked to see inside. Thierry was informing the rest of the intrigued Eurotunnel crew over the two-way that we were Australians on holiday, that the hearse had come from Ireland and that yes, we had sewn the curtains in the back ourselves. The crackly responses came thick and fast over the radio as Thierry answered more questions on our behalf. He had become quite the ambassador for our cause.

I opened the rear of the vehicle and introduced John to Wegs and Whitey. Without further ado, John jumped straight into the hearse and lay flat on his back on the coffin platform, playing dead. It had poor old Thierry nearly wetting his pants. These conductors were a two-man show, with Thierry the straight man to John's antics. I shut the rear door on John and he continued his lifeless charade for a few moments before his radio barked and jolted him back to life. He stood up through the open sunroof and spoke in his thick brogue over the two-way.

'That were the driver giving us our five-minute arrival notice. He's a Frenchy too. 'Ere, he wants a word wif ya,' and with that John slid his radio along the roof towards me.

''Allo,' I addressed the radio cautiously.

''Allo. We arrive at Calais very soon. Good luck on your vacation,' offered the French driver.

'Thank you very much,' I said, slightly shocked. Thierry was giggling away with his radio still held to his ear. He really was enjoying himself. So was I for that matter.

'It is OK,' signed off the friendly driver, hopefully now concentrating fully on the safe passage of the train.

I went to hand the radio back to John but he had somehow eased his round frame through the slender sunroof and was now clambering his way back along the roof of the hearse on his stomach. It was no mean feat as there was not much room between the top of the car and the roof of the carriage. John landed heavily next to Thierry and me and mopped away the flood of sweat on his brow.

'I could do wif a pint!' he said. I had no doubt he could.

Whitey took a photo of me with 'John the Geordie' and 'Thierry the Frenchy' before we said farewell to our new friends.

'Good luck. Bon voyage,' said Thierry, waving as they headed off to open the carriage doors for our departure.

Minutes later we were rolling the hearse out the front of the train, through the yard and onto the short motorway to Calais. It took less than five minutes for us to depart the compound. We didn't even have to leave the car, let alone talk to anyone. Despite our enthusiasm to get the show on the road we decided to look for a cheap hotel to bed down for the night. After all, we were in no hurry. It was a sensible decision. The excitement of our arrival in France had worn off, and I was becoming tired. Very tired.

We found a quaint little hotel in a dimly lit street on the outskirts of town. Wegs went to get the key to our room with three single beds while Whitey and I grabbed what gear was at hand, locked up the hearse and followed him inside.

It had been a long day. Lying on my thin and lumpy mattress in our cheap French hotel I felt I could finally relax. Life had been manic recently but now that all of the hard work and preparation had been done, we could look forward to the adventures that lay ahead. The journey had finally begun and we felt invincible. Warm in that knowledge, I fell fast asleep.

☻ ☻ ☻

After croissants and coffee we packed up our things and checked out of the poky room. It was only 8 a.m. but already the day had warmed up, it would be a beautiful start to our adventure. We wandered down the lane and as we approached the car I saw something hanging out of the driver's door. I remarked to Wegs that I mustn't have shut it properly when I locked the car last night.

'Probably didn't shut because that lead was hanging out,' Wegs observed as we arrived at the car to see a large black cable dangling out the door.

'What lead *is* that?' asked Whitey.

That question was answered by silence. Silence brought on by the sudden realisation that we had been robbed. Suddenly, I felt less invincible than I had last night. Wegs jumped in to inspect the damage. 'For fuck's sake,' he exploded.

The stereo had been unceremoniously ripped from the centre console of the dash, and the wires and leads were sprawled over the front seats. There was a gaping hole in the dashboard where the thieves had removed the entire centre section in order to extract the stereo. We could actually see down to the transmission and the road below. I ran around to the passenger's side and climbed in to inspect the scene.

'Bloody Froggies!' chipped in Whitey. There wasn't much more we could say or do.

It didn't take long to realise that the stereo wasn't the only item missing. Everything, and I mean everything, that had been lying around the inside of the car had gone. The car had been completely gutted of our belongings. It must have taken several thieves, or one very greedy thief with a shopping trolley, to make off with the following:

Stereo; Whitey's electric shaver; toasted sandwich maker;

kettle; power transformer; CDs; petty cash; paper towel; Wegs' socks; camera bag carrying leads and battery chargers; digital video tapes; tripod; Australian Rules football; twelve pack of toilet paper; my board shorts and towel (wet).

'Good thing we didn't buy that jack, hey Whitey,' Wegs chipped in cheekily. The day before Whitey had wanted to buy a car jack at the supermarket but Wegs and I had told him it would just be a waste of money as we wouldn't get flats.

'Mmmpphh', came his unamused reply.

So I guess things could have been worse. The only blessing was that our most valuable possessions were safe because we had taken the video cameras and my laptop into the room with us last night.

I sat in the back seat in silence, disturbed by the situation. Theft is a violation and one that I hadn't experienced before. I thought back to when, as a young lad, I had stolen a packet of Juicy Fruit chewing gum from the local store. I had fallen asleep that night with a mouthful of the stolen chewing gum, only to wake in the morning to find it stuck all through my hair. I haven't stolen since. I could only hope that fate dealt these thieves a similar hand to the one I had been dealt all those years ago.

'The secret compartments!' I blurted out. We hadn't checked to see if the thieves had emptied them as well. The lads swung around with expectant looks as I ripped open the compartment.

Our secret compartments had been constructed back in our Dublin garage when we were fitting out the hearse for the trip. Beneath the padded armrests of the two rear seats we had cut an opening, about a foot long and just wide enough for a hand, and had stuck the armrests back over the hole with double-sided Velcro tape.

With great relief I extracted the contents. In my hand I held all three of our passports and 2500 euro in cash. The cash belonged to Whitey and without it his trip would have been over before it started. We had learnt an important lesson. To avoid the risk of theft in the future we would need to thoroughly secure our vehicle at night, and leave tempting possessions, like Wegs' socks and my wet towel, out of sight.

3: CINQ OEUFS S'IL VOUS PLAÎT

After spending the morning painstakingly obtaining a police report at the Calais Police Station for insurance purposes, we happily departed Calais and set sail for the D-day beaches of Normandy.

Evening arrived quickly. We had spent the day at several of the D-day battle sites along the Normandy coastline, closing out our day at the Port Winston lookout to the east of the small town of Arromanches. We parked our big black hearse amid a long row of white RVs (recreational vans or campervans) at a cliff-top car park overlooking the township, and joined the hordes of fellow tourists who had congregated to watch the sun set over these historic beaches. It was a spectacular and memorable sunset – not just because Wegs peed off the large cliff – because it brought to a close our first, and highly memorable, day on the road.

With darkness approaching we decided to find a spot to 'free-camp'. The top half of the egg-yolk sun was rapidly descending below the horizon as we drove to the west of Arromanches and down a quiet country lane that turned into a rarely used grass track. The hearse bumbled along until the track opened out onto a small beach. It was a delightful location and we set up camp, the two tents and my swag, at the water's edge. The hearse was parked side-on providing us with a perfect windbreak. We gathered some driftwood and lit a small fire as the heat had long gone from the day. Tucked up warmly in our sleeping bags chatting around the fire, we dined on dry baguettes topped with wedges of cheddar, taking turns to slurp on a bottle of cheap red wine.

'Aaagh . . . yuck!' I winced as I downed a mouthful of the acidic wine. 'This stuff is terrible,' I said with eyes screwed shut. My mouth felt corroded, like I'd eaten an apple after brushing my teeth.

'What? It's all right. Can't complain for five euro.' Wegs loved a bargain and there seemed no limit to what he could endure and justify for the sake of saving a few bucks. This wine had cost only five euro for five litres and was sold in a large plastic container with handles, resembling those in which motor oil is normally found. It seemed entirely plausible that Wegs may have misread the label. He doesn't speak French.

'Well, it's all yours, mate,' I said, signing off from another pointless argument. Whitey was lying quietly, mopping up the last of a dubious pâté that Wegs and I had shunned, with his finger.

As the flames flickered I looked out to sea and tried to imagine what this coastline would have resembled on 6 June 1944.

'Can you imagine seven thousand boats out there, with guns

and bombs going off all over the place?' I asked the boys. 'And a hundred thousand-odd troops landing here on the beach to be picked off by the Germans?'

'Shit, no,' said Whitey, reflecting everyone's thoughts.

'I would've been no good in a war. I would've been shitting myself,' Wegs chipped in.

'You're not on your own there,' I added.

As a matter of fact, we all would've made terrible soldiers. I was the only one who had ever been in a fight, and that was some time ago. When I was ten years old I'd had an altercation with my younger sister Kate. She'd been annoying me at the time, so I grabbed a nearby hammer and 'tapped' her on the head, causing her to collapse in a screaming heap before running off to Mum and Dad. It was a fight won quite convincingly, although frankly, I thought she had overreacted. I'd only tapped her.

We didn't talk any more that night. The irony of camping on a D-day beach with a hearse by our side wasn't lost on any of us. Instead we lay there quietly, thankful for the efforts and sacrifices of the Allied troops that allowed us to camp here and enjoy this tranquil setting, in peace.

An hour or so later, teasing the last life out of the fire with a stick, I could see that Wegs and Whitey were both asleep. I didn't need to see Wegs as I could hear him snoring away. The low light of the fire showed him in his standard sleeping position: lying on his back, arm across his forehead and with his mouth wide open, knocked out by the cheap wine. Whitey was curled up snugly with his head buried deep in the sleeping bag, and there next to him, looking over us, was our faithful hearse. It was reassuring to have her close by us tonight. As she slept there beside us I felt there were four, not three, members of our touring team.

● ● ●

'What should we call this big girl?' I asked, patting the dash as we cruised along the N13 from Caen to Paris.

'I thought we had decided to name her after, you know, the first conquest,' said Wegs.

Exactly how we would name the hearse had been a recurring discussion within the team. We had agreed, in rather bloke-ish fashion, that she should be named after the first girl any team member got 'friendly' with in the car. This was, up until today, fine by me. But after last night, and the realisation that she was a fully fledged team member, I now thought this approach would be demeaning for her. Not to mention that I considered the likelihood of having relations with any female in the back of a funeral vehicle to be highly unlikely.

I explained this new position to the boys, who agreed in principle. Problem was, what to call her? Helga the hearse? Heidi? Helen? We seemed to get stuck on names beginning with 'h', and no further creative suggestions sprang forth. No name seemed to suit the big girl so, until we came up with a name we could all agree upon, she would be referred to by her default title: the Big Girl.

'What do you reckon about that, Big Girl?' I asked, talking to the dashboard.

'Beep! Beep!' came the Big Girl's happy acceptance, with the assistance of Whitey. I'm not sure this was the non-demeaning name I had in mind, but, in the absence of anything better, it would have to do.

A few hours later the Big Girl was in the Big City and things had become a little interesting. We entered Paris and made our way towards the River Seine. We figured it would be easiest to follow the river all the way to the centre of the city. Driving a six-metre-long vehicle, from the right-hand side, in any European city was always going to be a challenge, and Paris was proving to be just that. The traffic, despite the prolific traffic police, appeared to follow no basic rules.

Road markings at major intersections were non-existent and we regularly found up to five lanes merrily merging, indicator free. Whitey, after being cut off by yet another insolent little Peugeot, had had enough.

'Fuck this!' he said, throwing his hands up and acknowledging the traffic warden's outstretched palm by stopping. 'I give up.'

He undid his seatbelt, got out of the car and stormed around to my door, ripping it open, 'I'm the country specialist! You're driving.'

I obviously had no say in the matter so, as the recently appointed city specialist, I ran around the front of the car and jumped into the driver's seat. A whistle blared, a white glove flapped madly in front of me and with a poke of the accelerator we roared off down the Champs Elysées.

To succeed in this traffic I had to quickly learn to have the courage of my convictions. There is simply no room for indecision. If you wish to change lanes indiscriminately then you simply do it. The surrounding drivers, while not necessarily liking your decision, will accept it and take appropriate action. Such appropriate action normally involves swerving violently, blaring the horn and gesticulating madly. But strangely, it flows and it works. Don't even think about displaying courtesy to other drivers and pedestrians; it is simply not required or appreciated. Just do what you have to do in order to get to where you want to go, otherwise your nerves will be shot to pieces. When driving in Paris, do as the Parisians do.

The driving became considerably easier once I adopted this aggressive local style. After an hour or so cruising the city we discovered another ace up our sleeve that was assisting us greatly with our road craft. It was our size. At six metres long, two metres wide and over three tonnes in weight we were approximately twice the size of your average Renault. The Big Girl was also, for all intents and purposes, still a functioning funeral vehicle. This combination of size and function commanded a reasonable level of respect from the overwhelmingly arrogant French drivers.

However, our golden run through the city soon came to an end as we approached the Louvre. We had taken the liberty, as hearse drivers, to allow the Big Girl to travel in the 'Bus Only' lanes. God knows she was big enough. But it wasn't long before the gendarmes pulled up alongside us at the lights to inform us this was not allowed.

We didn't understand a single word that was yelled at us by the bespectacled officer, but we did appreciate the sentiment. It would seem that anger, like love, is a universal language. Anyway, we didn't really care. We were only here for a day.

❋   ❋   ❋

I had not spoken any French since arriving in the country two days ago. I'd studied it in my first year of high school but that was fifteen years ago. I asked Wegs, who hadn't studied French at even a year-seven level, how he had managed to book the hotel on our first night.

'Pictures. I drew three stick figures and three beds on a napkin,' came the reply. Wegs was nothing if not lateral.

'I wish I could speak French,' he lamented. 'Teach me a saying, Dav.'

Wegs' request forced me to think for a moment. My conversational French was appalling at best in year seven, and had dropped off significantly since. I was incapable of speaking French to any meaningful level. And the French spoke too quickly; it was even harder to understand than Irish. I could only read the words on signs or menus, and then join them together with basic commands and pleasantries, such as please and thank you. We passed by a busy cafe and my memory was jogged by a kerb-side sandwich board I'd seen that I think was advertising all-day breakfasts.

'Cinq oeufs s'il vous plaît,' I suggested to Wegs.

'What the hell does that mean?' he asked perplexed.

'It's a gentleman's greeting, a slightly more romantic version of bonjour,' I said straight-faced. 'One that the local women will definitely appreciate.'

'Good. Sank . . . erf . . . sill . . . voos . . . plate. I like it.'

'Yep. That's it, mate. You're a natural.' Wegs accepted the bogus phrase without further question. He is a trusting soul.

We soon arrived at a suitable hotel opposite the Gare du Nord in north-central Paris. I double-parked the Big Girl so that Wegs, the accommodation specialist, could run in and pleasantly order his breakfast from the receptionist before doing a sketch.

A car had pulled out from a parking spot just ahead of us and I took off towards it. Kerb-side parks were as rare as hen's teeth in Paris. I quickly moved the Big Girl alongside the vacant spot and prepared to execute a textbook parallel park. In my haste I'd failed to notice that the car which had departed the space was a SmartCar. This meant the space wasn't even large enough for the bonnet of the Big Girl. Whitey and I both cursed the SmartCar for its trickery. Whitey, being from a small country town, didn't need much encouragement when it came to abusing the trendy SmartCars and their city drivers. I didn't like them either. Just because they could fit into small places they thought they were smart, which inferred that the Big Girl was dumb. And I took exception to that.

Losing the park proved to be no great loss. In our travels around town we'd learnt that double-parking in Paris wasn't only accepted, it was as simple as a press of the button. Hazard lights. It seemed that as soon as the hazard lights were illuminated an illegal park suddenly legitimised itself. It appeared to be common practice in central Paris and who were we to flaunt local custom? I backed up to the front of the hotel and depressed the button with the orange triangle on it. Not a horn was tooted nor an eyebrow raised. We were getting away with murder, although it would take a particularly agitated driver or an overly officious parking officer to question the intentions of a double-parked hearse. It wouldn't be good karma.

Wegs returned to the car after successfully organising another room. He had even managed to get directions to a long-term security car park around the corner. It was an impressive effort.

'How did your French go, mate?' It was a loaded question.

'Yeah, still needs a bit of work. I tried your saying but it didn't work very well because she laughed and then spoke in English. So it was pretty easy in the end.'

I chuckled at the thought of Wegs sincerely ordering his 'five eggs, please'. She must have thought he was completely mad, if she even understood him. I preferred to think that she had.

At the car park we found a space near the security office. We unloaded our valuable gear before backing the Big Girl hard up against the concrete wall, making it impossible for anyone to open the rear door. We also removed all of the items from the front seats that were visible through the windows. We were not going to give a prospective thief any reason to violate our Big Girl again.

The hotel room was unquestionably Parisian. It was small and poky, with French doors opening out onto a tiny balcony. It had a double bed, a single bed and a small, portable cot bed.

It was not the Ritz but it was more than suitable for us. I opted to take first turn on the cot bed. I knew my turn for the double bed would come one day.

With the Big Girl and our accommodation safely organised we left the hotel and wandered off aimlessly. It was around dusk, too early for an evening meal in Paris, so we headed off for a pre-dinner walk. We lost formation as we ambled against the tide of smartly dressed men and women who crowded the footpaths as they made their way home. Most carried with them a bottle of wine or a small bag of groceries for their evening meal, reminding me that this was a normal working day in the real world.

We found ourselves walking along Rue La Fayette, the same road we had travelled along in the Big Girl earlier that day. The traffic seemed even more chaotic and less negotiable now in the evening rush. The wide road was a kaleidoscope of blazing headlights and blaring horns as impatient locals hurried home. I was thankful the Big Girl was safely parked for the night and we weren't driving along the road now. I was not half as glad as Whitey though.

We walked for an age, weaving through the pedestrian traffic. Looking left and right as we hurried across confusing intersections, looking up to take in the impressive architecture and looking down to dodge dog poo, another Parisian hazard. It wasn't until we stood away from the crowds, on the edge of the manic Place de la Concorde, that we regrouped. Ahead of us the Champs Elysées was lit up like a runway, outlining the long and wide path leading to the illuminated Arc de Triomphe that stood imposingly in the distance. Paris had been impressive by day, but was majestic by night.

'Righto, we've *done* Paris. Where to next?' Wegs yelled over the traffic.

Whitey and I just looked at one another and sighed. We had heard this classic Wegner comment before. Wegs had an annoying habit of referring to places he had visited in his travels as being *done,* which drove Whitey, in particular, mad. It meant that once Wegs had visited somewhere and ticked off a couple of the main sights, then that place offered nothing more of interest – to anyone.

'Piss off Wegs. Ya can't *do* Paris in half a day ya dickhead,' Whitey said, shaking his head in mock anger. I laughed. So did Wegs.

'I'm hungry,' I chipped in, changing the subject. I knew where this conversation was heading; I had heard it all before. Although admittedly this time Wegs did have a point, as earlier that day we had decided to depart Paris after sighting the Eiffel Tower and the Arc de Triomphe. However, even though we planned to hit the open road to Pamplona the following morning, I knew we hadn't *done* Paris. I would be back one day, older, wiser and wealthier – to *do* it.

We took a table at Brasserie Terminus Nord, around the corner from our hotel. We were tired from our long walk and ready for a large meal, even though it was approaching midnight.

'Trois bière s'il vous plaît,' I ordered, holding up three fingers to the waiter to supplement my poor pronunciation. I was sure that both my confidence and competence, certainly with this particular phrase, would eventually improve. The waiter returned with the three beers and then patiently waited as we ordered our meals: steak and chips for Whitey, tortellini and salad for me, snails and steak for Wegs, and a carafe of house red. Fortunately, with the Eurostar Terminal directly opposite the restaurant, our polite waiter had a reasonable command of English.

Before we knew it we had drunk and eaten our way through a couple of hours, and the crowd was starting to thin out. The tired waiter was dropping hints by removing rubbish bags to the side of the road, in full view of the remaining patrons who were smoking and finishing coffees, or picking at the remnants of a cheese platter, as we were. The streets were quiet save for the occasional pedestrian or street sweeper. Even the continuous line of taxis that had been servicing the train terminal had reduced to two; the drivers were standing outside their cars, smoking cigarettes and chatting to one another. It was late and, cot bed aside, I was going to sleep well tonight.

'Worked out where we're heading to next yet, mate?' Whitey asked across the table to Wegs.

'This sounds like just the place!' he said, stabbing his finger on the map excitedly. 'It's on the way to Pamps, too.' With his nose buried in the guidebook, he read: '. . . in an area renowned for excellent wine, impressive architecture, avenues and parks. Most importantly, it has a lively university community and vibrant nightlife.'

'Shit, yeah,' Whitey added.

'Sounds spot on, mate. What's it called?' I asked.

'Ummm,' Wegs scanned the map again with his finger. 'Bordecks.'

4: A PUBLIC DISPLAY OF AFFECTION

Pamplona was Wegs' baby. He was in charge of the itinerary for this leg of the journey. He knew where to stay, where to go and what to do, from stories told to him by fellow travellers during his days living in London.

Apparently, it was best to stay in one of the large tourist camp sites out of town, rather than finding accommodation in Pamplona – a near impossible task given the San Fermin (Running of the Bulls) Festival was due to start. These camp sites accommodate thousands of international revellers and, according to Wegs, they were where the action was. It also seemed the camp sites were so large that the Spanish authorities didn't feel obliged to signpost them.

We drove down dead-end road after dead-end road, and spent hours driving through a disorientating maze of small roads lined with lush fields of corn and olive groves. The corn was planted right to the road's edge and grew amazingly well in this hot, flat and dry region. It was growing far too well for my liking as the tall foliage blocked our view of the surrounding countryside, making finding the El Molino camp site almost impossible and adding to the mounting irritation within the Big Girl.

Whitey and I were too hot and bothered to oppose Wegs' 'process of elimination' style of navigation, so it was more through good luck than good management that we finally stumbled on the camp site just on dusk.

'Told you I would find it!' proclaimed Wegs.

I restrained myself from saying that locating the camp site was inevitable if you drove down *every* road on the map. His navigation was faultless in theory but slightly painful in practice. Never mind, we had made it successfully to the El Molino camp site.

As we passed through the entry gates it was clear this was where the action was. Before us lay a sea of inebriated antipodeans swilling down beer bongs and sangria. There were so many people that the party had spilled out of the pool complex and sprawled onto the road leading into El Molino. Things appeared to be getting a little messy.

To advance to the camp sites the Big Girl, like Moses before her, was forced to part the waters as Whitey cautiously edged her through the throng of revellers. Word soon spread among the crowd and our progress became even slower. There was a lot of pointing and laughing, and most of the slurred comments were incomprehensible. The Big Girl had her bonnet and roof thumped, no doubt feeling molested by these foreign hands all over her body. But it didn't stop there. Every inch of glass had strangers' sweaty faces pressed up against it in order to get a closer look. A couple of the guys pressed their nipples up against the glass and kissed the window passionately, only inches from my face. I felt like a freak sitting in the exposed rear seat as hundreds of sets of eyes focused on me. I wanted to get out of this crowd as quickly as possible.

Thankfully we emerged safely from the enthusiastic crowd. Whitey had to use the windscreen wipers to clean away the sweat and zinc that had been smeared all over the car. We'd driven through in silence, but there was concern within the Big Girl about just what exactly we'd got ourselves into. It wasn't that the environment was hostile; in fact, it was far from it – it was just a huge shock. These guys had obviously enjoyed a long day drinking in the sun and we, on the other hand, were as sober as judges and tired from our long and circuitous journey. El Molino was going to be an acquired taste.

I could sense the elegant Big Girl was as eager as we were to find a site to set up camp. A camping ground employee came to our assistance and led us to a vacant site. As we drove slowly along behind the guide, we passed row after row of colourful campervans anointed with stickers and flags. They ranged from the traditional Kombi van to out-of-service ambulances and ice-cream vans, and they all carried a hand-painted name: the Rusty Trombone, the Mean Machine, Mr Whippy, the Mole Patrol, Doggy Style, and the Mystery Machine.

We had come in contact with the infamous travelling institution known as the Van Tour. This is a tour that attracts up to one hundred vans laden with thirsty travellers, predominantly from Australia, New Zealand and South Africa. Their itinerary was similar to ours: starting at Pamplona and then travelling throughout Europe towards Oktoberfest in Germany, before returning to London. The Van Tour travelled in convoy, whereas we proposed to go solo. I was sure we would see these guys from time to time on the road; after all, you couldn't miss them, or us.

Thankfully our camp site was on the fringe of the Van Tour proper, which meant it was a less-public and less-trafficked location. Setting up camp only took us a few minutes. Unlike the well-planned members of the Van Tour, we had no camping equipment to erect apart from the boys' two small tents and my swag. With our site organised we decided we'd earned a drink so we headed off to join the poolside party. Within minutes we were deep inside the swarming mass of bodies, armed with large plastic cups overflowing with sangria and ice. As darkness moved in our sobriety moved out. We quickly learnt that sangria is a rather potent drink, despite its likeness to raspberry cordial. The night was chaotic and it wasn't long before we had lost each other in the crowd. It didn't matter though, as after four or five sangrias complete strangers rapidly became best mates.

After a lengthy drunken boogie, I left the dance floor to replenish my cup, concerned that I had not yet had enough to drink. I made my way across the dimly lit dance floor and, in one very cool move, I jumped over a small step to ground level. However, the step that I had so cleverly avoided didn't actually exist, and my foot landed on the ground much earlier than my brain expected it to, causing my body to stagger violently forward as my legs tried valiantly to catch up. They didn't, because they never do, pissed or not. My centre of gravity had moved so far forward it had passed the point of no return. Fortunately, despite my increasing speed, a verandah pole saved me from certain disaster. With the assistance of the well-placed pole I gathered myself up into a normal standing position and looked around at the thinning crowd to see if anyone had noticed. They had. I decided to head off to bed. Maybe I'd had enough.

I left the bar and headed back into the depths of the camping ground, walking alongside the rows of identical dome tents that had been erected prior to tomorrow's arrival of two thousand Contiki tourists. I decided to take a short cut through the uninhabited sea of tightly packed tents and wondered, if these people were to come home in a state similar to mine, how the hell they would know which tent was theirs. This observation distracted me from the task at hand and before I knew it I was struck in the throat by a sneaky guy rope. I staggered backwards, repeating the leaving-the-dance-floor scenario but this time in reverse. Sadly, there would be no happy ending. Within seconds I went careering backwards onto one of the small dome tents. As I fell awkwardly I heard the fibreglass support poles breaking under my weight. Thank goodness no one was in the tent. I lurched to my feet to flee the scene, but the tent had become quite attached to me and I had to frantically flap my arms and legs to free myself. I dusted off and looked around – this time no one had seen – and headed off towards bed again. I had *definitely* had enough.

❂　❂　❂

'We are a tent down. Repeat. Tent down!'

I woke up on hearing these words but it took me a few seconds to get my bearings and work out where I was. This was not made easy by the fact it was pitch black inside my zipped-up swag. I slowly recalled my whereabouts and the personal misfortune associated with getting there.

Did I really hear those words or had I just dreamt them? I was still intoxicated and thinking just made my head hurt even more. So I closed my eyes again and rolled over. I would need some more sleep before facing this particular day.

'Two-man dome. North sector!'

Shit. That voice again. My eyes shot open for the second time.

I unzipped my swag just far enough to peer out without arousing suspicion. A highly self-important tour guide was standing about ten feet from me, back turned, hands on hips. He was inspecting the flattened tent and his body language told me he was not happy. He muttered something into his two-way; I wondered if I should get out and own up to the accident.

'INCONSIDERATE PRICKS!' he yelled, as he gathered up the remnants of the tent into a tangled heap. It was clear this was more than just a tent to him, so I decided to stay in bed.

Within seconds a small van arrived and two other Contiki officers emerged. It must have been reinforcements from the Contiki Tent Rescue Unit (TRU). Whichever tactical response department they were from I could tell they were pros; they efficiently removed the damaged tent and erected an identical (prior to incident) replacement in a matter of minutes. Further hands-on-hips comments were passed between the three before they all roared off back to TRU headquarters, presumably to file incident reports.

I was amused by the serious attitude of these officious guides. After all, it was only a broken tent and, excluding my pride, there was no real harm done. It was an innocent mistake that anyone who had consumed four litres of sangria could easily make. I zipped up my swag and rolled over, thinking they could have been a little bit quieter at this hour of the morning. Inconsiderate pricks.

Try as I might I could not go back to sleep. My head was throbbing and I could feel the sangria pulsing through my veins. I unzipped my swag and sat upright to greet the day. As my eyes focused in the bright light I saw a girl leaving Whitey's tent.

'Morning,' I managed, with a gravelly throat.

'Morning,' she replied, in a funny sort of way.

I waited until she was out of earshot before yelling to Whitey.

'So?'

Whitey's grinning head popped out of his tent. Wegs, hearing the banter, also popped his head out of his tent. We wanted details. I gave Whitey twenty questions in order to extract all the juicy information about his overnight visitor. It turned out her name was Sharon and she was from New Zealand, which explained her unusual accent, and they had met at the bar after we lost each other last night. I was greatly relieved when he informed me that their union had been confined to the dance floor and his tent, and had not extended to the Big

Girl. Immediately I congratulated myself on the prudence of altering the naming procedure for the hearse. Imagine if something had happened between Whitey and Sharon in the Big Girl last night, and we were forced to travel Europe in a hearse called 'Shirren'! The thought sent chills up my spine.

We wasted little time in getting up and about. Today was the opening ceremony of the San Fermin Festival and we wanted to get into Pamplona nice and early. Wegs was particularly excited at the prospect of the large food fight that signals the start of the ten-day festival. He had armed himself with flour and eggs purchased from the camping-ground supermarket.

Whitey, the sober one, took the wheel for the half-hour drive into Pamplona. We parked the Big Girl and then walked into the heart of town along narrow cobblestoned roads with thousands of locals and tourists, all clad in traditional white clothing with red neck scarves. The atmosphere was one of excitement as people sang and danced, and necked bottles of sangria. I abstained for the time being. As we neared the town square the crowd had become so thick we could go no further. This was as close as we were going to get.

It was noisy as we waited for the ringing of the town bells that would signal the opening of the festival and start the food fight. We were packed into the narrow street like sardines and could barely lift our arms. When I bent over to pull my video camera out of our team backpack there was a sudden barrage of explosions ahead of us. I looked up to see flares shooting into the sky and the start of a loud chant. I couldn't see what was going on but word had spread through the crowd that Basque separatists were conducting a demonstration just metres ahead of us. Political tensions began to surface amongst the Spanish contingent and the situation grew potentially volatile.

More flares erupted as riot police entered the square to control the rally. Their arrival forced the Basque demonstrators to retreat en masse and we were swept away by the force of the crowd and thrown up against the wall behind us. I looked to Whitey who was the tallest and had the best chance to see what was going on. He had a concerned expression on his face. I'm sure I had the same expression and probably Wegs, who I couldn't see as he was squashed up behind me.

We were helpless to move against the avalanche of people, and I could feel claustrophobia closing in. I was starting to panic so I stared blankly into Whitey's t-shirt and breathed slowly. I was going to have to ride this one out.

The pressure eased after a couple of minutes as the demonstration was moved along. We regained some personal space but our position was still cramped, making it difficult to film the boys in the food fight. I noticed a large water truck to our left with two operators sitting on top of the driver's cabin.

'I'm going up there,' I yelled to the boys.

'Good luck!' They were sceptical.

I pushed my way over to the truck and managed to get the attention of one of the guys by grabbing his foot. He peered down at me with an angry expression and pointed a water hose directly at my head. I used my very best sign language to ask if I could join them on the roof to film. I was pointing enthusiastically at my camera and nodding my head to impress upon him that it would be a good idea. He then shook his head enthusi-astically to impress upon me that it would *not* be a good idea. It wasn't an argument I was going to win.

As I turned to head back to the boys I heard a shout from the rear of the truck. His partner was walking along the top of the truck, signalling to me to meet him at the back. I made my way to the ladder and began to climb up one handed, holding the camera tightly in the other. I made it onto the top of the water tank and he held up his hand, indicating that I could stay for five minutes only. I walked along the tanker with him to the rear of the driver's cab and sat down behind him. His grumpy hose-wielding mate turned to acknowledge me with a surly nod of the head.

After I got comfortable the church bells boomed through-out the town and the festival was under way. Red scarves began waving madly and champagne was spraying freely throughout the packed streets. I had a commanding and protected view from up on the truck and managed to get some great shots of Wegs hurling eggs and flour at complete strangers. I stayed on the truck for nearly half an hour before both men motioned to me it was time to go. I thanked them by shaking their hands.

Climbing down the ladder I suddenly became a focal point for nearby food fighters, and I was mercilessly peppered with eggs and champagne corks. Then came the champagne and the flour. I was starting to panic about my camera being dam-aged. I could only partially shield it from the onslaught because I needed my free hand to hold on – a task not made easy by the increasing amount of egg white on the ladder. I was forced to stop, duck my head into my chest and place the camera inside my t-shirt, otherwise I was certainly going to fall. And I didn't fancy that. I hate pain. It hurts.

The scenario, while entertaining for the throwers, was quite enraging for the target, me. It appeared there was no way out and I was starting to get really pissed off. What was more annoying was that I couldn't return the fire to defend or strengthen my position. I would have given anything for a hammer. However, as it turned out, I wouldn't need my weapon of choice. My previously unfriendly mate with the water hose had noticed the futility of my situation, and had dragged the hose to the back of the truck and begun to hose away the troublesome food fighters. Their champagne bottles were no match for his powerful water cannon and they retreated hastily. This allowed me to safely continue my descent to the ground where Whitey was waiting with the backpack. I shoved the camera in and we raced away to the front of the truck. I looked up to see my saviour grinning sadistically at his handiwork. We firmly saluted one another in sync. The battle was won.

We ran off in the direction of Wegs and found him wearing even more pancake mix than I was. He was white from head-to-toe and appeared to have no eyes as his sunglasses were covered in a thick layer of congealed egg and flour. As a team we beat a hasty retreat to the sanctuary of the Big Girl. Wegs and I needed to get out of the heat of the day and back to the camp site to have a thorough shower and hair wash, before we turned into bread.

❀ ❀ ❀

That evening was spent in much the same fashion as the previous evening. The only exception on my part was that I managed to stay upright for the entire night. Perhaps my body was becoming conditioned, through over-exposure, to sangria. We slept in until lunchtime the following day as we had no plans to go anywhere beyond the camping ground pool. The bull run was not for another day and we all had horrendous hangovers.

I managed to catch more than just a few rays by inadvertently falling asleep for a couple of hours by the pool. I had of course forgotten to apply any sunscreen and my back was now brutally burnt and pretty painful.

'Ouch. I'll go and get you something for that,' offered a compassionate Wegs, after he had stopped laughing. He returned a few minutes later. 'Here you go, mate. This will help ease the pain,' he said with a smile.

I reluctantly accepted the familiar plastic cup of sangria and ice.

'Here we go again,' said Whitey dryly as we clashed our cups together.

'Cheers,' came the chorus.

After a couple of rounds the conversation began to flow freely between all of the poolside drinkers. Wegs and Whitey were chatting away merrily with the girls from the Mole Patrol van that was parked adjacent to our hearse in the camping ground, and I had struck up a conversation with a lovely girl called Loren, from Cape Town. We were getting along famously, and as the afternoon merged into the evening we adjourned to the bar for the next few hours. I wasn't at all concerned I'd once again misplaced Wegs and Whitey. I had the pleasure of Loren's effervescent company and we were having a great time chatting and joking with one another. It wasn't all that late in the night when we decided to head upstairs to her room for a bit of privacy.

I was dismayed to learn that her room was in fact a twelve-person dorm. Privacy would be at a premium but, never mind, I was sure we could improvise. We turned on the light to check that the dorm was empty, and it was. Loren flicked the light off and took me by the hand. We walked over to her bottom bunk bed and drew together in a passionate embrace. I pulled her tightly towards me and we fell together onto the bed.

'Aaaggghhh! FUCK!' I screamed. I had landed heavily on my sunburnt back. Poor Loren withdrew, wondering what had gone so horribly wrong. I composed myself, told her of the sunburn and rolled onto my side. I grabbed her by the hand and we moved into a side-on position, relieving my discomfort. We renewed the embrace and our hands began to roam freely.

Just as things were gaining momentum the door burst open and the light came on. Actually it took some time for the light to come on because the pissed intruder was fumbling around trying to find the switch. I watched her stagger about and hoped she had just returned to the room to grab something. She made her way towards our bed and yawned; the pissed room-mate was sleeping in the bunk above Loren. Things were not looking good. She commenced her clumsy ascent to her bed, oblivious to our presence.

Great. Just great. Why had she chosen this moment, out

of all possible moments, to retire to bed? Why ...? Silently I grieved and cursed her lack of consideration, she was snoring away within minutes.

Loren and I lay there snugly before once again beginning to get intimate with one another. However, it seemed that the gods were conspiring against us as the door burst open yet again. This time it revealed a pissed bloke, in search of his bed. Behind him followed a further two well-lubricated occupants. It was clear nothing was going to happen tonight.

'Let's go back down,' suggested Loren.

'Good idea.'

We straightened our clothing and headed off to find Wegs and Whitey. My return to the bar with Loren was unexpected and the boys were overjoyed to have the team reunited. This was cause for celebration, so we ordered repeated shots of tequila to mark the occasion.

Wegs, Whitey, Loren and I enthusiastically celebrated for a few more hours until, at midnight, Whitey decided to retire to bed. He was being characteristically sensible, as we had to be up at 5 a.m. to get into town to run against the bulls. Loren was starting to fade, and she also said goodnight and headed upstairs. It had been a long day but Wegs and I thought one more drink would be appropriate before retiring. While he was ordering our nightcap I had the foresight to set the alarm on my mobile phone for 4.30 a.m., just in case I forgot when I got into bed. It was critical that we got away at the specified time to get a good position for the run. Wegs returned with the beverages.

'Heressh to usshh!' he said.

'To usshh.'

❂ ❂ ❂

Beep . . . beep . . . beep-beep-beep . . . beep . . . beep . . . beep-beep-beep . . .

'Wegsh. WEGSH,' I shouted. 'Ish time to get up! WEGSH!'

I wasn't surprised Wegs didn't respond. After all, he was on the other side of the dance floor, and the music was bloody loud. Our nightcap had turned into nightcaps, and the time had really got away from us. I muscled my way through the heaving dance floor to him and pointed to the time on my phone.

'Sshhit. Whitey'll be crossh wiff ussh!' he spluttered, his shiny forehead dripping with sweat.

We politely finished our drinks before leaving the pumping party to return to the campsite. It was dead quiet. The Big Girl was resting and Whitey was sound asleep in his tent. It had been over twelve hours since our first drink by the pool, and now that we had left the crowd and music behind we were bloody tired. I flopped down on top of my swag fully clothed and passed out. Wegs got the first half of his body into his tent and did the same. It was lights out for us.

Five minutes later I felt Whitey's shoe in my ribs. I opened one eye and looked up at him. I wanted to protest but no words would come out. I was too tired to argue.

'For the last time, GET UP!' he roared. Slowly I dragged my heavy body to my feet.

I grabbed my bedding and clambered into the back seat of the Big Girl and made myself comfortable.

I watched out the window as Whitey stormed over to Wegs and repeatedly booted him in the backside while issuing the same aggressive instructions. His ranting and raving had little impact, so Whitey wrapped his large man-hands around Wegs' ankles and dragged him over to the passenger door of the Big Girl.

'Whitey . . . I'm gunna belt you.' Wegs delivered his hollow threat with a tired smile.

'Shut up you fool and get in the bloody car!'

I giggled a drunken giggle to myself before resting my head on my pillow.

'For the last time, GET OUT!' screamed Whitey through the window. I looked at him and slowly he and the surroundings came into focus. I had passed out in the car and now we were in Pamplona. Wegs was still asleep in the front seat, mouth open.

It took us a few minutes to remove ourselves from our warm and comfortable seats. During this time Whitey had extracted the gear we needed for the day and packed it into a small backpack. It had been decided last night that Wegs would be the only runner. The run wasn't as important to Whitey and me, so we put our hands up to film and take photos. Given the way I was feeling this morning I wasn't at all concerned I was going to miss the run. Anyway, I don't like running much. I find it tiring.

We dropped Wegs off at the start of the course, and Whitey and I moved off to fight our way through the heavy crowds heading to the arena. We wanted a good position to film the end of the run so we split up and took seats on either side of the bullring to get opposing perspectives. Our late arrival meant we didn't have to wait long before the first of the runners entered the arena. The first to enter the ring are booed by the crowd for being cowards; they are so far in front that often they have entered the arena before the bulls have even been released. Most of the early guys just do it for a cheap laugh and run in with their hands in the air as if they have won a footrace. I was recording every wave of runners hoping that some bulls, and Wegs, would soon appear. It was a difficult task as my sangria-fuelled body was shaking violently, and I was feeling dizzy from having to concentrate. I drink well. I recover badly.

Soon there was a sense of urgency amongst the entering runners. Gone were the guys running in casually and looking around the arena for friends. They were replaced by a wave of people looking apprehensively over their shoulders as they ran flat out. The crowds made it impossible for them to see beyond their immediate surrounds, so the majority of runners were actually running from imaginary bulls. I delighted in watching these panic-stricken entrants enter the arena only to realise that there was not a bull within one hundred feet of them. Cowards! I thought to myself from the stands.

I had become a bit savvy with the camera and had stopped recording every false alarm, but I was quick to hit the record button when I caught sight of a wave of red and white runners breaking the sound barrier. These guys were genuinely shitting themselves, and with good reason – behind them two angry black bulls thundered through the entry tunnel and into the arena. The packed bullring moved as one as frightened runners toppled over the perimeter fence and into the sanctuary of the crowd. To everyone's relief, a couple of matadors entered and distracted the incensed beasts out of the ring before they did some serious damage.

It wasn't going to be easy to find Wegs in the large and bustling crowd. I scanned the arena but my eyes were sore and focused poorly after looking through the camera for the previous hour. Wegs looks Spanish with his dark hair and bushy eyebrow, and with thousands of people all wearing the same traditional colours it was futile. I gave up and decided to head back to the car for our scheduled rendezvous.

It was early afternoon when we arrived back at camp in the Big Girl. The camping ground was pretty deserted as most people were still in Pamplona waiting for buses to bring them home. We hurriedly packed up our tents, tidied up our rubbish and drove over to the El Molino office to pay our bill. I left the boys to deal with the paperwork as I wanted to do one last thing before our departure. I wanted to say goodbye to Loren. I headed towards the ever-busy pool area to have a look around. As I wandered through the packed cafe a hand grabbed me by the arm and I turned around to see Loren's smiling face before me.

'Hey, sweetie,' she said, with her cute South African lilt. She leant forward and gave me a strong kiss on the lips.

'Hey, there.' I was surprised to find her so quickly. 'We're heading off now. We've decided to hit the road. I just wanted to come and say goodbye.'

'Right now?'

'Yep.' I explained that we just had to leave. Our bodies simply couldn't handle another night of abuse and we didn't trust ourselves. We didn't seem able to avoid a party.

We stood closely together saying our goodbyes. She was four or five back from the front of a long queue at the BBQ and stood on a step in front of me. She looked gorgeous in her floral bikini and we shared a long goodbye kiss.

As the kiss progressed I could sense that my attraction for Loren had registered downstairs. Rather unfortunately, I had chosen that day to wear my board shorts without underwear. As my shorts tightened I began to panic. The romantic farewell had created a difficult conundrum. Do I pull away from our final kiss and offend Loren, or do I risk the embarrassment of a dozen strangers witnessing my full appreciation for her? I chose to continue the kiss. Surely if I didn't think about it the swelling would just go away. Who was I kidding? It just made things worse. After a minute or so we pulled away from one another.

'Seeya, sweets,' was her parting offering.

I can't remember what I said in reply. I wasn't thinking straight. Now that the kiss had ended I had to face the cold hard reality of my situation. I released Loren's hand and took a deep breath to calm myself before heading off. I forced myself to suppress the desire to run and hide. I am a man, as was plain for all to see, and real men take responsibility for their actions. So,

I walked straight-faced past the remainder of the lunch queue and through the crowded cafe, with the most public and highly inappropriate erection of my life.

I didn't turn around to wave a final goodbye to Loren in case I cleared one of the tables. I was sure she would understand. Goodbyes are always hard.

5: A DEFLATING EXPERIENCE

'Ticketa.'

'Sorry. Don't have one, mate,' Wegs calmly informed the intrigued toll officer, who had leant out of his booth to look down into the Big Girl. I'm not sure if he was bemused because Wegs was a passenger instead of a driver, or by the fact that we were in a hearse.

'Ticketa!' he repeated.

'We just got on, back there. We got on at Avee-r-ios? Avee-ros? Av-eer-ios?'

'Ticketa!' he repeated sternly.

'Pass me the map, Whitey.' Wegs was getting flustered. In a bid to explain why we didn't have the required ticket, he wanted to show the officer where we had recently entered the N1 motorway in northern Portugal. He found the town on the map and showed the officer.

'Ave-rio . . . ? Av-ireo . . . ? Aveiro!' said Wegs, pointing furiously at the map as he struggled with the pronunciation. He was getting testy, still tired from the rigours of Pamplona and the two long days in the car since.

The officer then barked something in rapid Portuguese, which was met by silence. It was Wegs' turn to furrow his brow and cock his head to one side. They looked blankly at each other as they shared the same thought: what the *fuck* is this bloke talking about?

They both held this thought for some time.

'No-a-ticket?' The officer finally appeared to understand Wegs and pressed a button on his computer that flashed the toll up on the screen in front of us.

'Fifty euros!' Wegs was outraged. We'd only crossed into Portugal from Spain half an hour ago. He was fining us for not having the ticket from the previous tollbooth to present here for payment, but this was the first tollbooth we'd encountered since joining the N1 and we genuinely had no ticket. The toll systems between Spain and Portugal were obviously very different. The language barrier, however, was the same.

'No-a-ticket!' the officer said, pointing vehemently to the inflated figure on his screen. He too was getting flustered, as a long line of cars stacked up behind us.

It was a hopeless situation. He was explaining his position in Portuguese, and Wegs was explaining our position in English. We had reached a stalemate.

'We-a-saw-no-a-tollbooth,' Wegs tried to reason in Portuguese.

The officer replied with a torrent of waving arms. He'd lost his patience. He pointed back and forward and yelled at Wegs. The slanging match continued as Wegs yelled back at volume.

'Averio? Avireo? AVEIRO! NO-A-TOLLBOOTH!' Wegs

roared, a vein bulging in his neck.

We had no choice but to pay the fine and move on. Fifty euros was a lot of money to us. We operated on a shoestring budget, and with nothing to show in return this charge was aggravating to say the least, especially when we'd not been at fault. The boys were swearing angrily and, sensing the tension, I prepared a round of sardine sandwiches to lighten the mood. The culinary delight soon removed the bitter taste of our financial misfortune and we settled back into cruise-mode on the N1 heading towards Lisbon.

However, the tension returned as we confronted another tollbooth half an hour later. There was apprehension within the Big Girl. What would happen? Would they fine us again? Would Wegs converse at volume? I didn't think I could survive another painful exchange. At least we had a bloody ticket this time.

Whitey manoeuvred the Big Girl into the only lane of the five without a queue, and slowed down from fifty miles an hour to around twenty as he approached. I could see the uniformed attendant lean over in preparation for our arrival. Moments later I saw him imitating a sideshow clown. With eyes wide open and mouth agape he watched helplessly as our long black hearse sailed regally through his post. I was as shocked as he was, but waved to him cheerily, out of instinct.

'Take it off the tab, fellas!' Whitey yelled back over his shoulder and raised two fingers in the air.

Wegs and I were dumbfounded by Whitey's nonchalant drive-by, made possible by the lack of boom gates at the toll point. This action was most out of character for the conservative Whitey.

It reminded me of our funeral drive-by back in Ireland. The conservative and unflappable Whitey had shown that, if pushed, he could push back. It just took a bit more pushing than most.

I looked back to see if anyone had given chase, but the coast was clear. We'd taken the law into our hands, run the gauntlet and survived. Should we be questioned or detained by the authorities then, as in Paris, a plea of ignorance would be the cornerstone of our defence. Nobody could disprove that.

'Ticketa?' mocked Wegs, and we burst into laughter.

This was a small victory for our financially embattled unit, for we now had some return on our fifty-euro investment. The self-administered justice called for a celebration, so I delved into the car fridge and again called upon the most decadent product we had at our disposal: sardine sandwiches.

As we cruised along I gazed blankly out the large rear window, my hair blowing freely in the strong wind. The road noise was loud with the windows down and, without any competition from the stereo or chattering voices, it was pleasant.

We soon passed through a mountain range and the wind delivered a familiar scent. This time it was cool and refreshing and not warm and reeking of second-hand sardines. It was sinus clearing as opposed to room clearing – and there was no giggling coming from the front seat. Eucalyptus? The context was completely wrong, so it took me a while before I recognised we were passing through commercial blue-gum plantations. Here I was driving through eucalyptus plantations as a tourist, in a hearse, in Portugal, as opposed to driving through them as a manager, in a 4WD, in Australia.

The invigorating air rushing in the open window combined with the gliding motion of the Big Girl into a strangely therapeutic mix, and we drifted off into our own personal headspaces for an hour or two as we progressed slowly along the fast-moving motorway. I like these moments. I've always been a daydreamer.

The blue gums flicked hypnotically before me, stimulating a long and involved daydream. It was one of those detailed and complex visions that sit on the fence between the conscious and subconscious mind; comprised of jumbled and illogical images, yet delivering its message with absolute clarity. This particular vision delivered a new objective for our burgeoning adventure. It now seemed obvious that we should take the Big Girl home with us, to Australia. I returned from my trance-like state and decided to keep the idea to myself for a while. I would tell the boys later. It wasn't the right time: we had no beer.

❀ ❀ ❀

Later that day we drove into the windy coastal township of Cascais, about half an hour west of Lisbon. I was forced to pilot the Big Girl with the steering wheel at forty-five degrees because the wind howling off the Atlantic tried to push her out of her lane. Despite the ferocious breeze the relaxed vibe of Cascais appealed to us. We pulled into a camping ground opposite the main beach and hired a small bungalow for a few nights. It was time to set up camp and consolidate our washing, and our sleep. The Big Girl was also in desperate need of some care and attention.

We unpacked the entire contents of the Big Girl and sprawled everything out on the lawn in front of our bungalow. Whitey took control of the laundry, Wegs went indoors to prepare some food and I set about cleaning and repacking the dishevelled Big Girl. We worked well as a team.

A couple of hours later Whitey sat beside me on the edge of our small porch. His long limbs touched the grass below, while mine dangled freely.

'Good work, Mum,' I said to him, admiring his domestic handiwork.

'Ha ha, not bad though is it?' Whitey replied, proudly. He had just finished hanging out our washing on the world's longest makeshift clothesline. The temporary structure was tied at one end to the flower racks on top of the Big Girl and, at the other end, to a tree branch. In between it was looped around verandah posts, a power pole, a window latch and several tree branches. The zigzagging length of cord was probably twenty metres long and colourfully adorned with two weeks' worth of team washing. Our mothers would've been impressed. My mum would've been doubly impressed by the fact it was also such a perfect 'drying day'.

'Impressive!' Wegs had emerged, beers in hand, to join us on the porch. 'Good work, mate.'

'About time too. The man odours were getting a bit much,' said Whitey, referring to our stinky laundry.

'Bloody oath. I was starting to recycle my jocks,' I added.

'Me too!' exclaimed Whitey. 'Sniff testing.'

'Don't know why you bother with them, fellas,' Wegs chimed

in, swigging on his beer. 'Waste of time.' He never wore underwear. Wegs, in his own words, liked to 'go commando'.

'Disgusting!' Whitey was not impressed.

'Why?' asked Wegs.

'Mate . . . it's just *wrong*,' I agreed. Like Whitey, I was not a fan of 'riding rough'. It was too breezy for my liking, and it made me feel vulnerable. Not only is the extra layer hygienic, it's also supportive. Loren had taught me that much.

Thankfully there was a pause in the conversation. I went inside and returned with more snacks and refreshments. I handed the boys a Corona each, complete with sliced lemon, and sat down between them. We sat side by side on the narrow timber porch, peering out underneath the laundry towards the roaring ocean. On the beach the last of the tired windsurfers packed away their gear, silhouetted against a crimson Atlantic sunset.

'Let's take the Big Girl home,' I blurted out to the boys.

My words were met by perfect silence, save for the gentle flapping of clothing overhead. We all continued to stare straight ahead. It was Whitey who spoke first.

'To Australia?'

'Yeah.'

'It's a bloody long way.'

'Yeah . . . and which way would we go?' Wegs queried.

'Dunno really. I was sort of thinking about heading through Russia to China and down through Asia. I don't really care. As long as we avoid the Middle East and any country ending in "stan".'

'Mmmm, good idea. I don't fancy Iraq much,' Whitey quipped.

'Can we drive all the way through Russia?' Wegs asked. 'Surely we couldn't drive through Siberia ... in winter. The engine would freeze.'

'Not if we kept the Big Girl running twenty-four/seven,' I said, without a lot of thought. No response from the boys. 'In all likelihood we won't be able to drive every step of the way. We'll have to improvise. Trains ... tractors ... boats ... donkeys. Fucked if I know really. Whatever it takes.'

The boys were directing all the questions to me, in much the same way that Whitey and I'd done to Wegs back in Dublin, when we wanted to know more about hearses. I was about as much an authority on driving through Siberia and across the world as Wegs had been about the specifics of funeral vehicles. It was nothing we couldn't work out in good time though, I reckoned.

'It's going to need a shitload of planning, which I'm guessing won't be done,' Whitey said.

'Yeah, probably not. A minor detail,' Wegs conceded dismissively, with a wave of the hand.

'And how are we going to get all the way back to Australia without a *jack*?' Whitey added, smirking as he awaited our predictable response.

'Another minor detail.' I looked at Wegs and we shook our heads, smiling. Whitey was still going on about the bloody car jack. It had become a battle to see who would give in first.

'Well, it will either work or it won't,' Whitey accepted. 'Some of us might run out of money before then though . . .'

❀ ❀ ❀

After three days in Cascais we hit the A2 motorway for the five-hour drive south to Lagos, refreshed and ready to take on all that lay ahead of us. Lagos was an old town on the Algarve that we'd heard a lot about from fellow travellers. It had a reputation for golden beaches and a lively nightlife, and catered for young backpackers with a host of cheap hotels and camp sites, in con-trast to the large holiday resorts lining the coast outside of town. This relaxed young vibe appealed to us, being too young, slim and non-English to contemplate a package-holiday resort. We were looking forward to checking out Lagos.

And check it out we did. Four days later our bodies were beginning to resemble the same battle-weary ones that had departed Pamplona, and we simply had to leave. We had spent four solid nights frequenting the likes of the Red Eye Bar, Whytes Pub and Phoenix Club. It had been a non-stop party that was only interrupted by our daily recovery swim in the freezing cold Atlantic Ocean. It was fun, but it was time to go. The late nights had once again taken their toll.

On the final morning I awoke as I'd done the previous three mornings – in a pool of sweat in my swag. We hadn't arrived back at the camp site before 5 a.m. from our nights out on the town, which invariably resulted in me waking up to the hot Por-tuguese sun beating down on me. Adding to my discomfort was the fact that I had not managed, on any of the nights, to actually take my clothes off before climbing into my swag. I would wake up literally in a canvas oven, sweating like a bastard.

When I got up on our final morning I noticed that Whitey was already awake and sitting in his camp chair at the rear of the Big Girl. It took a little while for my pupils to adjust to the harsh light but I could see that he was grinning.

'What's so funny?' I enquired as I opened the boot of the Big Girl.

'Oh, you'll see.' he replied.

Not through these eyes I won't, I thought to myself. I had caught sight of my reflection in the back window and I looked dreadful. My hair was all over the place and my eyes were like piss-holes in the snow. I grabbed a bottle of water from the rear of the Big Girl and tipped it down my dry throat. No sooner had the water hit my lips that I spat the near-boiling liquid out. It was definitely the worst start to a day I'd ever experienced. I was hot and bothered, tired and still very drunk. I sat down in the shade of a tree and prepared myself for the onset of a ripping hangover. Just as I felt death approaching, something made me feel immeasurably better: Wegs.

Wegs stuck his head out of his tent to greet the new day. And I thought I looked bad! He was sweating profusely, his face was bright red and his eyes were even narrower than mine. He looked like he'd been stung by a swarm of bees. Staggering to his feet he moved to the back of the car, feeling his way with outstretched hands. He located the same water bottle I'd found and repeated my actions of a few minutes ago. Then he sat down next to me, equally unimpressed with the day so far. Still Whitey grinned.

'What are you laughing at?' Wegs asked.

Whitey grinned and pointed.

'Aaahh, fuck it!' Wegs and I yelled in unison. Whitey was pointing at a flat rear tyre.

'Who's eminently more sensible now?' asked Whitey rhetorically. 'Won't get flats, hey?' he added smugly.

This was inconvenient to say the least. Wegs and I had tempted fate by not buying the car jack in Calais. Deep down I always knew we needed a jack because getting a flat tyre was inevitable, but it was just so much fun for Wegs and me to watch Whitey get upset when we dismissed him every time he'd suggest getting one. The shoe was on the other foot now and we would pay dearly for our stupidity.

Wegs and I set to work changing the tyre. The only tool we had with us was a cheap all-in-one gadget that we'd bought in Ireland. It had a whole raft of impractical applications, but fortunately it did have an adjustable spanner at one end. Wegs used this spanner to make a start on the wheel nuts. It was futile. The hopeless tool was too small and weak for the job. We would have to approach this problem another way.

While Wegs and I sat staring blankly at the flat tyre Whitey had begun recording the moment on his video camera, which he had set up on the tripod facing him. He pressed record and sat back down in his chair, cracked a beer and started talking to the camera.

'I'm sitting here drinking beer because we have a flat tyre, and even though I had my hand on a jack in Calais I was told not to buy it because we won't get flats, and if we do, then these two, being Wegs and Dav, will fix it, while I sit here and drink beer. Which is exactly what I'm doing!'

'Whitey . . .' I started.

'Whitey . . .' Wegs started.

'Shut up!' we finished.

He raised his can and winked.

'Cheers, boys.'

It took two hours, but Wegs and I successfully changed the tyre of a three-tonne 1985 Ford Granada hearse, with a car jack borrowed from a one-tonne 2002 Renault coupé – no small feat.

As Wegs and I rested our sweaty and fatigued bodies, we were forced to acknowledge that we'd learnt an important lesson. If we seriously planned to get the Big Girl back to Australia, then we would have to avoid getting flat tyres when we had hangovers. It was just too hard.

DAV WEGS WHITEY

6: EASY DAYS

Leaving Portugal and the Atlantic we headed inland to Seville and across southern Spain towards Marbella and the Mediterranean Sea. The trip took a couple of days as we nursed the Big Girl along in temperatures hovering above forty degrees Celsius. We regularly stopped to rest in the shade of an olive tree in one of the numerous groves we passed. It was a preventative measure that allowed us to enjoy the delightful, yet harsh, rural surroundings of the region. The black exterior of the Big Girl was too hot to touch during these stops, and I regret we didn't try to fry an egg on the bonnet. I've always wanted to do that.

It wasn't just the bodywork that was hot. We regularly burnt ourselves on the interior metal trimmings and vinyl seats. Dressed only in board shorts, our every move was fraught with danger. Exposing bare skin to parts of the boiling hot seats or resting an arm on the steel coffin rollers regularly had us squealing like kids. Eventually we placed towels beneath us to prevent being burnt and also to mop up the relentless sweat we were producing. Even with the windows down the conditions inside the Big Girl were sauna-like. Unlike Wegs and Whitey, I'm not normally known for my sweating; however, as I sat in the front of the Big Girl with no air conditioning, I was sweating for Australia. Sweat was running down my forehead and dripping off my eyebrows, accumulating on my upper lip, flowing down the insides of my arms, pooling in my lower back and streaming down the back of my legs. The towel covering my seat was nearly soaked through. Wegs and Whitey were on their second towels. The Mediterranean could not come quickly enough.

The profuse sweating and the stifling heat inside the Big Girl had finally addled Wegs' brain. While sitting in the back seat waiting for Whitey to return from refuelling the Big Girl, he started to think of ways to improve our comfort.

'I think we need a bigger sunroof, Dav. This one's too small.'

It was a ridiculous suggestion. We'd installed our current sunroof at great cost and installing a larger one would just be an unnecessary expense. I was surprised by his suggestion. It wasn't odd for Wegs to come up with a stupid idea, but it was odd for him to suggest a stupid idea that would cost a lot of money. I deemed his suggestion unworthy of a reply.

'Actually,' Wegs continued, thinking aloud, 'when we get back to Darwin, I reckon we should remove this whole top section and make it a convertible.'

I turned around to shoot Wegs a disapproving look, expecting him to be grinning stupidly. Instead he was clambering around the back of the Big Girl, tapping away at the supporting arms of the fibreglass canopy.

'Yep. It'd be a piece of piss. We could do it in four cuts with a

chainsaw. Imagine that, a convertible hearse.' He was dead serious. The heat was making the poor bloke delirious.

'That is, without doubt, the single most *stupid* idea I have
ever heard!' I looked Wegs straight in the eye.

'Piss off. It's not as stupid as your theory on running the Big
Girl twenty-four/seven through Siberia – *that* was fuckin' ridiculous!' he countered. Bugger, he had a bloody good point. Wegs
had trumped me with my own stupidity. Cheeky bastard.

Mercifully, Whitey's return stopped this conversation from
reaching an all-time intellectual low. He jumped back in behind
the wheel and passed a large cardboard box over to me. I opened
it to see a shiny new car jack with a sticker proclaiming its three-
tonne rating. I turned to Whitey.

'Stop. I don't want to hear one bloody word from you fools,'
said Whitey grinning. 'This jack business has gone on for long
enough.' He was wagging his big finger at me and looking at
Wegs through the rear-view mirror.

We departed the small township in silence before laughter
broke out when Whitey saw a small sign by the side of the road.
It informed us that we had just left the small Spanish village of
Moron.

❀ ❀ ❀

The Mediterranean was a welcome sight. This was the first
time we'd seen the sea that we had heard so much about. The
Big Girl was particularly relieved as the big blue swimming
pool revealed itself from our position high in the mountains.
She stopped her continual moaning and audibly sighed as she

began to coast down hill for the first time that day. Reaching the top of this gruelling climb in the oppressive heat had been a great accomplishment by the graceful old lady, and I rubbed the dashboard supportively.

'Well done, Big Girl.'

Once again our faithful chariot had pulled her weight, literally. Below us was a shimmering concrete blob – Marbella – our beachside destination and resting point for the Big Girl. I hoped it was not a mirage. When we wheeled into town half an hour later my opinion had changed; now I wished it had been a mirage. The concrete metropolis that presented itself was not the exotic Mediterranean town we had dreamed about during the sweltering journey from Seville. The town had a contrived and tasteless feel about it and the waterfront was littered with characterless buildings as far as the eye could see. It reeked of package holidays. We decided we would stay only long enough to rest the Big Girl, have a long overdue swim and tend to some emails. This wasn't really our sort of place.

Emerging from our refreshing dip in the salty Mediterranean water we were treated to the horrific site of fat, bald men swanning along the beach in speedos, dick togs and lolly bags. There was not a topless chick in sight. We dried off quickly and left these guys to show off their wares. This was definitely not our sort of place.

We found a funky Internet cafe one street back from the beach to attend to personal correspondence. Some interesting emails grabbed my attention, pushing the unpleasant mental image of middle-aged men in brief swimwear out of my mind.

The first one I opened was from the editor of *TNT*, a popular travel magazine in London inviting me to audition for their weekly 'On the Road' column. She wrote that one of their photographers had mentioned us to her and that *TNT* was fascinated by the concept of three guys travelling around in a hearse. I vaguely remembered a conversation with a bloke named Rob, a *TNT* photographer, at the bar one night at El Molino. Poor bloke, I probably bored him to death with my drunken sangria ramblings. I had forgotten the conversation entirely until this email jogged my memory. Rob, true to his word, had forwarded our details.

This was an exciting development as we all had friends in London who would enjoy following our exploits in their weekly travel bible, *TNT*. I immediately replied that I would be delighted to apply. I had two weeks to draft an audition article. I thought that should be plenty of time, although I'd never written before. How hard could it be?

After sending the obligatory emails to family and friends we climbed aboard the freshly detailed Big Girl in high spirits, and steered her towards the open road once again. Our rough plan was to skirt the Mediterranean all the way to Barcelona, before heading inland to the tax-free shopping haven of Andorra, where we hoped to right a significant wrong by replacing our stolen stereo. After all, a road trip is not a road trip without bad eighties music.

DAV WEGS WHITEY

7: GUANDONG-STYLE CHICKEN WITH CASHEW NUTS

As the crow flies, the distance from the alpine perch of Andorra to the almost sea-level township of Montpellier is only a couple of hundred kilometres. Despite this, our descent from the Pyrenees had taken most of the day. The day had started slowly, waiting for a young apprentice to fit our new car stereo, and continued slowly as the Big Girl negotiated the tight, winding roads around Andorra. These roads demanded cautious and patient driving at all times, but we were being even more careful as the Big Girl had been running very roughly. We nursed her along as she coughed and spluttered her way down the mountain, concerned she may have a serious problem. It was the same problem that had surfaced on our way up to Andorra, a few days earlier.

Mysteriously, as we entered the foothills of the Pyrenees, the problem disappeared. Now that we were out of the mountains the Big Girl was back running on all cylinders, much to our relief. Given our lack of mechanical knowledge, it was impossible to pinpoint the exact cause of the problem. Our best guess, after initially blaming the alternator (the only engine part we all knew), was that the Big Girl was struggling in the thin, high-altitude air. We understood enough about cars to realise that, like humans, they need sufficient oxygen to operate properly. Whatever the cause, we soon forgot about the Big Girl's problems, and focused on our need to refuel. We were all starving.

Our ultimate destination for the day was Nice. Normally when we still had a distance to travel we chose to eat on the run; however, it had been a tiring and stressful day on the road so we opted to stop and sit down for dinner. We pulled into a well-patronised Chinese restaurant on the outskirts of Montpellier, very glad to get out of the car.

We took a table outside and perused the extensive Chinese menu, written in French.

'Reckon they do sweet'n'sour bolognaise here, mate?' I asked Whitey.

'Probably. I hear it's a pretty popular dish,' Wegs interjected, knowing I was having a dig at him. Wegs had cooked an improvised spaghetti bolognaise using a sweet and sour sauce on our last night in Dublin, to use up the remnants of our pantry cupboard. It had tasted absolutely disgusting. Even Wegs couldn't eat it.

'I doubt it. Cor, that was fuckin' terrible,' recalled Whitey. Although he was the only one to actually eat, and finish, the experimental dish. The big fella would eat anything if he was hungry.

It was at least half an hour before a busy waitress came to take our orders. Wegs eventually succeeded in placing an order by pointing at meals on other tables that looked desirable. He then pointed randomly to a chicken dish on the specials page of the menu for himself. The waitress nodded and ran off to the kitchen; she was working alone and, judging by the speed at which things were operating that evening, she was the chef as well.

Normally a leisurely experience like this would not concern us, but tonight we'd stopped for just a break and a quick bite, as we still had some miles to travel. The meals, when they finally arrived, were of a remarkably poor quality and small quantity, given the length of time they'd taken to prepare and serve. After a three-hour dining ordeal we eventually said our farewells to Lee Lim, the busy Chinese waitress who had fussed over every detail except the actual delivery of the meal. We were still hungry.

'Gracias and adiós,' I thanked her in perfect Spanish, continuing my annoying habit of speaking the language of the previous country for at least the first two days after our arrival in the new one.

After dinner we refuelled the Big Girl and purchased some additional road-trip snacks (potato chips, chocolate, Coke) for the drive down the N7 to Nice. Four hundred kilometres is a long way to drive in a day when you're travelling in a hearse, irrespective of delays along the way. It was just after midnight when we arrived in Nice, much to Whitey's disgust as it meant we would have to sleep the night in the Big Girl. We went in search of a safe area to free-camp in town, instead of heading to a hotel.

When we arrived in a city late at night, we would often sleep

Eurotunnel officials John the Geordie and
Thierry the Frenchy with Dav the Aussie

The Big Girl's scratched duco after
her violation, Calais

The Big Girl high in the Pyrenees, Andorra

'*Ticketa*' demands the enraged
Portuguese toll officer

Whitey makes the most of a great
'drying day'— Cascais, Portugal

Dav, Whitey and the Big Girl, France

Relaxing at a French camping ground

Wegs struggles with the Big Girl's tight
wheelnuts – Lagos, Portugal

Finally the last stubborn wheelnut gives way

Two hours later a sweaty Wegs and Dav
complete their arduous task

Dav at the helm, Spain

Whitey in undertaker mode in the back of the Big Girl, France

Whitey navigates with beer in hand, France

An incriminating photo from the 'watermelon incident', Nice

Wegs cruising, Nice

Whitey cools off, Marbella

Servicing the Big Girl, Naples

Dav in his best 'Top Gun' pose, Sorrento

A romantic dinner by candlelight, La Barca

Posing for a team photo for *TNT* magazine, La Barca

Whitey cooks a bbq as 'Huckleberry Finn' wets a line in the background, La Barca

Caught in the act, Rome

Cruising in the Big Girl, Italy

Wegs gets a budget haircut, Athens

An annoyed Wegs at the
Romanian Embassy, Athens

Vertigo kicks in 2900 metres up
Mt Olympus, Greece

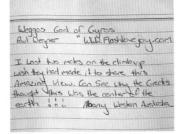

Wegs' logbook entry at the
summit of Mt Olympus

A useless Dav watches the helpful Mick – Skopje, Macedonia

in the car. Wegs preferred to do this because he thought there was little value in paying for a hotel room to sleep only for a few hours. He loved to save money on accommodation. I didn't fancy it much. Whitey, as a large man, hated it. But as we were on a tight budget, we begrudgingly accepted that it would happen on occasion.

'If you hadn't ordered your bloody Guandong-style chicken with cashew nuts we would have got here early enough to find a cheap hotel,' Whitey complained.

'Mate, blame Lee bloody Lim, not me. How was I to know the chicken had to come from China?' Wegs responded.

I was in the front seat navigating under the dim glow provided by the Big Girl's interior lights. These small lights ran the entire length of the hearse; the lights in the front were much weaker than the rear ones, which lit up the coffin platform, and any occupants, brightly. Tonight it was Whitey who was on display and lit up like a Christmas tree as we rolled past the airport towards Nice.

I had the window down in the front as I stared hard at the map. As we got closer to Nice the warm air began to taste salty and, even though it was too dark to see clearly, I could sense that the Mediterranean was just a stone's throw to our right.

A few kilometres from the centre of Nice we spotted a vacant car park that seemed well suited to a free camp in the Big Girl. It was quiet enough to get some peace, dark enough (once curtains were drawn) to sleep, yet light enough to feel safe and secure. Perfect. Wegs backed the Big Girl up to the wall in the far corner of the lot and killed the engine.

We were well drilled in this procedure and within five minutes we were all tucked up in our respective sleeping bags, in our respective positions. Wegs was in the reclined driver's seat, Whitey was in the reclined passenger's seat, and I was in my swag up on the coffin platform with my head at the rear of the car. Up front I could hear Whitey groaning and complaining under his breath as he shuffled around trying to get comfortable. The front seats needed a couple of well-placed towels, otherwise the springs in the worn seats would stab painfully into the groin area. It wasn't exactly a bed of feathers up on the coffin platform either. Six large coffin rollers, like domestic rolling pins, were embedded in the platform and prodded through the thin mattress, at my feet, knees, waist and, for good measure, in my ribs. It was more of a tolerable resting position than a comfortable sleeping position. I had to be very tired to be able to sleep when free-camping.

That particular night we must have been very tired, as it was nearly daylight when I was awoken by Wegs winding down his window. As I slowly came to my senses I detected a strange odour. In the front Wegs was tossing and turning, and when I heard his stomach growl angrily I knew instantly what the odour was: Guandong-style chicken with cashew nuts.

Whitey was awake now and had begun sniffing his own armpits.

'Geez, few man-odours getting around,' he observed, his bones cracking as he stretched out.

Finding a hotel was an immediate priority. Whitey needed a shower, Wegs needed a toilet, I needed a soft bed and the Big

Girl needed some fresh air. We drove out of the car park and headed for the sunbathed Promenade des Anglais, the wide road lined with palm trees that hugs the rocky beaches fronting the Mediterranean and runs straight through central Nice.

It was early in the morning but the street was already alive with shiny convertibles and scooters, and the footpaths awash with joggers and roller-bladers dodging for position. Beneath the palm fronds and through the traffic the sun glistened ominously off the millpond Mediterranean. It was going to be a warm one and I was keen to park the Big Girl and find a nice airconditioned hotel room.

From the Promenade I turned down a narrow street that took us to a large open space with impressive water fountains, encircled by chaotic laneways and roads. The guidebook informed us we were in the heart of Espace Masséna, but to reach the hotel precinct near the train station we needed to head up Nice's main shopping street, Avenue Jean Médecin.

Wegs was complaining loudly, as he always does when he's slightly ill. I may fight young defenceless girls with hammers but I'm tough when I'm sick. Wegs is not a good patient. I reckon his mum spoilt him when he was young. I could just imagine him as a child, too 'sick' to attend school, sitting up in his bed watching television and ringing a little bell for his mother to come and refresh his bowl of ice-cream. Never mind, we would just have to find a hotel without our accommodation specialist, who we left slouching in the back seat of the Big Girl. This was fine by Whitey and me, it allowed us to escape his moaning and preliminary bowel movements.

It was at least two hours before Whitey and I returned to the Big Girl. It had taken us longer than expected to find a hotel that was within our budget, and that had a vacancy. On our third try we found the affordable Hotel Belle Meunière on Avenue Durante, near the train station. Opposite the hotel was a neat little Internet cafe and we dropped in for a coffee and cake, and a cursory email check. Time had got away from us, and when we returned to the car Wegs was nowhere to be seen.

It was unusual for Wegs to move an inch when he was feeling unwell. Then I noticed him lying beside another car a few metres away, hugging a pot plant for dear life. We rushed over just as he let fly with a torrent of chicken and cashew nuts into the neatly potted petunias. Wegs is a particularly loud vomiter and this latest gush caught the attention of some alfresco diners nearby. They looked up from their omelettes with disdain. I'm sure they thought he was dying, or perhaps they were just willing him to hurry up and do so; they certainly didn't appear to be prepared to help the poor vagrant lying in the gutter. Once the convulsions had eased Wegs looked up. Tears were streaming down his gaunt and pale face and he had a couple of flecks of vomit on his chin.

'Where the fuck have you blokes been?' he spluttered. It was clear it wasn't just his stomach that was upset. He was angry and slightly delirious, but relieved that we'd returned to help.

He wiped his chin with the back of his hand and got to his feet. He walked gingerly over to the car, his gait indicated that his food poisoning had progressed to the stage when every action was fraught with danger. One sudden movement could result in a terribly sticky situation. We had to get Wegs to a toilet, fast.

Back at the hotel Wegs grabbed the key and waddled towards our room, leaving Whitey and me to deal with the luggage. In a cruel twist of fate our hotel actually had an ensuite, instead of the shared facilities usually found in our standard of accommodation. This was a pleasant revelation for Wegs, but given that the extraction fan didn't work, a fairly unpleasant one for Whitey and me. It was an hour before an emaciated Wegs emerged from the bathroom to join us, shaking his head.

'Not pretty, fellas. Not pretty at all.'

'Yeah. We could hear!' said Whitey.

'So, where were you blokes?' Wegs wanted answers. He held us responsible for his misfortune, despite the fact we were acting purely in the interests of the team by organising the hotel. It was hardly beer and skittles for us either.

'Having a latte and cheesecake,' I answered truthfully, knowing it would give him the shits.

Which it did.

● ● ●

By the following morning a state of equilibrium had returned to our embattled team. We joined the refreshed Big Girl in the car park and headed off to Cannes for the day, arguing the entire drive about whether Cannes was pronounced *Can, Cans, Carn* or *Carns*. There was no definitive resolution to the argument and we stubbornly continued to call it by our preferred interpretation. It didn't really matter though, as everyone we'd met, the French included, pronounced it differently. For the record though, I reckon it's *Carn*.

Cannes was unlike any other place we'd ever seen. It positively reeked of money, and lots of it. It was the sort of place that made country boys like us realise that the local car dealer back home was actually not the wealthiest man in the world. We parked the Big Girl adjacent to Vieux Port, and set off on foot to tour the impressive marina and waterfront, gawking at the huge yachts bobbing before us.

'Wouldn't fancy backing that down a boat ramp, mate,' I commented, as we passed by *IRS*, a yacht from the Caymans.

'Yeah, might struggle,' Wegs responded.

IRS wasn't a boat or, by definition, probably not a yacht either. It was more like a small ship. On board it had a helicopter, two speed boats, half a dozen jet skis and a crew of around ten people immaculately decked out in white uniforms. I couldn't even begin to guess how large this boat, yacht or ship was. It was huge, and what was most amazing was that it was just one of about twenty similar vessels, moored side by side along the marina. It was Beverly Hills on water.

From the marina we wandered along the palm-lined Boulevard de la Croisette, a promenade that revealed the style and class of Cannes on land in the same way the marina had done on water. Expensive hotels lined the boulevard, expensive cars drove along the boulevard, and expensive people adorned the boulevard – present company excluded. As budget travellers, wandering along in board shorts, we were well and truly out of our league in this environment, without a designer label to bless ourselves.

'Fancy a dip?' Whitey offered.

'Yep, bloody oath,' I replied, and we walked the twenty metres to the water's edge, throwing our shirts on a deck chair en route. Watching people was hot work.

'Excuse me! Excuse me!' a waiter called out in perfect English. 'You can not swim here. This beach is for guests of the Grand Hotel *only*,' he said graciously enough, and pointed to the monolithic hotel over the road.

'Oh sorry, mate,' Wegs said. Someone owning a beach, or part of it, was a novel concept for us. As far as I'm aware, you don't need to be rich to use a beach in Australia.

'You may swim over there.' He waved us towards an overcrowded section of the beach, no larger than a postage stamp, before returning to serve his paying guests martinis, shaken not stirred.

Not being wealthy enough to swim was no great loss, as the Mediterranean is rarely the most pleasant bathing experience. I found the water tepid, salty and, around the resorts and coastal centres, of an unattractive appearance, like pre-loved bathwater. The attraction of this part of the world is more about what happens *along* the Mediterranean, not what happens *in* it.

I turned to the boys.

'We've *done* Cannes.'

'Yep.'

'Yep.'

We spent the afternoon back at our hotel's pool before heading to Cours Saleya in Vieux Nice and treating ourselves to an opulent seafood banquet for dinner. It was a balmy night, and we sat at a small table in the middle of a packed outdoor dining area, washing down our crayfish and oysters with some chilled Stella Artois. There were hundreds of tables and chairs in front of the numerous restaurants, cafes, pizzerias and bars that filled the cobblestoned street. It was difficult to tell where one restaurant finished and the other began. We often tried to gain the attention of waiters to refresh our rapidly disappearing drinks, only to find they were from the adjacent establishment.

Dining on the Cours Saleya was loud and colourful in a fun and relaxed way, and a great spot to tap into the vibe of Nice. There was an easy-going blend of students, locals and tourists, which was a contrast to the aristocratic air and pretension of Cannes. That's not to say Nice was without flair and style, it was just that Nice is to Cannes what Calvin Klein is to Versace.

Street buskers with guitars and violins stopped at tables and played romantic tunes for hand-holding couples. Strangely, these buskers would solicit the three of us for a request, and from nowhere ladies with baskets of roses would appear hot on their heels, trying to flog their romantic offerings. After the fourth combined approach I felt it best to interject in my politest French.

'Pardon. Je ne comprends pas.' Which I soon learnt was the wrong thing to say when trying to dismiss a pestering Frenchman or woman. Saying 'I don't understand' in perfectly delivered French actually achieves the opposite result, prompting the annoying touts to believe you *do understand* French, and continue their spiel even more enthusiastically.

'Non ménage à trois, non!' I delivered this with a strong shake of the head and it seemed to work, the musicians and rose-lady finally departed, laughing.

After dinner and a couple of wines we decided to head to Chez Waynes for a nightcap. Chez Waynes was a small bar nearby that was recommended in our guidebook as having a great atmosphere. It was renowned for its live bands and healthy mix of travellers and locals, which sounded like just the ticket for us. Tonight though, Whitey was feeling a little off-colour and he decided to head back to the hotel for an early night, leaving Wegs and me to tackle the glamour of Chez Waynes on our own. I could have done with an early night myself, but being a Friday I was keen to check out the local nightlife. I would just have a couple.

❀ ❀ ❀

I awoke to the sound of slamming doors, heavy breathing and stomping feet. I sat bolt upright in bed to see what all the commotion was about. Whitey was storming around the room, obviously quite worked up.

'What's up, mate?' I enquired with a furry tongue.

He swung around and looked wildly at me.

'You're fucking kidding aren't you?' he said in a level yet deliberate tone. It sent a chill up my spine. I'd never seen Whitey angry before. Wegs was now sitting up in bed.

'Consider this team reduced to two!' Whitey delivered this message with a finger firmly pointed at Wegs and me. Then he stormed out of the room, slamming the door.

I was in shock. I looked over at Wegs to gauge his reaction. He was in shock too, and we sat there in silence. Despite the seriousness of the situation I had to smirk when I noticed that Wegs' sheet had stuck to the side of his face and shoulder. There were also a smattering of watermelon pips stuck to his chest.

'What was all that about?' Wegs asked.

'Not sure.' I stood up to go to the bathroom and dragged my bedding onto the floor. Wegs laughed. My sheet had stuck to me also. I peeled it off my leg and tiptoed over the sticky floor to the bathroom.

The scene in the bathroom brought back vivid recollections of the previous night, and put Whitey's mood into some perspective. What lay before me couldn't have been achieved quietly. I called Wegs over to survey the damage. The bathroom was not as we left it last night. The sink was blocked, the bidet was blocked, the toilet was blocked and the bath was blocked – with watermelon. The walls, floor and mirror were also covered with watermelon.

On the way home from Chez Waynes, after more than a couple, Wegs and I had purchased two watermelons, initially bought for their nutritional benefit. However, once we returned to the hotel room something, and I couldn't say what, brought out the boarding-school boy in each of us, triggering a food fight of rather epic proportions. It had been largely, but not totally, confined to the bathroom.

'Mmmm.'

'Mmmm, indeed.'

Wegs and I immediately set to work cleaning up the results

of our wild night. Wegs tried to unblock the sink and bath by creating a makeshift plunger with his hands. I was very sceptical but his lateral approach worked like a charm. Sadly this approach couldn't be applied to the toilet so I was forced to place a bread bag over my arm and unblock it manually. This did not go down well with a hangover. I sensed I was being taught a lesson.

Two hours later Wegs and I had cleaned the bathroom to an acceptable level. We'd also showered and freshened ourselves up so that things were no longer sticking to us. In reality the cleaning of the bathroom was the least of our concerns. We had a far more important problem to resolve: Whitey.

Wegs and I left the hotel room and went in search of a cafe for lunch. Over coffee and baguettes we had a crisis meeting about our situation. Whitey had sounded very serious this morning and his comment about the team being reduced to two worried us. Whitey is a particularly stubborn character and a man of his word. There was a very real risk that he would follow through with his threat. He had proven that if pushed, he could push back. The question was: had we pushed too hard? This was the first time tension had surfaced amongst our easygoing team. Would the team, the journey and the friendship collapse because of some errant watermelons?

We sat there and debated, deliberated, theorised and hypothesised about the situation and the range of possible outcomes. Would Whitey really leave? What would we do? Would we continue? Would we go home? We left the cafe and spent the afternoon wandering around town, doing some basic sightseeing, but we weren't really concentrating. Around five o'clock we headed back to the hotel to hopefully catch up with Whitey. Wegs and I could talk and theorise all day and still be no closer to a resolution. It was time to speak to Whitey and sort things out.

Whitey was lying on his bed reading a book when we returned. He looked up without saying anything and Wegs and I sat down. The peace negotiations had started awkwardly, and a silence fell upon the room.

'Feel like a beer, mate?' I asked Whitey after a couple of minutes. He lowered his book and looked over at me with an expressionless face.

'Yeah. OK.' He got to his feet.

'Wegs?' I asked.

'Not just yet. I'll join you later.' Bloody wimp. I would have to mend the bridges myself.

Whitey and I headed to the backpackers bar across the road. I didn't think the glitz and glamour of Chez Waynes was appropriate for this drink. We entered and took a seat at the bar.

'Deux bière s'il vous plâit,' I said, without raising two fingers. Practice had made perfect.

We each took a sip before Whitey broke the deadlock.

'You blokes were a bit rowdy last night,' he understated.

'Yeah. Sorry about that, mate. Things got a little out of hand.'

A busload of German girls entered the bar, causing the subject to change.

'Shit, she's all right!' I said, nodding in the direction of a gorgeous Bavarian blonde.

'Bloody oath. Her friends aren't bad either,' Whitey added with an appreciative eye. He was slowly coming back to life.

We slugged on our beers in unison as the girls continued to pour in through the door.

'Wegs will kick himself for not coming!' Whitey said. And as we laughed into our beers I realised something important had just happened, the team had returned to three. Conflict resolution, it would seem, was pretty easy for blokes: just add beer and girls.

8: LOSING THE MIDAS TOUCH

The village of La Barca was exactly as I had imagined it to be from Wegs' description. He had visited it on a previous trip to Italy, and had organised for us to stay in a house in the village belonging to Italian friends of his from Perth. Wegs had done an amazing job of navigating us to La Barca, and getting us there on the same day we departed Nice, including a lunchtime stop in Monte Carlo.

La Barca was nestled away in the hills of northern Tuscany, near Lucca. Life in this quaint town ticked over at its own slow rhythm, oblivious to the hectic pace of the twenty-first century. Driving into La Barca was like driving back in time. The town was old, the people were old, and the tradition of life in these parts was even older still.

The road into town followed the bends of a stream that flowed through its centre. We drove along the winding road slowly or, as we had taken to saying, at hearse pace. As we crawled into town it seemed that every member of this ageing community had noticed our purposeful approach. La Barca was, without doubt, one of God's waiting rooms. We definitely raised a few eyebrows, not to mention heart rates, on our entry that day. Each time an elderly local looked up from tending their tomatoes or drinking their coffee they'd hurriedly make the sign of the cross, either as a sign of respect for a departed friend or, more likely, in the hope that we hadn't come for them. It felt like we were back in Kinsale again. With the Big Girl calling La Barca home for the next week, I dearly hoped these elderly Italians appreciated irony.

The first street we came across happened to be Via del Mare, the very street we were looking for. We shouldn't have been too surprised, given there was a one in four chance it would be. Things now became increasingly familiar to Wegs and he directed us to Maria Maroni's house on the top of the hill. Maria Maroni was our contact in La Barca for the key collection. Wegs had met her before and he was confident she would remember him, and that his Italian would be sufficient to organise the delivery of the key. We pulled the Big Girl up outside and Wegs fired himself up for the meeting.

'I can do this,' were the parting words of our accommodation specialist. He seemed strangely confident for a bloke whose knowledge of Italian was limited to basic greetings and counting from one to ten.

He knocked loudly on the door, though I doubt he needed to knock at all as I was sure the Tuscan grapevine had already informed Maria Maroni that we were in town. The door quickly opened to reveal a short and matronly Italian woman wearing an apron. We couldn't hear the conversation between Wegs and

Maria Maroni, but there seemed to be a lot of head nodding going on as they stood on the doorstep. After a couple of nods and a smile that suggested she had no idea what he was talking about, Maria invited him inside. I knew he would have trouble. I bet he was either shouting at her in English, drawing a sketch or relying on sign language. Being able to say hello and count to ten wasn't going to be enough.

Sitting outside in the Big Girl, Whitey and I noticed that the presence of a hearse at the Maroni's had stimulated a flurry of activity. Suddenly people were walking dogs, feeding cats, pruning rosemary, potting geraniums and driving tractors back and forth. An elderly lady was walking her dog and I thought it would be nice to break the ice with a polite greeting. I wound down the window as she drew level with the Big Girl.

'Bonjour,' I said, accompanied by a friendly wave.

'Buongiorno,' she replied, without breaking her stride.

'Bugger.' I'd done it again.

I watched the old lady in the rear-view mirror as she continued past the car, and then stopped to join a group of locals involved in a deep discussion. She was obviously a scout sent out on reconnaissance and was now reporting back to command about the foreign hearse. I wondered what they could possibly be talking about. Perhaps they were planning Maria Maroni's funeral. If so, I bet they were pretty upset the Maroni family had chosen to use French undertakers for the job.

Plans for the funeral were soon put on hold though, as Wegs and Maria emerged. The locals seemed relieved to see Maria alive and well, and quickly broke up their conversation and dispersed. Wegs said his thank yous to Maria, in English, and made his way over to the car with six semi-ripened tomatoes, two jars of fig jam and, most importantly, the key. He'd done it. Wegs placed the home-grown produce on the floor in front of him.

'Well done, mate. Took a while though,' I said.

'Yeah well, my Italian was a bit rusty,' he confessed. He pulled a piece of paper out of his pocket. 'But I had my cheat sheets!'

'Hey?'

He grinned as he showed us the piece of paper. On it were some key phrases in Italian that had been emailed to him from his friend in Perth. That's why he'd been so smug about speaking with Maria Maroni.

'You must've made a good impression,' I said, referring to the tomatoes, and the fig jam.

'Mate, if I eat any more fig jam, I'll explode,' said Wegs with a sickened expression. 'I never want to see fig jam again. Ever!' However, with his bowels still in a relatively tender state, I had a hunch it may not be long before Wegs would experience that fig jam for a second time.

❀　❀　❀

Wegs twisted the large key in the old lock, fumbling around before finally hearing a loud click. He turned the solid timber doorknob and pressed his hip and shoulder against the heavy door, pushing it open.

'Could do with a bit of oil,' remarked Whitey as the door squeaked open.

'I don't think it's been opened for a while, mate,' I observed, stating the obvious.

A dank and musty odour greeted us as we stepped into the kitchen.

'Cabbage?' Wegs offered cheekily, reminding us of sitting in the Big Girl in Donal's Cork stables for the first time. It was dark and it smelt old.

Next to the kitchen was the living area, where a couch and a couple of armchairs were arranged around a low coffee table. Dustsheets covered the furniture, giving the house the feeling of a deceased estate. We bumped our way towards the windows and Wegs and I heaved open a stubborn window and pushed open the external timber shutters, sending them crashing loudly against the building's stone facade.

'Shit, that's better!' said Whitey, as fresh Tuscan air and sunshine streamed in.

'Bloody oath!' yelled Wegs as he walked purposefully to the bathroom. I smirked – fig jam.

Whitey and I explored the rest of the house, opening windows and ripping off dustsheets as we went. We folded the sheets neatly and dusted down the unprotected surfaces in each room before unpacking our bags.

Our mothers would have been pleasantly shocked at our domestication. God knows we were. Speaking of God, the light from the open windows showed us that he'd been integral in the decoration of the house.

'Better be on our best behaviour,' I noted, drawing Whitey's attention to the decor.

On every wall there was a print of 'Saint Someone', and in each room there was a religious statuette casting a watchful eye over the proceedings within those four walls. I felt sorry for the one in the toilet. He must have been very concerned for Wegs.

After neatly laying out my clothes on my chosen bed I headed to the dining room to set up a temporary workstation. With Saint Christopher on the wall behind me to provide some travel-writing inspiration, I hoped to knock up a respectable audition article for *TNT* in the week ahead.

❂　❂　❂

I woke up the following morning to a scream coming from the bathroom. Whitey came storming out of the bathroom clad in a towel, his big hair only half wet.

'No fuckin' hot water,' he complained, shaking his head and jowls from side to side.

'Really? Bugger. We're off to a bad start,' I said with a smile. During the night one of the neighbourhood cats had crept in through my open window and launched itself onto my bed, landing square in the middle of my back. I'm not sure who was more scared, the cat or me. I sprang up and flapped around in a frenzied tangle of sheets and blankets, squealing as if shot. I knocked the light switch on just in time to catch sight of a chubby white cat with ears pinned back, bolting back out the window.

'Don't worry about the shower, fellas, we can wash down at the swimming hole.' Wegs was awake now and gathering his

toiletries. Whitey and I did likewise. We opened the back door
to head to the river and nearly tripped over the mountain of
fresh local produce stacked neatly on our doorstep. During the
night half of the town must've visited and left us something
from their garden or pantry. There were bottles of jams and rel-
ishes; home-bottled olive oil; knotted bunches of garlic; onions;
ripened tomatoes; and, of course, figs.

'The figs are all yours, fellas,' said Wegs.

We carried it all into the kitchen and stacked it neatly on the
table. We were honoured.

'Let's go swim!' Wegs declared.

It was around nine in the morning and already extremely
hot. We skipped barefoot down the hot bitumen path towards
the river, regretting our decision not to wear shoes. A woman
stood at the doorway of a small corner deli and laughed as
we tiptoed gingerly past. She was in the same mould as Maria
Maroni – large and maternal, friendly and welcoming.

A slow tractor passed by, forcing us to hop from foot to foot
as we waited to cross the road. Ahead, a leafy vine grew over
a pergola, shading a table of elderly men and women. They
looked up from their espressos and conversations and, to a person, waved and smiled and nodded, which we returned with
interest. These men and women could well be responsible for
the produce that had mysteriously landed on our doorstep. We
threw in a few more cheery waves and continued the short distance to the river.

'Down here,' said Wegs, disappearing down a rocky path.
Whitey and I followed and soon the path opened onto a huge

rocky expanse leading to the edge of the deep, dark green swimming hole. We ran across the large grey rocks worn smooth by the stream's passage, dropped our toiletries and jumped into the inviting water.

'Not bad, hey!' yelled Wegs, surfacing from a dive. 'Can't touch the bottom here. Let's jump off that rock.' We raced him to the 'jump rock'.

We spent the next few hours tending to our ablutions, jumping off rocks, sliding down rocks and skimming pebbles. Wegs, who had morphed into Huckleberry Finn, even rigged up a fishing pole from a branch and a length of errant fishing line retrieved from a tree. It still had the hook attached, to which Wegs baited a handful of cherry-flavoured corn kernels.

'You won't catch a fish with corn kernels, you wanker!' Whitey stated.

'Yeah, especially cherry-flavoured ones,' I added wisely.

'Just you wait. There was a picture of a fish on the can I found, so I reckon that's what they use for bait around here,' said Wegs, convincing only himself.

This became our daily routine for the next week. Each morning we'd open the back door to collect our anonymously donated produce on the way for our morning wash at 'jump rock'. Around lunchtime we'd head back into town, stopping for a coffee and pastry with the elderly locals in the shade of the cafe. From the cafe we'd stop at the deli, run by the matronly lady who we discovered was Mrs de Rosa, Maria's neighbour. She'd motion us into her shop with flailing hands and arms, before wrapping up a fistful of prosciutto and a selection of local cheeses in the blink of an eyelid. Shopping in her aromatic store was great value because Mrs de Rosa's servings were, along with her build, extremely generous. As a result the fridge not only contained a lot of beer, but loads of enticing parcels of olives, pancetta, salami, mozzarella and parmesan; which was really quite refined for us country blokes.

The afternoons were spent reading, listening to music, writing and napping before our evening meal. Mostly we dined on a meat-sauce pasta and red wine, but on the third night we were forced to break with tradition because earlier that day Wegs had managed, God knows how, to catch two good-sized mountain trout on a hook full of cherry-flavoured corn kernels. Huckleberry had had the last laugh.

The daily activities were just the tonic for our travel-weary team. However, after six thoroughly enjoyable days in this Tuscan village, the call of the road could once again be heard. On the seventh morning we woke up and packed our bags, replaced the dustsheets, closed the shutters and locked the big back door for the last time. On the back doorstep we left a card addressed to Maria Maroni, thanking her and the townsfolk who'd delivered the fresh produce to our door over the last week. It was written in English and basic Italian, and I drew a few smiley faces to help convey the sentiment our words so confusingly communicated.

La Barca was deserted as we passed through early on our final day, except for an elderly lady walking her dog. It was the same old lady I'd said hello to, in perfect French, the day we'd arrived. I slowed the Big Girl and wound my window down as I drew up alongside her.

'Arrivederci!'

⊛   ⊛   ⊛

It was a good thing I was behind the wheel as we motored into central Rome. The lanes and intersections were poorly marked, if marked at all, and the traffic moved quickly and haphazardly across the wide roads. Like Paris, it called for decisive and positive driving. It goes without saying that Whitey, the country-driving specialist, wouldn't have coped. Wegs, while not a bad driver, is unpredictable in pressure situations, making his city driving a rather unnerving affair for Whitey, me and the Big Girl. So I was glad to be at the helm, fighting for road position with the Fiats and Alfas, with Whitey beside me navigating, and Wegs advising from the back.

'Where are we going, mate?' I asked Whitey, as I pulled up at a red light.

'Dunno . . . to find a hotel I guess.'

'Let's just cruise around for a while . . . it's only early,' suggested Wegs.

'OK. Which way?' I was happy to drive around and get a feel for the city.

'Right,' said Whitey, consulting the map. 'The Colosseum is up this way a bit, then we'll find a hotel.'

'Hotels will be bloody expensive in —' Wegs started, before being cut off by vicious looks from Whitey and me. He raised his hands, surrendering to our desire for a decent bed, hot shower and parking for the Big Girl. After free accommodation in La Barca and another night spent free-camping in the Big Girl, Whitey and I had a strong case for a hotel.

Whitey did a sterling job that morning of navigating us around and through the chaos of Rome. We would often forego the well-worn tourist paths in the major cities, as we had done in Paris, because they're usually overrated, overcrowded and, as sacrilegious as it sounds, pretty boring. Churches, museums and art galleries held little appeal for three single blokes on the road exploring life. For Rome though, we were prepared to grant a temporary exemption.

I slowed the Big Girl as we approached Piazza del Campidoglio. Ahead the traffic had come to a standstill so I put the gear into park and sat back to wait for the congestion to clear. Suddenly Whitey started laughing and pointing to his left.

'Ha ha. Check out these blokes. They think we're one of them,' he said in an unusually high pitch.

Beside us two Italian undertakers were leaning against their hearse, which was parked outside a small church, and smoking cigarettes. The big back door was wide open and backed up to the entrance, obviously waiting for a funeral service to conclude.

'Wonder if they think we're competition?' Wegs asked.

'If they do they don't seem very worried ... nor should they!' They were whacking each other on the arms and pointing at the Big Girl.

'G'day fellas,' Whitey yelled, accompanied by a double thumbs-up. The traffic ahead cleared and I moved the Big Girl forward, as our fellow undertakers waved us a loud goodbye, even returning Whitey's double thumbs-up.

Our interaction with the real undertakers seemed to raise our profile amongst the locals: girls on scooters smiled and flirted as they passed, bemused pedestrians stared blankly and speeding cars slowed for a better look and a wave. Smiles all round. A normal working day in Rome was coming to life and I liked the vibe. Rome and the Romans wore their cultural heritage with stylish continental flair. They were warm, relaxed and welcoming and they were treating us like rock stars!

'Nice one, Rome,' I thought to myself.

Around lunchtime we checked into the Hotel Pensione Dolomiti near Stazione Termini, Rome's central train station. It was only a modest hotel room, but it had three single beds, airconditioning, a functioning shower and secure underground parking for the Big Girl. It was all we required. After unpacking, we each showered and lay down in the cool room for an after-noon nap (known as a 'nanna nap') before waking, later than expected, around dinner time. Even the excitement of being in a new city couldn't combat the fatigue from a poor night's sleep in a hearse.

Rising from our snooze we wandered a couple of blocks along Via Varese before being corralled inside Trattoria Da Bruno by a vivacious tout. We ordered a large pizza with the lot (which in Italy means cheese, tomato and salami) and a Coke each. For once, none of us felt much like a beer.

I sat next to Whitey, and Wegs sat opposite with his head buried in the omnipresent guidebook.

'Apparently the train station, the number 64 bus and the Colosseum are full of pickpockets. We'd better be careful tomorrow,' warned Wegs.

'I couldn't get pickpocketed if I tried,' I said.

'I don't know about that. Sounds like it's pretty common around here.'

'Nah, those guidebooks talk shit. They're written for tourists who don't know any better – you know, the ones on package holidays. Older people, with floral shirts, high-waisted pants and sandals,' I added, confident I was too travel-savvy to be relieved of my wallet.

'You've got a floral shirt and sandals. You should wear those tomorrow and see what happens,' Whitey said absently.

'What . . . and see if I get pickpocketed?'

'Yeah, why not? We'll follow you with the cameras,' Wegs joined in, warming to a bit of irreverent adventure.

'OK. Done.' We shook hands. At the very least it would add a fun dimension to our big day of sightseeing. All we had to do was to set up a scenario to attract any self-respecting pickpocket.

After dinner we retired to the hotel room and, despite our earlier nanna nap, slept soundly through until morning. Uncharacteristically, I sprang out of bed more eager than most to become a victim of theft. It was time for me to throw the camera around the neck, don the floral shirt, the aviators and souvenir cap, pull the socks and shorts up as high as breathing would allow, strap on the sandals and hang a tempting five euro note out the back pocket. I admired myself in the mirror and thought I made a pretty good textbook tourist. The boys, however, thought my tourist uniform was incomplete.

'Something's missing,' Whitey said, rubbing his stubbled chin.

'A bumbag!' Wegs added. He was right, without a bumbag, Tourist Dav was incomplete.

I departed the hotel with the boys not far behind. The plan was that they would follow me at a distance with both video cameras, and hopefully capture me being pickpocketed. But first, I needed the bumbag. I was in luck, as just around the corner from the hotel were some street stalls selling bumbags. Whitey stood away from the stall and started the film rolling for the day.

It took a couple of minutes of searching before I spotted a large red bumbag that I could imagine my mum or dad wearing on holiday. I leant forward to ask the surly stall attendant how much it was. She spat an answer back, but I didn't have a chance to hear it because I was tapped on the shoulder. I turned around to see a small man in a green shirt smiling as he handed me my wallet. It had fallen out of my pocket onto the ground.

'Thanks, mate,' I said with a wave, as the kind gentleman disappeared into the bustling crowd. I returned the plastic wallet to my back pocket, making sure the five euro note was sticking out.

I'd completed the transaction for the bumbag when it occurred to me that perhaps the incident with the honest local wasn't as honest as it had appeared. I shot Whitey a quizzical glance out the corner of my eye and raised my eyebrows.

We moved to a bench to review the tape. We cleared away the pigeons, rewound the tape and hit play.

The footage started by showing me leaning forward to inspect the bumbags, with Wegs next to me. Then the man in the green shirt entered the shot. His head turned sharply when he noticed the money sticking out of my pocket and, with a glint in his eye, he thrust out his hand to pluck the money from my wallet. It was the perfect scenario for any pickpocket, or so he thought. What he hadn't banked on was the money being stuck to my wallet with a large knob of Blu-Tak. His eyes really widened when the entire wallet fell out of the pocket and onto the ground. His swift move had become a clumsy and fumbling affair. A seasoned professional, he recovered quickly and, instead of running away, he calmly picked up the wallet, tapped me on the arm and handed it back to me with a smile that said, 'Here, you dropped this, mate. You can't be too careful around here . . . someone could have stolen it.'

'The cheeky little bastard!' I roared, with a smile. There *was* merit in the guidebook warning. It had taken us less than five minutes to be pickpocketed.

With my lesson learnt I tucked the money safely away and we moved on to visit the Forum and the Colosseum, before catching the stifling Metro to the Vatican City. The open space of the Vatican was a welcome relief after the tiresome crowds at the Colosseum and on the packed underground trains. Unfortunately, Whitey and I were wearing shorts, so when we arrived at St Peter's we had to wait outside while Wegs, who was wearing jeans, was allowed to go inside. We sat and waited in the huge piazza, dwarfed by the architecture that surrounded us.

We were both annoyed at the clothing oversight; we'd read the previous evening that full-length pants were required to enter St Peter's but had forgotten this morning when dressing for pickpocketing and the hot day ahead. As a result we had sacrificed our opportunity to view and experience Michelangelo's masterpiece first hand. We sat in silence, knowing that you can't *do* Rome properly without a visit to St Peter's. This was one cultural icon we'd really wanted to see.

Our peace was soon interrupted by an officious member of the Swiss Guard. He came and stood beside Whitey who was holding our two video cameras and tripod.

'No tripod allowed here! Only camera. Do you have authorisation? No film here!' he boomed. Beneath the bright and whimsical uniform of this famous security force was a stern, no-nonsense professional.

Whitey was stuck for words.

'No film here! You journalista?' the guard continued the barrage.

'No. Home video,' Whitey said pointing to the camera.

'No film here! You professional?' the guard pressed. Whitey didn't seem to be making much impact. I stood up to address the guard. He leant forward, peered over the top of his sunglasses with a furrowed brow and looked me up and down. No explanation was required.

'OK, you can go,' he laughed, prompting me to remember my ridiculous state of dress. It was blatantly obvious that anyone associated with someone dressed in my tourist uniform couldn't possibly be a professional of any kind. We were free to go about our business, as tourists.

Wegs materialised shortly afterwards.

'Righto, we've *done* the Vatican. Well at least I have!' he said, teasing us.

'Piss off, mate!' I laughed back.

'Where to now then, or have we *done* Rome?' Whitey asked Wegs, who was in charge of the itinerary.

'Nuh, we're not done yet. One more stop.' And we headed off back to Ottaviano station and descended into the sweaty depths of the Metro once again, en route to our last destination for the day: the Trevi fountain.

It was very busy when we arrived in the late afternoon and it was difficult to get through the crowds to the fountain's edge. I didn't know much about the Trevi fountain, and because of the swarming and impatient crowds I immediately wanted to leave. I was hot and bothered after our whistle-stop tour but Wegs, who had read about it in the guidebook, said there was an important reason behind us coming here.

'Relax, mate,' Wegs said smugly.

At his command, I pointed the video camera at him as he sat on the wall of the fountain.

'You filming, mate?' he asked.

'Yep. Action!'

Wegs then delivered a carefully crafted piece to camera, as only he can.

'Well, here we are at the fountain of . . . Trevally? Apparently, if you throw one coin over your shoulder here, into the water, it means you'll come back to Rome. So, here goes.'

Splash.

'If you throw a second coin over your shoulder, you can make a wish. Here's hoping that we get the Big Girl, and ourselves, all the way safely back to Australia.'

Splash.

❀ ❀ ❀

Pompeii, two days later, would round off our list of must-visit tourist locations in Italy. It held particular appeal for Whitey, and he'd championed its inclusion in the itinerary. It was therefore terribly poor timing that, swinging the Big Girl into an all-day car park near the Pompeii ruins, Whitey's bowels began to move rather violently. He'd gone home early from the pub in Sorrento the previous evening complaining of a sore stomach. It'd been Wegs' turn in Nice, and I knew that eventually my time would come, but, for now, it was Whitey's. He accepted his fate philosophically and trudged off carefully, yet purposefully, towards the conveniences with toilet roll in hand.

'Had to happen sometime I guess. Better get it over with.'

'Righto, mate. We'll wait out front,' I said, in a concerned tone. I wasn't laughing; I didn't want to tempt fate.

We'd parked in the grounds of a large caravan park and, luckily for Whitey, right next to the toilet block. Wegs and I unpacked the camera gear into our daypacks and then leant against the bonnet of the Big Girl and waited, and waited, and waited. Whitey must have been having a pretty thorough cleansing. Poor bugger.

It was another half an hour before Whitey's head poked out from the toilet block. His long mane of unkempt hair swung wildly as he looked quickly from left to right, like he was crossing a busy road. He then bolted out the door at full speed and raced straight past us, without saying a word. We watched in amazement as he continued his arm-pumping run right out the exit before turning to the left and out of sight.

'What the . . . ?' Wegs and I looked at each other. We walked off in bemused pursuit. This was really out of character for the laid-back Whitey. He likes running about as much as I do.

We found a pale and puffing Whitey around the corner.

'What's the matter, mate?' Wegs asked.

'I didn't want the owner to see me.'

'Why?'

'I made a bit of a mess. He won't be happy.' Whitey sighed, and shook his head. 'He won't be happy at all.'

'Why? How? It's only a dunny!'

'Well, if it was a proper dunny it would've been all right, but it wasn't, it was one of those stupid hole-in-the-ground jobs.' He shook his head again and sighed, obviously having a flashback.

After leaving us he'd raced into the cubicle and immediately removed his shorts to accommodate the urgency of his situation. Whitey is a tall man, which means that it's a lot further down to a hole-in-the-ground toilet than it is for most people. When this additional height above the hole is combined with a violent explosion, the likelihood of all the contents hitting the target is quite low, very low in this instance. After the initial violent movement, Whitey reached behind him to place his unsoiled toilet roll on top of the cistern, out of harm's way. Unfortunately, there was no lid, resulting in Whitey plonking the entire toilet roll into the cistern water.

Whitey was forced to substitute the sodden and irretrievable toilet paper with his underwear. He cleaned himself as much as possible under the circumstances, and disposed of his jocks into the toilet. He then turned to survey the extensive damage his spray painting had done to the surrounding walls and floor. Pro Hart would've been proud (if not slightly jealous). There was nothing the luckless Whitey could do about the walls, so he tugged on the chain to flush the contents of the bowl away once and for all, but to no avail. Both the toilet and the cistern were totally blocked.

'Tonight, when we come back, you guys'll have to bring the car out to me.' He'd regained his breath, but his voice was still shaky. Wegs and I couldn't stop laughing. At the start of the day Whitey had been as keen as mustard to get to Pompeii. Now he was more concerned about leaving.

I contemplated what this unpleasant incident meant for me. Would I have to vomit in the streets, or spray-paint walls and destroy public property? I only hoped that when *my* time came, things would be dealt with in a far more dignified manner.

❂   ❂   ❂

On our journey to date, excluding the robbery in Calais, pretty much everything we'd touched had turned to gold. We'd had no bad weather, no mechanical problems, no run-ins with the law, and no medical concerns beyond bad hangovers and upset stomachs. Even without an itinerary, things had repeatedly fallen into place. Perhaps we were getting overconfident, too big for our boots, and beginning to believe we were above the law, for, as we prepared to depart Italy, our alchemist's touch deserted us.

Whitey's innocent destruction of public property seemed to precipitate an extended sequence of misfortunes for the team. These problems would not prove to be life or journey threatening; they were just a few hurdles thrown into the trip to keep us honest.

On the night of Whitey's Pompeii experience, which became known as the 'Poo-peii incident', we left our camp site on foot to go to dinner in nearby Sorrento. Before leaving we'd been warned that heavy rain was forecast and that we should consider relocating our tents to avoid the risk of flooding. We decided against this sensible course of action and headed into town for the night. The general consensus was 'she'll be right'. Predictably, on our return in the wee hours of the morning, we found that our camp site had captured the majority of the run-off from the steep hill above us, and had been partially washed down the hill. There was little we could do other than weather out the storm, in the car.

What we found the next morning was not good. Our clothes, tents, bedding, mattresses and backpacks were soaked and covered in mud and assorted garden debris. Fortunately, our electronic equipment had been safely locked away in the Big Girl.

Wegs decided to take a photo to record the moment for posterity, only to find that his new digital camera he'd taken to the pub last night wasn't working. It'd been damaged by the rain, or by a vodka and Red Bull. Either way, it was ruined. I surveyed the damage and assessed the work needed to redeem the situation, and was reminded of one of my mother's maxims: when all is said and done, lazy people take the most time.

With no break in the gloomy weather apparent, we decided to load up the Big Girl with our sodden belongings and hit the road. There seemed little point waiting around in the muddy camp site. It was time to head to Greece. A new country would surely bring about a change in our fortunes. However, Italy was not done with us just yet.

While rapidly traversing Italy, from Sorrento in the west to Bari in the east, Whitey spotted the flashing lights of the Carabinieri in the rear-view mirror. Although our progress along the autostrada was rapid relative to our normal hearse pace, it wasn't rapid enough to warrant the attention of the police. We were unsure why we'd been pulled over. An officer emerged from his Alfa Romeo, with blue lights flashing brightly, and approached Wegs in the passenger seat. Realising, in the absence of a steering wheel, that the driver was on the other side of the car, he walked around the front of the Big Girl without saying a word, before calmly asking Whitey, in perfect English, to step outside the vehicle and show his licence. Whitey obliged. The officer inspected the Australian licence and then instructed Whitey to follow him to the rear of the car.

He explained to Whitey that we'd been pulled over because we'd failed to display a 'GB' (Great Britain) sticker on the back of our car. In Italy this is an offence punishable by an on-the-spot fine. The sticker informs fellow motorists that our car is an English vehicle and therefore right-hand drive. They'd noticed us because Wegs' feet were hanging out of the passenger's window. He made Whitey very aware that this was a potential safety hazard because, without a GB sticker, fellow motorists would think someone was driving the Big Girl with both feet out the window. We paid the one hundred euro fine, unable to argue with the logic.

An hour later we arrived at the bustling port of Bari, keen to get the team loaded onto a ferry bound for Greece. Our resolve was tested when we entered the packed ferry terminal and discovered that all ferries scheduled for Patras or Athens were fully booked. I was quite aggrieved that this was the case. *Why* were there no ferries able to take us? It didn't make sense. Normally our good fortune would see us arrive in perfect time for a connecting ferry irrespective of our lack of planning. I threw my head back and looked to the heavens for direction, but none was forthcoming.

Other travellers in the terminal were ranting and raving about how they would need to wait two full days before the next connecting ferry to Athens would arrive. Clearly we weren't the only people who expected the planets to align at all times and in any situation. We took a seat and wondered what to do. I sat and listened to the pathetic complaints of the other disorganised backpackers, and the more I heard, the more pathetic they became. I realised that we sounded exactly the same, and I wasn't proud of it. The ferry schedule was inconvenient but it was definitely not going to change for any whingeing backpackers or for a bunch of disorganised blokes in a hearse.

We retreated to the bonnet of the Big Girl to formulate a plan. Whitey had the map, Wegs had the guidebook, and I had a ferry timetable.

'From here the car ferries go to Patras, Athens and Igoumen-itsa. Patras and Athens are full, what about this Igou . . . menitsa place? Is it in Greece?' I enquired.

'It doesn't get a mention in here,' Wegs answered.

'Here it is.' Whitey found it on our road map. 'Yep, it's in Greece, looks as though it's a few hours north of Patras.'

'Well, let's do it then,' Wegs said. Now that we knew the full range of options, the obvious course of action became clear.

A lack of public transport from Igoumenitsa to Patras or Athens meant that the average backpacker, without a car, could not use this service. But we could, because we had an ace up our sleeve: the Big Girl.

Within the hour we had the Big Girl safely on board a sturdy ferry bound for Igoumenitsa. As we stood watching the diminishing Italian coast, we cracked a cold can of Mythos. It had been a long and testing day for the team, one that was now thankfully behind us. Tomorrow we would wake up to a fresh new day, in Greece.

DAV WEGS WHITEY

9: A MAN DOWN

The repeated blaring of the ferry horn startled me awake. I had slept surprisingly deeply in my damp swag and sleeping bag on the exposed deck. From my position on the edge of the upper deck I looked straight into the morning sun that revealed the brilliantly blue Mediterranean waters, and, as I hoped, a fresh new day full of promise.

I had one concern though: the source of an unpleasant odour that was at odds with the stunning day presenting itself. I rolled over and saw Whitey next to me in his sleeping bag, and between us the source of the dubious odour. We were covered in garbage from head to toe. During the night every empty beer can, greasy kebab wrapper and cigarette butt had rolled and wobbled its way over to our low-lying corner of the deck. I hate the smell of garlic sauce at the best of times, but when combined with the stench of stale beer and pre-loved cigarettes it becomes truly hideous. I had to restrain myself from dry retching. It was an unpleasant start to an otherwise glorious day. Things could only get better.

The ferry horn blared again and Whitey and I looked out from the deck to see that we were pulling into Corfu, a scheduled stop for the Igoumenitsa service. The long line of recreational vehicles and campervans below deck started up their engines in preparation for departure. We leant on the railing and took in our first impressions of Greece.

Ahead of us was a quaint village overlooking the port. White stone buildings lined the streets and the cliff tops surrounding the sheltered inlet. The small port was a flurry of activity, with ferries of all shapes and sizes coming and going, and blaring their horns. The town's small fishing fleet was heading out to the still blue waters for the day's catch. On the wharf another long line of campervans were waiting to exchange positions with the ones about to depart. It was exactly as we imagined Greece would be. It was blue, it was white and it was idyllic postcard material. We grabbed three coffees and headed down to see Wegs, who had slept the night in the Big Girl. It was time to organise our belongings, which had been loosely hung out to dry, and prepare for departure. Igoumenitsa was the next stop.

On schedule, the ferry delivered us to Igoumenitsa mid-morning. It was a beautiful clear day but already fearfully hot, and the vinyl seats of the Big Girl once again needed to be covered with towels. The Big Girl fired up first time and exited the hull of the large ferry, scraping her exhaust on leaving before touching Greek soil for the first time. With no customs' formalities to attend to, we simply drove off the ship, out the gates of the port and into Igoumenitsa.

'Whitey, pull in here, mate – breakfast,' said Wegs, rubbing his hands together. He'd spotted a kebab shop on the main road out of town. Whitey dutifully pulled the Big Girl up to the side of the road and we clambered out and over to the kiosk window.

'Three please, mate,' Wegs ordered, pointing and holding up three fingers. It worked, the 'chef' grunted and pulled out three pita breads. Wegs and Whitey sat down and waited, while I stood watching the kebab preparation, wondering how I was going to ask for one without garlic sauce. I can't stand the stuff. It gives me terrible indigestion, and it gives *everyone* bad breath. I've never understood the attraction of eating garlic. I mean, why would you knowingly give yourself bad breath?

'Aaaagh,' I yelled at the kebab chef, just as he was about to slop a large dollop of the objectionable sauce on the third kebab. He understood my animated language, and returned his ladle with a loud plonk back into the trough. I thanked him and then paid for all three, handing the tainted ones to the boys.

Before I was halfway through mine Wegs had finished, downing his kebab in four aggressive mouthfuls.

'I love kebabs. I could eat two for every meal,' Wegs declared, wiping garlic sauce off his chin with his palm.

'No you couldn't,' I said, conveying my disapproval of his puerile claim.

'Could so. I could do it easy!' Wegs continued the schoolyard banter.

'OK then. I bet you can't eat two kebabs per meal between here and Athens. That's two days at six a day . . . twelve kebabs in two days,' I challenged.

'Too easy. Make it fifteen,' he countered, 'for a box of beer.'

'Done.' We shook on it as Wegs stood up and approached the kiosk again. I would win this bet for sure, and Wegs would learn a valuable lesson in thinking before speaking. It was a win-win situation.

'Three kebabs, thanks!' He ordered for himself. He was going down fighting.

* * *

After the kebab breakfast our first priority was a wash. We drove for an hour along a scenic road that skirted the coast at a great height. It eventually returned to sea level where we found a secluded beach adjacent to a camping ground. Whitey and I raced each other across the rocky beach to the inviting blue water. It was heavenly to rid our body of the filth from the night before. We'd had little quality sleep and no quality showers since the flooding in Sorrento a couple of nights ago and as we flapped around in the warm and salty water we began to feel human again. It's not every day that your bathtub is the Mediterranean.

After our cleansing dip we jumped back in the Big Girl and pushed on towards Athens. The drive was spectacular and full of contrasts. The road scaled barren and rocky mountain passes before descending into rich and fertile river valleys. Occasionally we found ourselves back near the coastline before heading inland once again to negotiate the harsh mountains. It was already the afternoon, and as we descended into yet another fertile valley we realised that making Athens that night was unlikely. We drove for a while longer before Wegs turned down

a gravel lane that led to an unfenced field. It seemed like a perfect place to set up camp. We parked the Big Girl in the shade
of a large tree and then removed every piece of luggage that she
carried.

An hour later our corner of the field resembled a patchwork
quilt. We had laid out two tents, three sleeping bags, three pil-
lows, three mattresses and all of our towels and clothing to
dry in the sun. It was just as well we'd stopped, as during the
unpacking we'd detected mould on some items, and there was
a dank and musty odour attached to the luggage. In this warm
weather another day would have seen entire colonies of bacteria
thriving. We'd done our mothers proud once again.

❂ ❂ ❂

Athens materialised before us through the grimy windows of
the Big Girl. The traffic was intense and unrelenting like in Paris
and Rome, but that was where the comparisons ended. Unlike
these heavyweight cities, Athens didn't have the beautiful architecture to distract you from its congestion and pollution. Athens
was ugly. It was a hot and dirty, sprawling concrete jungle.

Cars drove aggressively and there wasn't a traffic policeman
to be seen. Yellow taxis and large buses ruled the roads, billow-
ing smoke from poorly maintained engines. The hot, sweaty,
humid and polluted environment reminded me more of an
Asian capital than a European one.

We cruised past the open space of Syntagma Square and, with
considerable relief, finally wheeled the Big Girl into Plaka, the
old Turkish quarter, to find a hotel. The streets were narrower

here, and lined with hotels, restaurants and street stalls. It was a lively and leafy oasis tucked away at the foot of the imposing Acropolis. Plaka was a welcome respite from the hustle and bustle of downtown, and would make a perfect base for our stay in Athens.

Our early arrival meant that even Wegs was comfortable with us staying in a hotel; however, it seemed Wegs' desire to save money hadn't completely abated. His first action upon arrival in our airconditioned room was to ask Whitey to give him a haircut outside on the balcony. I wasn't surprised; I'd long since ceased to be amazed by Wegs' unusual decision-making processes. What did surprise me was the excellent job Whitey did with an electric shaver and a Swiss army knife. He showed a deft touch with these instruments that I wouldn't have thought possible, given the large size of his man-hands.

Shortly after the completion of Wegs' serviceable haircut we found a cafe down a nearby lane where we could consult our guidebooks. An important decision needed to be made. Our journey to date had been a simple matter of driving from one EU nation to the next, but Greece was the end of the line as it bordered no EU nations. After returning from our planned week in the Greek islands we wanted to travel from Greece to Germany overland, so we had to decide which was the best, and safest, route to take. We'd identified three options, each with their own pros and cons.

The first option was to head from Greece to Bulgaria, Romania, Hungary, Austria and then into Germany. This meant we could visit new and interesting Eastern European countries while avoiding the unpredictable and dangerous territory of the former Yugoslavia. This route was the most preferable; however, we would need to organise a visa for Romania prior to our arrival at its border. This meant a visit to the Romanian embassy in Athens and the associated headaches and delays that come with organising visas, especially in a non-English speaking country. According to the guidebook, visas for the other countries on this route could be arranged upon arrival. If we could arrange the Romanian visa, this preferred option seemed a pretty safe bet.

Option number two was to head from Greece to Macedonia, Kosovo, Montenegro, Bosnia, Croatia, Slovenia, Austria and then into Germany. This was the riskiest of the three options. We understood little about the current political situation of those countries that previously made up Yugoslavia. Fighting in these areas had ceased in recent times, but we appreciated that relationships between the ethnic factions were still volatile. It was a world beyond our comprehension, one that we'd heard of only through news bulletins during war times. These bulletins had done little to promote the Balkan Peninsula as a potential holiday destination. The positive aspect of this option was that we wouldn't require advance visa organisation, therefore avoiding logistical headaches. We could simply do a cannonball run straight through the region, stopping only to cross borders and refuel, enabling us to reach safe ground in Croatia within a day. This was the high-risk, high-return option.

The third option was to return to Italy and enter Germany via Switzerland or Austria. This route required no visa organisation and it was safe and secure, but it involved backtracking, and none of us were in favour of that. We'd already painted the Italian section of our canvas. Option three was the boring, blue-chip investment.

We ruminated on the possibilities over an early lunch of frappes and Greek salads. Each alternative was vigorously debated as we munched on pipped kalamata olives and cool, crunchy cucumber.

'So what do you reckon?' I addressed the boys.

'Through Romania,' Wegs answered.

'Yeah, me too. Whitey?' I asked.

'Huh? Oh yeah, Romania sounds best,' he replied in a distracted fashion. He'd been away with the pixies all day.

'Well, let's do it then,' I said, bringing the meeting to a close.

Whitey popped up to the room to grab the passports and, with some difficulty, Wegs and I flagged a taxi. We were off to the Romanian embassy. Surprisingly we'd all been in favour of organising a visa for Romania. Normally the thought of advance planning would be a deterrent; perhaps we'd matured in recent times.

Successfully flagging a taxi had been hard enough, but successfully directing the taxi driver proved to be an even more difficult task. Despite everything, we eventually arrived at the Romanian embassy in suburban Athens, exhausted from the protracted journey, which was made worse by the driver's overpowering body odour. I was relieved to get out of the car and suck in a few deep breaths of fresh air. I couldn't have lasted much longer in that taxi.

'Geez . . . phwoar . . . pretty stuffy in there,' I said as I shut the door.

'God. You're not wrong,' agreed Whitey, laughing. Perhaps body odour was a barometer of manliness in Greece.

We composed ourselves and approached the tall steel gates of the Romanian embassy. Wegs pressed the buzzer on the intercom. There was no response. He depressed the button again and spoke.

'Hello? Anyone home? We here to get VISA for ROMANIA,' he boomed, rendering the intercom superfluous.

'No, you may not!' came the terse response, delivered with a heavy accent. We looked at each other, shocked by the odd reply.

'We AUSTRALIAN. VISA for ROMANIA,' Wegs yelled again, a vein in his forehead bulging.

'No, you are not!'

'Yes. AUSTRALIAN. VISA. ROMANIA!'

'No, you can not!' All the responses varied slightly on the same negative theme.

'VISA. ROMANIA?'

'NO!' Then the line went dead. We were completely baffled. We were definitely at the right place and we'd even come at the correct time. In my past experience these two factors were generally the most difficult to coordinate. Getting motivated and actually getting *to* the embassy are normally the biggest hurdles involved in obtaining a visa. Getting *in*, assuming you have fluked your arrival to coincide with the opening hours, is normally only a formality.

Wegs tried a few more times but received no reply. We stared up helplessly at the mirrored windows of the large building. I wondered what was going on behind that glass. Very little it would seem.

'What do we do?' asked Wegs.

'Go back to the hotel, I guess.' There seemed nothing else we could do. We had reached a diplomatic stalemate.

We turned back to the road to hail another taxi and spotted one approaching in the line of traffic. Wegs prepared to flag it down, but as it came closer I realised it was our aromatic driver from the trip out.

'Fuck. Quick, look busy. We are *not* getting back in *that* taxi!'

⊛ ⊛ ⊛

We'd decided to have an afternoon on our own, so we could attend to some personal errands. I wanted to research our trip to the Greek island of Ios, Wegs wanted to get his digital camera repaired and Whitey said he needed to visit a bank. Whitey had seemed distant and unenthusiastic during our discussions about visiting Ios. He just didn't seem himself. It must have been the heat.

The afternoon of 'private time' was a success, and we met back at the hotel room with our respective goals achieved. We showered and adjourned to the rooftop bar of our hotel to have a light meal and a couple of beers before turning in for the night. The roof of our hotel towered over the surrounding buildings and afforded us a majestic view. With the setting sun casting a golden blanket over the neighbouring rooftops and the nearby Acropolis, we drank some of the most enjoyable beers of the trip to date.

I sipped on my beer as the boys talked amongst themselves. I was thinking, which I do on occasion. Our unsuccessful attempt to get a visa meant some tough decisions would need to be made, and made soon. Would we avoid the headaches of bureaucracy and chance our luck driving a hearse through the former Yugoslavia? How were Whitey's finances travelling? We planned to escape these concerns for a while by relaxing on a Greek island, but I knew they would be waiting for us on our return – along with the Big Girl.

❃ ❃ ❃

Ios was billed as our holiday within the holiday. We had planned to stay for five days, but that soon became eight, or maybe nine. I think it was nine but I couldn't say for sure: it felt like one long night to me.

Our team of three rapidly became a posse of eight after we combined forces with a group of blokes trawling Europe in a Kombi van. Quincy, Rosy, JB, Ryan and Neddy were a mixed bag of Aussies and Kiwis who were also en route to Oktoberfest. There was an immediate rapport as our travelling teams merged into one, and each day and night was spent partying as if it were our last.

We hired a bungalow in the Purple Pig camping ground, a haven for backpackers. The bungalow was sparsely furnished: four bunk beds, a sink, shower and toilet. However, it was all that was needed as precious little time was spent within its confines.

Each day we would head straight for the camping ground pool, where our afternoons were spent with hundreds of other travellers: listening to tunes, drinking cold beers and having an occasional swim to combat the oppressive heat.

The expanded team was inseparable and if one member was down and out with a bad hangover, the other seven could be relied upon to throw him in the shower, get him dressed and drag him out on the town against his will. It was one in, all in.

But it wasn't all about the booze and blokes. Our time on Ios was greatly enhanced by the fact that I met a lovely Australian girl called Georgie, Wegs met a loud Irish girl called Caroline, and Whitey met, well, Whitey met no girls. Poor bloke – on Ios that was nearly impossible to do.

Although there were more reasons for us to stay than there were for us to leave, we knew that great champions always quit while they're on top. Sadly, this wasn't to be the case for our team. The consumption of the entire cocktail list at the Underground nightclub on our final night ensured that we didn't depart Ios as champions. The knockout punch was delivered in the eighth round. We'd trained well over the previous months and managed to put up a respectable performance, but with our party-weary bodies screaming for mercy, it was time for us to throw in the towel.

The final word was left to an exasperated Whitey as we tried to rest before catching our ferry for Piraeus.

'I can get my body tired . . . and I can get my body pissed . . . but fucked if I can get my body to sleep!'

The ferry steamed out of port on the morning of the ninth day, leaving the excesses of Ios in our wake. We waved goodbye to our mates and our holiday, and walked to the front of the slow-moving vessel. Ahead lay reality, adventure and the Big Girl.

❀　❀　❀

The reality of our situation presented itself on our first night back in Athens, much sooner than expected. We had each spent the day on our own, doing various personal chores ahead of the planned departure, and had regrouped in our hotel room to have a cold shower before our evening meal. There was no air-conditioning in our budget suite. Whitey was sweating more than normal and fidgeting as he paced the room, before finally sitting down on his bed. When you know someone well you can tell when bad news is coming. Something was up.

'Um, fellas,' Whitey began cautiously, pausing before continuing, 'I've gotta go home. I'm outta cash.'

'What?' I asked, surprised.

'Already?' Wegs said, with both voice and eyebrows raised.

'Yep. I was hoping to at least make it to Oktoberfest, but I went to the bank today and it's all gone,' Whitey stated in an apologetic tone. He looked tired; it had obviously been concerning him for weeks, probably ever since Portugal.

'We'll loan you some,' I offered.

'Yeah, mate. We'll find some cash for you. You can't go home now,' added Wegs.

'No.'

'Sure you can. You can pay us back when we get home. We know you're good for it,' I pushed.

'No!' Whitey's tone was serious. 'Thanks, but no.'

I knew he wouldn't borrow the money, but it was worth a try to keep the team together. Whitey is a proud man, proud to the point of being stubborn at times, but proud nonetheless.

'Sure, mate?' Wegs pleaded. 'We don't mind loaning you the cash. We want to.'

'I know, mate, but I'm sure. I saw a travel agent after the bank today and my flight back to Australia is booked. I leave the day after tomorrow.'

Whitey was handling the situation as best he could, by saying very little. There are times to speak and times to be silent. This was the latter. With mates, some things don't need to be said; they speak for themselves. His mind was made up.

❂ ❂ ❂

The next evening we sat down for our last supper at a crowded Plaka restaurant, reminiscing about the events of the previous two and a half months. It was a subdued gathering by normal standards, as we came to terms with Whitey's leaving. Before we knew it tired waiters were sweeping around our feet and packing up the tables and chairs. We had been deferring the end for long enough, so we downed our last beers together as a team before making the short walk back to our hotel.

The following morning we reunited ourselves with the Big Girl. We had left her on the top floor of a long-term car park, parked so she could see the Acropolis in our absence. We emerged from the lift to see her beaming with delight at our arrival. She'd been detailed by Con, the friendly level-seven attendant, and looked fantastic. However, she would be dismayed to learn that the team was soon to be a man down.

It took us hours to sort through the accumulated gear to isolate Whitey's belongings. Over the course of the trip everything in the car had officially become communal property – with underwear, toothbrushes and girls the only exceptions.

'You want to take Wegs' Madonna CD with you, mate?' I said, smiling as I sorted out the CDs.

'Ha ha. It's all yours!' Whitey approved of nothing other than rock and roll.

'Westlife?' I queried again, knowing full well Whitey would prefer a slap in the face with a wet fish than to listen or be seen in possession of such music. I was just trying to lighten the mood – and to offload some of Wegs' terrible CDs. I slipped both of the CDs into Whitey's music folder anyway, knowing he would get a laugh on the plane when he discovered them.

After what seemed like an eternity, Wegs and the shirtless Con combined to squeeze the Big Girl into the car lift so she could descend the seven floors to freedom. Whitey and I were on hand to film a very relieved and very sweaty Wegs drive the Big Girl out of the lift. On seeing the video camera the effervescent Con, with a big smile and even bigger wave, yelled through his thick moustache, 'Thank you! Welcome . . . next time . . . Greece.'

We paid Con, tipping him heavily, before nosing out into

the snarling Athens traffic. Whitey was behind the wheel for his last drive in the Big Girl. More silence. I decided to turn on a few tunes and quite accidentally put on the Skunkhour song 'Home'. The line '. . . my time to return has come – I'm coming home' caused Whitey to note in his classically understated manner, 'Hmmm, appropriate.'

Normally our departures were exciting times, and although this remained the case for Wegs and me, the atmosphere was tempered by Whitey's imminent departure. We pulled over to the side of the main road to the airport. Whitey had decided to get a taxi so the goodbyes weren't prolonged and awkward. Men are not good at saying goodbye.

Wegs pulled out Whitey's backpack and helped him put it on; it was poorly packed and much heavier than when we left Ireland nearly three months ago. I set about flagging down a taxi. If Athens' taxi drivers don't like the look of you they don't stop; if they do stop and they don't like or don't know where you're going, they don't take you. So I was genuinely surprised when the first taxi I waved at actually stopped. However, this was still no guarantee that he would take the fare. It really depended on his mood.

'Air-a-port?' I asked in my best Greek.

'OK. OK. OK,' he said in a typically agitated manner. But this was no time to question his manners for he had stopped, known and accepted the proposed destination. I couldn't speak for his body odour though.

'Got him!' I called out triumphantly to the boys.

Wegs and I thrust out our hands for the final goodbye, and

each handshake was returned with interest. No man-hugs. No tears. It was just an old-fashioned masculine goodbye.

'Enjoy it, boys,' Whitey said, 'and I don't want to see that fuel tank fixed by the time you get home either!' These were the last words we heard from a whimsical Whitey as he piled into the taxi. Wegs and I had ignored the hole in the fuel tank in the hope it would go away. As yet it had not. Good old Whitey: sensible to the end.

With the roar of an overworked engine and a thick plume of smoke, he was gone. We watched the taxi drive off into the jungle of traffic and managed to catch sight of Whitey's large man-hand sticking out the window. Slowly, an index finger emerged from the large fist and remained in a raised position until the taxi vanished from sight. Wegs and I returned our official team salute.

'And then there were two,' I said.

'Three,' corrected Wegs, pointing to our ever-reliable and faithful chariot.

'Three, indeed.'

It was time for Wegs and me to put the recent disappointment behind us and regain our positive focus on the trip.

With the windows down and the sunroof open we left the concrete metropolis of Athens behind and headed off towards the former Yugoslavia. I inserted our *Best of Bon Jovi* CD, selected track three and cranked up the volume. Wegs and I became a lame male version of Thelma and Louise, with hair blowing and fists pumping, belting out the wrong lyrics to a Bon Jovi classic.

Invigorated by what lay ahead, we shook hands firmly and said, 'We're back!'

10: BACK ON TOP

'Wegs, how would you feel if, instead of paying you in beer, I made a payment of a spiritual nature?' I enquired.

'Hmmm?' Wegs was tired and brain dead after the long drive from Athens.

'Our kebab bet,' I said.

'Hmmm?'

'I owe you a case of beer because you won the kebab bet.'

'Yeah, but what do you mean by a spiritual payment?'

'Well, I was just reading the map and saw that we're about to pass Mt Olympus, the centre of the mythological Greek universe. I see they have twelve gods, so I'm proposing we climb Mt Olympus to crown you as the thirteenth Greek god: Weggos – the god of Gyros. What do you reckon?'

I wasn't overly serious, I was really just trying to get out of buying the beer by appealing to his ego. Given my knowledge of his ego I shouldn't have been surprised when he immediately responded by taking the Olympus exit from the Athens–Thessaloniki freeway.

Climbing Mt Olympus is for some people a life goal; for us, it was undertaken in a typically lighthearted fashion. How hard could it be?

Before we left the base-camp car park we quickly ran through a checklist of our mountaineering supplies.

Map – no. Torch – no. Compass – no. Water – no. Warm clothing – no. Tent – no. Fitness – no. Dunlop Volleys – yes.

So, with everything in order, we set off towards Mytikos, at 2917 metres the highest peak on Mt Olympus.

Hours later the ascent had taken its toll on us, not the least of which was our pride. We had been continually overtaken by groups of people who shouldn't have been fitter than us. Even the heavily laden donkeys that supply the mountain's refuges with supplies had passed us, twice. At least Wegs benefited from the climb in the sweltering conditions, as he managed to sweat out the majority of his fifteen kebabs. By late in the day we'd begun to hallucinate, thinking that we had reached the summit only to be presented with another thigh-burning climb, and another, and another. Why were we doing this?

The end of the first day's climb saw us just make the overnight refuge before dark. Never have I been so happy to enter lodgings that had no alcohol and no hot showers. Walking into this mountain refuge was as close to heaven as I had ever been: literally, but that was all going to change as we planned to climb the remaining 800 metres the following day, or die trying.

But for now it was time to rest and eat. We had only consumed a Mars Bar each and were exhausted. We took a small table in the dining area as close to the fire as possible. The temperature had dropped significantly since the sun had set, and now we'd stopped the feverish exercise we'd become quite chilled. I could finally appreciate why the guidebook had recommended warm clothing. I'd overlooked this requirement given that I'd read this information when the mercury was hovering around forty-two degrees Celsius and the fan was on the blink. It just didn't seem relevant at the time. Now it did.

There was only one thing left for us to do and that was to warm ourselves up with a hearty dinner, so we ordered two bowls of vegetable soup from the menu. Not because we like vegetable soup – I actually hate it – but because vegetable soup *was* the menu and God knows our bodies needed some nutrition and sustenance. As we waited for our meals I took particular notice of the other residents. It was clear that Wegs and I were the only mountaineering virgins in the room. Surrounding us were a dozen boring-looking European couples who had that look of health and youthful exuberance. They were all wearing branded outdoor gear and the irritating rustle of Gore-Tex jackets accompanied their every movement.

These were the type of people who climbed mountains for fun, and not because they've eaten a record number of kebabs. I could tell we had absolutely nothing in common, so there wouldn't be much idle chit-chat for us tonight. Even if we had wanted to stay up there was nothing to do. Signs boldly stating 'You are not allowed to play cards' adorned the walls, so for me it would be dinner followed by bed. Wegs planned to stay up and read as there was no fine print on the draconian signs saying '. . . or read books either'. He felt that it was too early to go to bed. I knew he would pay for that decision tomorrow.

The warmth of the fire began to soothe our aching muscles, muscles I didn't know I had, and I soon became very, very tired. We'd been told that a 5 a.m. start was required in order to reach the summit and return to the car within daylight hours. I'm used to being up at 5 a.m., but normally I am getting home from a club and climbing into bed, as opposed to getting up out of it. I left Wegs reading his book and headed off to bed. I brushed my teeth before climbing into my bunk bed and sliding beneath four heavy blankets. It was only 7.30 p.m. but within minutes I fell into a deep sleep. I was soon snoring heavily, mouth open, and dreaming vividly of cushioned chairlifts and courtesy helicopters.

I awoke to the sound of rustling plastic bags and hushed German voices. I figured it must have been a fraction before 5 a.m. because only one couple was up and about. I'd been camping and hiking once before, and I instinctively knew it was time to get going. 'Be prepared' I thought to myself. My six months in the boy scouts had stood me in good stead.

I stealthily crawled out of bed so as not to wake the rest of the mountaineers in the room. This wasn't through a desire to be polite or considerate, but because I wanted to prove a point by beating those fitness freaks up the mountain. I tapped Wegs on the top bunk to wake him but he was already up and gone. I thought that Wegs must've been a boy scout too. I dressed in record time and left the room ahead of the German couple who had woken me. I was so proud of myself. I met Wegs as he was coming out of the toilets.

'Sshh. Let's go. I've got all the gear from under the bunk. I want to beat these poofs,' I said eagerly.

'What are you doing, Dav?' Wegs looked surprised. 'It's 8.30!'

'Shit. We're late. Come on.'

'8.30 P.M!'

'What?' I'd only been in bed for one hour. I turned away and could hear Wegs sniggering with delight. I chose to say nothing and returned to the dorm, in time to see the German couple climbing *into* bed.

I undressed and lay in bed embarrassed and wide awake, and spent the next few hours listening to every turn of the body, every breath, every snore and every passing of wind. Eventually I must've fallen asleep, as Wegs and I both awoke at 8.30 a.m. to an empty dorm. Not even the relentless early-morning scrunching of plastic bags that had tormented us in hostels the world over had woken us. Begrudgingly, I climbed out of bed and dressed for the day, again.

Outside the refuge we caught our first glimpse of Mt Olympus. It was an amazing sight in its morning splendour. A long and wide mountain, it had eight peaks; the highest, Mytikos, was our objective. We set off briskly. Three hours later our brisk pace had slowed as the terrain became steeper and the air thinner. An hour from Mytikos our lungs and thighs were burning. Why were we doing this?

We continued our ascent to the summit and soon passed our German mountaineering colleagues, as they continued their *descent* from the summit.

'Guten tag,' they offered cheerily.

'G'day,' we replied in insincere unison.

'Smart-arses,' I muttered to myself.

We pushed on for a further forty minutes but sadly, with the summit in sight, I could go no further. The last section had become more like a rock climb rather than the walk up a mountain it had been. The summit is long and thin and the final one hundred metres to Mytikos is truly terrifying. I got to within twenty metres but could go no further. Vertigo crowded my thoughts and all I wanted to do was return to the safety of the previous peak. Just a few feet to our left was a vertical drop of over 2000 metres. One false step would result in certain death. I clung tightly to the rock in front of me as the unsettling wind howled through the narrow section where Wegs and I were on high alert perched. Our senses were on high alert and for the first time in a long while we were deadly serious.

'Shit. This is the scariest thing I have ever done in my life,' yelled Wegs, and he doesn't suffer from vertigo. I could see in his eyes that he wasn't just saying it to make me feel better. 'C'mon Dav, you're nearly there. You can make it,' he encouraged.

Despite his desperate pleas for me to continue, it was the end of the road for me. My phobia was becoming a dangerous liability, and I needed to keep moving – backwards. If I didn't move soon I could feel I wouldn't be able to move at all. I was terrified and could only look at the rock right in front of me. By focusing on this rock I was able to temporarily trick my phobia into believing I was no longer standing so perilously close to possible death. I left Wegs to climb the remaining section as I crawled back down and across the narrow escarpment to the safety of the ledge below. It wasn't the perfect climbing technique but I was concentrating hard and taking particular care with my foot and hand placement. I was *not* going to fall. I remained in this focused mind-set for the forty-five minutes it took me to reach safe ground, a very relieved man.

Taking a seat, some ten metres back from the edge, I looked across to the summit to see Wegs filming me. I waved shakily as if I were stranded on a desert island. He gave me the team salute and then finished filming the amazing view before he too had to negotiate the treacherous passage between summit and safety. I sat back and relaxed while the adrenalin rushed through my body, and managed to stop shaking after about five minutes. In my solitary position above the clouds, high on life, I felt on top of the world.

Half an hour later Wegs arrived safely back to sit by my side. He was still experiencing the high of scaling Mytikos and the relief of making it back to tell the tale. A tale he'd recorded on camera. We played back the footage he'd filmed just minutes earlier and I was able to view his entry into the Mytikos log book:

Weggos God of Gyros
Paul Wegner
I lost two mates on the climb up wish they had made it to share this amazing view. Can see why the Greeks thought this was the center of the earth!!!
Albany Western Australia.

Wegs' ambiguous entry in the summit book read like an obituary, but his recording of the moment did serve to highlight a very important fact: even though Whitey was no longer with us physically, he was most certainly not forgotten.

I sat with Wegs at the centre of the universe and enjoyed a rare moment of clarity. I realised that climbing Mt Olympus had provided us with a galvanising experience, one that we needed in order to confront the remainder of our ambitious journey, a man down. It had taken a couple of days of putting on a brave face and singing forgettable eighties music, and a walk up a really high mountain for us to understand the impact of the change to the dynamics of our team.

Now I *knew* we were back.

11: 'MACEDONIAN PAPERWEIGHT?'

Wegs and I received this email in a smoky Internet cafe in Thessaloniki. It seemed poor old Whitey couldn't take a trick at the moment.

'Poor bugger,' I said to Wegs.

'Yeah. Poor bugger,' agreed Wegs.

I returned to my inbox and there was an email from the *TNT* editor in London. I hastily opened it to receive the exciting news that I'd been offered the gig to write the 'On the Road' column for the magazine for the next three months. All I had to do was supply four hundred words about our exploits by 3 p.m. every

Tuesday, and I was going to be paid to do so. This was huge news. I read the email aloud to Wegs, hardly able to contain my excitement and bulging pride.

'Good work, mate,' said Wegs, patting me on the back.

I was now a legitimate travel writer and an international hearse adventurer. I liked the sound of that.

A brief email check was all we had time for because we wanted to hit the road and make the Macedonian border by lunchtime. We had heard some horror stories about delays crossing this border and we wanted to get through Macedonia and across to Croatia as quickly as possible.

It wasn't long before we found ourselves passing through the green fields of northern Greece towards Polikastro and the Greece–Macedonia border. The green pasture and healthy crops were in stark contrast to the polluted concrete mass of Athens. The steady cruise through the rolling countryside had a peaceful Sunday drive feel to it.

We arrived in a relaxed state of mind only to find a line of goods trucks stretching as far as the eye could see. We sighed and reluctantly accepted our position at the tail end of the queue. The Sunday drive had hit peak-hour traffic. There was no way we were going to get through the border today. The truck drivers were out of their vehicles and standing around in groups smoking and chatting amongst themselves. We pulled up short of the rearmost group and killed the engine. It was an hour or so before our arrival was noticed. Then the nearest group of drivers approached the car and started yelling in Greek or Macedonian, I wasn't quite sure which. They appeared genuinely concerned about something, and as they came closer they became much louder. However, despite their wild gesticulations they didn't appear threatening.

'What are they saying, Wegs?'

'How the fuck should I know!'

Were they reacting to the hearse? How the different cultures reacted to the hearse was always unpredictable and of concern. Could it be that the Macedonians were the first nationality who didn't appreciate the innocent and light-hearted notion of a couple of blokes holidaying in a funeral car? I was no longer relaxed. I was confused.

A toothless truck driver stuck his head in Wegs' window and yelled, 'Car. Go!' Or at least that was what it sounded like. We liked the idea of 'go' so I started up the Big Girl and pulled out from the line of trucks. This action was met with smiles from the group of truck drivers, who parted to make way for us. They began to point enthusiastically towards the border and a couple of them even started clapping. We continued to cautiously queue jump around the outside of the stationary truck convoy. As we rounded a bend we became aware of a cars-only lane next to the trucks-only lane. We'd been unnecessarily waiting in the truck lane for over an hour. The truck drivers had actually been trying to help us and weren't abusing us. We sailed straight up to a booth where a gorgeous Greek policewoman enthusiastically stamped our passports. With a smile and a wave we were sent off to the Macedonian entry point. It was as easy as that. The confusion and tension departed and we drove off in high spirits.

'She was smiling at me more,' I said.

'Piss off. It was all me!' he insisted. The banter had returned.

Crossing for the first time from an EU country to a non-EU country was easier than we expected and we predicted that, at this rate, we would drive straight through Macedonia and reach Croatia later that night. Pulling up at the Macedonian booth we confidently handed over our passports. We knew this would take longer as we had to buy an entry visa. Macedonia is one of the few European countries where visas can be purchased on entry at the border. Luckily for us, because installing a CD player, a sunroof and a car fridge in the Big Girl had been the extent of our forward planning.

'Papers,' requested the border official.

'Wegs,' I said, expecting him to hand over the Big Girl's insurance and ownership papers. The Big Girl is a right-hand-drive vehicle and therefore in the left-hand-drive world of Europe it is the passenger that deals with the paperwork at any tollbooth, car park or border crossing.

'I don't have them. You've got them. Haven't you?' Wegs asked.

We often played these little tricks. I gave Wegs the token laugh he expected so he would stop fooling around and deal with the paperwork.

'I seriously don't have them, Dav. *You* must have them!' he stressed. I began to think he wasn't joking.

'No. Why would *I* have them? Look in the glove box.'

Wegs began frantically tearing through the glove box and centre console. He was working himself into a panicked frenzy.

This was classic Wegner behaviour so I just let him go. Normally it's his misplaced passport or wallet that triggers this type of reaction, before he finds he's been sitting on it or that it was in one of his pockets. However, it's usually not found until he's proclaimed it lost or stolen half a dozen times after the most cursory 'boys' search. I watched as he stuck closely to his 'lost personal items' script.

'Papers!' the official repeated impatiently.

'Where are they, Dav?'

I rolled my eyes to reflect the stupidity of this question. Wegs was now in the back seat ripping open our secret compartments. I felt sure they would materialise and that Wegs would learn a valuable lesson about the importance of remaining calm. However, they failed to magically appear.

'Whitey's got them!' he exclaimed. 'He put them with his travel documents after we got that driving ticket in Italy.'

I realised that was the last time I'd seen them also and I became alarmed. This could be very inconvenient.

'Move. Move!' the official had left his booth and appeared at my window. He motioned for us to move ahead and pull over outside the control point as we were holding up dozens of cars. I obliged and Wegs and I got out to check the back, as that was the last place they could possibly be.

Despite only having luggage for two, the rear compartment of the hearse was surprisingly full and, unsurprisingly, poorly packed. I tried in vain to remove my large backpack but it wouldn't budge. Wegs came over to assist and we both started pulling at it with all our might. Finally the massive pack came free and landed on the ground with an audible and lifeless thump. God only knows what the assembled crowd of police and civilians thought we were trying to remove. I waved to the intrigued crowd and received many waves and friendly smiles.

The border official had also become highly amused by our manic actions, now that we had stopped obstructing the flow of traffic. With all of our personal effects spread out on the ground it was clear we didn't have our papers.

'OK. You buy insurance. Fifty euro. No worry no more,' he offered. It was a short-term fix to a long-term problem, but it would have to do for now.

We went inside and paid the insurance with our last fifty euro. Our next problem quickly arose when our passports were handed back with freshly stamped visas: we no longer had the twenty euros required to pay for our entry visas. We had absolutely no cash, and with no bank in sight it seemed we had finally run out of options. Our day that had started on a high at Mt Olympus appeared destined to finish on a low at the Macedonian border. Then our friendly official pulled us aside and we discovered we did have an option: the kindness of the Macedonian people.

'You make us all laugh,' he said with a sweeping action that indicated he was talking on behalf of the twenty onlookers. 'I will make conversation with boss and when I do, you go. It is good. Have fun. Enjoy Macedonia.'

We thanked our new friend and quickly snuck away from border control as he distracted his boss. Little did we know that this wouldn't be the last time that the kindness of the Macedonians would save us from a difficult situation.

Despite successfully making it into the country we were still without the Big Girl's insurance papers. With further border crossings between Macedonia and Croatia still to be negotiated we needed to try and get the original paperwork back into our possession. We pulled over up the road, Wegs got out the guide-book and found a phone number for a hostel in the Plaka. With fingers crossed we dialled the number in the hope that Whitey was staying there. It took me seven or eight attempts to dial the correct sequence of numbers as I struggled with the confusing international dialling codes. Finally it rang and a female English employee answered the phone and, even better, there was a J. White in residence.

'I think he's at the bar,' she added. I was confident it would be our J. White.

'Hello?' Whitey's familiar voice greeted me on the line.

'G'day mate. It's me.'

'G'day. How's things?'

'Good mate . . . listen. I'm sorry but I have to be very quick, the battery is about to go flat any second. Just wondering if you've got the Big Girl's papers?' I asked hurriedly.

'Well, funny you should ask. I do!'

'Thank God for that.'

'Yeah, I found them in my stuff this morning. I've given them to Quincy, they're going the same way as you blokes.'

'You beauty!' I exclaimed, punching the air. 'How will they get them to us?'

'Where are you?'

'Heading to Skopje, the Macedonian capital.'

'OK. They're leaving for Macedonia in the morning. I've given Quincy your number, and the boys should be through in the next couple of days.'

'Excellent mate, that is —' The line went dead, but we knew enough. Whitey was well and the boys would bring the papers through soon. We could relax.

Wegs was filming me as we drove off towards Skopje and I turned to the camera he was sticking in my face and said: 'We always, always, land on our feet!'

It was midnight when we arrived in Skopje and booked ourselves into a reasonable hotel. The Hotel Ambassador was a block or two south of the Vardar River, on the new side of town, and seemed central enough.

Wegs joined me at reception with our bags as I finalised the registration and collected the key, before bundling into the lift and ascending the three floors to our room. We flopped down on the squeaky twin beds. It had been a testing and tiring couple of days and I was looking forward to some quality rest and relaxation. Wegs fell asleep instantly, while I lay contentedly on top of a lumpy mattress with my head resting on an equally lumpy pillow. Staring at the ceiling I ran through the recent highs and lows in my mind. What if this? What if that? Before long I too was sound asleep. We were both fully clothed.

We awoke to bright morning sunshine streaming in through the window. I opened the double-glazed windows to reveal the sights and sounds of a lively city that had been hidden under the cover of darkness. Seeing things in daylight for the first time is always a strange sensation, and it was impossible to believe the lively intersection three storeys below was the same deserted one we drove through last night. Dourly dressed pedestrians walked haphazardly through the intersection chocked with boxy little cars and overcrowded buses. Vehicles jostled noisily for position, tooting horns and revving engines but with little effect in the grid-locked morning chaos. It appeared to be much quicker to walk to work in this city, than to drive. Clothing and food stalls lined the bare street of the night before providing the only colour in the crowded scene below, but despite the pollution and congestion I was strangely invigorated watching Skopje come to life for the day. I drew in a deep breath of exhaust fumes and felt alive.

After breakfast we jumped into the Big Girl to have a look around. Typically, we knew very little about the history, culture and politics of Macedonia – apart from a few brief paragraphs in our guidebook. It informed us that due to its natural resources and strategic position in the centre of the Balkan Peninsula, Macedonia had often been regarded as a 'political powder keg'. Over the centuries it had been conquered by a succession of foreign armies, making modern-day Macedonia an interesting blend of cultural influences. The guide gave us a very basic appreciation of a complex country but that didn't overly concern us; we figured we would work the rest out in good time.

Shortly into our drive we were struck by the contrast between life in Macedonia and life in Greece, given their geographical proximity. The guidebook mentioned that Macedonia's neighbouring countries had significant historical and political differences, but to us the main difference between the cultures was obvious: the women.

Macedonian women are tall and slender and have an Eastern European beauty not evident in the matronly Greek females. The Eastern European look is largely due to the Slavic occupation of Macedonia in the seventh century, which was pivotal in changing the ethnic character of the region. As we toured through downtown and suburban Skopje we thanked the Slavs for invading and occupying this fertile land, all those centuries ago. The women were truly amazing. I made a mental note that if I were ever to live in this part of the world I would have a Greek wife, and a Macedonian mistress.

A few hours later our impromptu tour of greater Skopje was cut short by a sudden thunderstorm. We found ourselves driving through axle-deep water as the drains overflowed, unable to deal with the sudden deluge. The narrow country lanes turned into streams and, despite enjoying driving through the big puddles and creating large splashes, we thought it best to return to town.

On the main arterial road into Skopje I noticed the Big Girl was running a bit rough. I put the foot down, as all bad drivers do, to blow away the cobwebs responsible for this problem. With this action the Big Girl died instantly. We'd lost all power. I moved across to the service lane, without power-assisted steering or brakes, and safely rolled to a stop. Wegs and I looked at each other blankly.

'Alternator?' Wegs asked. People who know absolutely noth-ing about cars think any mechanical problem is always the fault of the alternator.

'Yeah, I reckon so.'

'What do we do?'

'Sit here and turn it over every couple of minutes and hope the problem goes away.'

'Good idea.'

We did just that. After a couple of hours of trying this approach the problem didn't go away as hoped. It was still pour-ing with rain and any attempt to get out to inspect the engine would be futile. Actually, in any weather an attempt by us to inspect the engine would be futile. But it would help our peace of mind. We resolved to have an engine inspection if and when it stopped raining. Meanwhile we sent an SOS SMS to Wegs' friend's father back in Perth. He's a mechanic, and while we realised it was unlikely he could come and assist us, he might have a suggestion as to how we could approach the problem. A reply came through immediately.

Dry distributor cap. Dry plugs.

To which we replied:

Will it just dry itself?

Answer:

No. Use a drying agent or hair dryer.

Practical advice, but sadly Whitey had taken his hair dryer with him so we would have to improvise and use some paper towel instead. The rain had let up somewhat and the time had come to be proactive. Once under the bonnet we discovered we had to remove the air filter in order to access the distributor at the rear of the engine. We used the same all-in-one gadget we'd used on the flat tyre in Portugal, the one that had everything from a spanner to a corkscrew. Fortunately it also had a Phillips head screwdriver, finally justifying its purchase, and we were able to remove the filter. We then removed the distributor cap and all the plug leads, drying them as best we could.

We held little hope that our effort would resolve the problem. Sure enough, I turned the key again to no avail. As we sat back to reconsider, a common boxy little Macedonian car pulled up behind us and, much to our surprise, only one man emerged from it. We'd observed that most cars in Macedonia, no matter how small, carried a minimum of six people, because owning a car appeared to be a luxury afforded by very few. The man came up to the passenger's window as no doubt he, like many before him, thought this was the driver's side. We got out to greet him, and thankfully his limited knowledge of English exceeded our non-existent Macedonian. He identified himself as 'Sashko the Mechanic' and promptly stuck his head under the bonnet and started playing with the connections and leads. He worked systematically as he tried to identify the source of our problem. After an hour or so he repeatedly tapped a part of the electronic ignition system and turned to us, proclaiming it to be 'bad'.

'We take to Ford. You come with me,' he said, pointing to Wegs. Wegs squeezed himself into the front seat, with his knees up around his ears, and the car roared down the wide arterial road towards Ford.

I watched the nondescript car merge into the throng of traffic and noticed our surroundings for the first time since we'd broken down. We were beside a busy main road connecting suburban and downtown Skopje. It was eight manic lanes wide and was lined as far as my squinting eyes could see with large concrete apartment buildings – conforming exactly to my stereotype of suburban Eastern-bloc existence. Life in this part of town appeared bleak, although my perception wasn't helped by the sleeting rain and the incapacitated Big Girl.

I returned from my musings to the Big Girl, and got chatting to an interested bystander who had been watching Sashko the Mechanic work. He implied, through broken English, that he would like to try and fix the car. I nodded acceptance and he handed me his umbrella and dove under the bonnet. I stood by his side holding his umbrella over him, feeling like a golf caddy. He worked in a similar diligent and systematic fashion to Sashko the Mechanic.

Twenty minutes later Wegs and Sashko the Mechanic returned and I rushed to greet them. Wegs informed me that Ford had shut for the day and we would have to wait until tomorrow to get the car towed to the workshop. Sashko the Mechanic offered to give us a lift to our hotel.

'You not sleep in car. Police think you terrorist. Especially with elections coming up,' he informed us.

We appreciated his sincere advice but we couldn't leave the Big Girl stranded alone by the side of the road. We would either have her fixed and move on, or sleep with her on the road. This part of Skopje didn't appear to be the safest place for a lady to be out on her own at night.

Sashko the Mechanic apologised for not being able to do more for us and promised that he would check on us in the morning. We had no doubt we would see him tomorrow.

We returned to see how Macedonian mechanic No. 2 was going. I noted ashamedly that he was now quite damp. I had temporarily neglected my caddying duties and assumed the umbrella to be my own. With the umbrella back over its rightful owner's head he informed us, as best he could, that he would head home and then return. At least that was my understanding. He shook my hand and promised he would be back. As he departed he asked my name, I think.

'Nem?' he asked and pointed at me.

'D-a-v. And this is P-a-u-l,' I said, as if he were retarded.

'Me A-m-e-c-k,' he replied, as if we were retarded.

'Ah, Mick,' I said as he headed off without his umbrella. 'Don't forget this'.

I wouldn't have blamed Mick for not returning, as it was very cold, very wet and soon it would be very dark. We jumped back into the car and felt helpless again now that our good Samaritans had departed. Even though we hadn't fixed the Big Girl that day there was something reassuring about Sashko and Mick's presence in this unfamiliar environment.

Half an hour later we received a knock on the window. The

windows had fogged up so I opened the door to see Mick standing there in his overalls and carrying a toolbox. I was delighted
to see him and we set to work immediately. He was on the tools
and I was back on the umbrella. What a team. Soon we were
ready to test the leads. Wegs was in the driver's seat control-
ling the ignition and I was standing at the edge of the bonnet
between him and Mick. It was raining hard and difficult to
hear, particularly under *my* umbrella. Mick would first yell
an instruction to me, I would then yell it to Wegs who in turn
would yell confirmation back to me.

'Cornetact!' Mick would yell, trying to say 'contact'.

'Cornetact!' I would pass on, giggling.

'Cornetact!' Wegs would reply, also giggling.

'Sterat!' Mick would yell, trying to say 'start'.

'Sterat!' I would parrot.

'Sterat!' Wegs would reply.

'Stoop!'

'Stoop!'

'Roger that. Stoop!' said Wegs, occasionally throwing in a bit
of two-way radio jargon for my amusement.

It was great comic relief. We repeated this procedure for all
six of the engine leads but still had no joy starting the car. Mick
even tried, without success, a replacement distributor cap he
had brought from his home. He, like Sashko, apologised for not
doing enough to help and promised to return in the morning.
It was dark and all too apparent that we would be sleeping in
the Big Girl by the side of the road. We would have to run the
risk of being suspected as terrorists. It was an educated risk in

my book, surely we could never be confused for being terrorists, that would be absurd.

I set off for a nearby shop to buy some comfort food for our unscheduled sleepover and returned with standard slumber-party fare: chips, chocolate, marshmallows, bread, bananas, sardines and a couple of stubbies. We moved into the back seats, put the food in the fridge between us and slid into our sleeping bags.

We sat the video camera on the centre console in front of us and for the next three hours we played back several of the tapes we'd recorded throughout Europe. In those few hours we could have been anywhere; we certainly didn't feel that we were stuck in a broken-down hearse by the side of a busy road in a strange and distant country.

The following morning I awoke before Wegs and snuck off to get us a couple of coffees. Mercifully it wasn't raining. I entered a small cafe and ordered a couple of coffees by holding up two fingers and pointing to the espresso machine. While the coffees were being prepared I went to the toilets and, like the vagrant I was, had a wash in the sink. Walking out of the bathroom I could hear a Dandy Warhols' song about cars not working playing on the radio. It continued my recent run of hearing highly relevant song lyrics. I couldn't help but smile. I was confident we'd be back on the road soon.

Soon after downing our sweet coffees both Mick and Sashko turned up to see how we were. Sashko thought we were mad to have slept in the car. It turned out he was an interpreter for the NATO-led KFOR peacekeeping force and he knew, from experience, that we were very lucky not to have been arrested. We'd been blissfully unaware of the dangers but made a mental note not to push our luck too far. We would take such advice more seriously next time.

We relayed to Mick, via Sashko, that we planned to push the Big Girl the two kilometres to the Ford workshop. He thought it was a silly idea and he was right, it was a silly idea, but it was a silly idea that would save us some money. They said their final farewells and wished us luck. We thanked them earnestly. Despite not fixing the car they'd helped us beyond words.

We decided to take it in turns to push the Big Girl, and Wegs was to take the first turn.

'Push! Push!' I bellowed from the driver's seat with my foot firmly planted on the brake pedal. When the throbbing veins in Wegs' forehead threatened to burst I took my foot off the brake, breaking into fits of laughter, and we slowly began to gather momentum. We successfully negotiated a busy intersection, reaching the other side as the lights turned red. Wegs was totally exhausted so we exchanged positions. I also pushed to exhaustion before we both collapsed, with chests heaving and lungs burning. We had progressed eighty metres.

We had grossly underestimated how difficult it was to push a three-tonne vehicle up a slight incline. There was no way we would make it to the Ford workshop, so we resigned ourselves to flagging down a tow truck. This was not a difficult task; tow-truck drivers, like crows to a carcass, tend to have a knack of finding you. Within minutes a large flat-tray tow truck came to our rescue.

Sol, the driver, was friendly and before long we were riding up front with him on the way to a workshop of his recommendation. It was a local workshop run by a bloke called Akim whose quick and clinical inspection of the Big Girl confirmed Sashko the Mechanic's diagnosis: a problem with the electronic ignition and a new part would have to come from Athens. This would mean a wait of at least three days. There was nothing more we could do so we headed off to collect our thoughts over a pint, or two.

We took up residence at the Penguin Pub in the heart of Skopje. It was a new bar with a nice atmosphere and friendly staff. Dean was our enthusiastic young barman whose angular features were softened by a beaming smile, which wasn't marred by missing a front tooth. He was enjoying the new clientele as it gave him a rare opportunity to practise his English. He was enjoying the tips too, given that his daily salary equated to the cost of three beers. After we'd been at the bar for only a few hours he'd already managed to earn his weekly salary a few times over.

Later that evening Dean introduced us to his boss, Hugo. He was only twenty-three, but at around six foot four and twenty-odd stone in the old measurements Hugo already had the build of a seasoned publican. Like every other Macedonian we had encountered, he was a bloody good bloke. Upon hearing we were Australian Hugo called over his new business partner. Vlad was born in Macedonia but had spent the last ten years managing nightclubs in Sydney, catering to the local Macedonian community. Vlad was a suave and polished host and was excited to meet some Aussies to whom he could extend some local courtesy.

He quickly had us seated at the VIP table and within five minutes he'd even offered to get his mum to do our washing for us! Our polite refusal was unconditionally and summarily rejected. We were to bring our washing to the pub tomorrow night and that was final. The remainder of the night was spent telling stories and drinking numerous shots of rakia (the local digestive), tequila and anything else that took Hugo's fancy.

The following night was much the same. We sheepishly dropped off our washing for Vlad's mum and sat down in the same seats, drank the same range and quantity of alcohol and most probably told the same stories. I certainly suffered the same hangover.

Within just two days, life at the Penguin Pub in Skopje had become very familiar and very comfortable. Hugo, Vlad and their staff made us feel like a part of their family, which was fine by us because it meant we got to live in a pub.

On my third day in Macedonia, with my second hangover, I was woken by the familiar beep of an incoming text message on my mobile phone. It was from Quincy. They'd made great time and were driving into Skopje at that very moment. I sent a message back suggesting we rendezvous at team headquarters, the Penguin Pub, in one hour.

An hour later Wegs and I were taking great pride in introducing Hugo, Vlad and Dean to Quincy, Rosy, JB, Ryan and Neddy. With the car not due to be ready for another day we indulged in another lively session at the Penguin Pub.

The next morning I awoke with the same dry mouth I'd had the previous two mornings, and therefore found it difficult to speak when Akim called to tell us that the part for the Big Girl hadn't arrived yet.

'Maybe tomorrow,' was the best he could offer.

In light of this information we rescheduled our departure, in as much as we had a schedule, for another day or possibly two. Quincy and the boys were happy to stay as long as it took the Big Girl to be fixed as we had planned to travel in convoy through Kosovo. Safety in numbers. The prospect of another day and night in the Penguin Pub scared our now feeble bodies, so it was decided to head up into the hills to Lake Matka for a day of swimming and sightseeing. However, I had my first deadline looming and chose to remain in the hotel to complete my article for *TNT*. I would meet the others later at team headquarters.

A day on my own seemed an enchanting prospect after our recent excesses. I headed downstairs to enquire about Internet access. We were now staying at a hotel run by Vlad's cousin, Igor, and were receiving mates rates – or should I say family rates. Igor was at reception and vacated the hotel computer for my personal use. He assured me it was no problem and asked if I could keep an eye on things for an hour or so while he popped out to run some errands. It was one of my more productive hours of the trip. I finished my article as well as collecting room keys from departing guests and answering the phone.

When I returned to my room for a brief nap, my phone beeped with a new message. It was from Quincy:

slight delema, we r in a millatary police cell, wegs has not got his passport. will inform u when we know whats going on. hows the big girl?

Did they really think I was born yesterday? They were obviously pulling my leg at Wegs' request, so I replied:

 Bullshit. Find out tomorrow am about big girl. By the way u spelt military rong!

There was something about the tone of his reply that made me take the second message more seriously:

 No joke, please bring wegs passport to police station, get taxi, georgepetrov, bring yours as well, no cameras, this is serious, asap.

If I had known that Quincy had an armed Military Policeman looking over his shoulder at these messages I would have worded my reply differently:

 OK. Will mobilise contacts.

The situation was serious, and in this time of need I turned to my family. I caught a taxi directly to the Penguin Pub. It wasn't yet open for business but fortunately all of my new relatives were present. I briefed Hugo and Vlad on the situation, saying I was surprised they'd got into trouble as they'd only planned to go for a swim in Lake Matka.

'Matka! What?' Hugo's tone alarmed me. 'Why they go there? Who said go there? You should ask me! That is Albanian area. No go!'

We had been blissfully unaware that, although there's no

war at the moment, regional tensions still run high in Macedonia and pockets of localised unrest are commonplace. The complex history of the turmoil of the former Yugoslavia had been explained in detail in our nights at the pub, but the alcohol consumption meant that it was forgotten as quickly as it was heard. What I remembered though was that Macedonians and Albanians don't particularly like each other, and the Lake Matka district was an area controlled by rebel Albanian forces.

Hugo took a moment to calm down and then grabbed me by the arm and pulled me towards the door. As we departed, the ever-relaxed Vlad called out some words intended to comfort me:

'Don't worry, Dav. Your washing will be ready in the morning.'

Hugo told me to climb aboard his motorbike and hang on. There was no time to put on helmets as we roared off in the direction of Georgepetrov Police Station. The next ten minutes were some of the most terrifying of my life as we sped down the wrong side of the road to avoid the slow-moving traffic. Occasionally we were forced to brake suddenly and pull over to avoid oncoming trucks. Hugo, laughing like a madman, roared through red light after red light. Through my watering eyes I could see the speedo hovering on the wrong side of 130 km/h, which was pretty good going in suburban Skopje. I held on to Hugo as best I could, given that my arms couldn't reach around his chest, and buried my head into his back.

I looked up from behind Hugo when our pace finally slowed. We were pulling into the Military Police (MP) compound and I could see Quincy standing at the back of their Kombi van.

Its contents were spread out on the ground and were being thoroughly inspected by armed officers. He didn't return my smile or wave. Things were serious.

Hugo introduced himself to the plain-clothed detective who approached us, and they spoke in a serious tone. I went over to speak with Quincy but two of the officers had other ideas and pushed me into MP headquarters. They quickly relieved me of the two passports I'd been brandishing as my 'get-out-of-jail-free' cards and hustled me through the office towards a large steel door. The door opened to reveal five sets of expectant eyes focused on me. The door quickly closed behind me and I sat down on the floor to join a despondent Wegs, Rosy, JB, Ryan and Neddy. We'd expected my arrival and the presentation of passports would end this unnecessary detention, but we were wrong.

The lads were buoyed by my arrival. They'd been in the cell for over three hours and were becoming increasingly concerned as no one had been able to effectively communicate with the officers. The confidence of the group was bolstered knowing that Hugo was outside negotiating on our behalf. We would have to sit and wait. This gave me plenty of time to hear the team's combined report on how a swimming trip had landed them, and now me, in hot water.

The boys had been following crude directions to Lake Matka from an out-of-date map they had purchased. On the way out of town they'd stopped to ask directions from an official they described as looking like an army reserve officer. He was very helpful and pointed them in the direction of Lake Matka.

Further up the road they pulled over to ask a group of kids. The kids laughed when the boys mimed their intention to go for a swim but they too pointed them in the direction of the lake. They headed off, following the river as instructed, only to be confronted by two gun-toting military officers minutes later. They were told to leave the vehicle and hand over their passports.

'Five passport. Six men!' One guard shouted as his colleague stood by his side with machine gun at the ready. 'You wait. Big problem. Police come.'

Wegs, typically unprepared, was without his passport and they were forced to wait. Rosy noted it was after fifteen minutes of waiting that the guards relaxed enough to switch their weapons to the safe position. The boys weren't overly concerned at this stage. They sat by the side of the road patting the neighbourhood goats that had come over for a look.

The police arrived and four armed officers emerged from a van. They searched the Kombi and found our video cameras and tripod that Wegs had taken with him for the day. The discovery of the camera equipment aroused suspicion amongst the police. They confiscated all passports and told the boys to follow them into town to MP headquarters. The police stormed off into town at a frenetic pace. The police van weaved in and out of traffic with lights flashing and sirens blaring, ignoring every road rule along the way. The boys followed, flashing their lights and blasting their horn while actually *chasing* a police car, and being forced to speed and run red lights in order to do so.

Once at Georgepetrov they were immediately taken to the holding cell and received no further instructions, until Quincy was asked to accompany the police while they conducted a thorough search of the Kombi.

⚉ ⚉ ⚉

It was quite some time before the door opened allowing Quincy to rejoin the group. He had spent the last hour and a half assisting the police on a painstaking search of their luggage. Every bag had been searched. They had found cameras in each of the backpacks, a discovery that further aroused suspicion. Fortunately they weren't confiscated. The only other discovery that concerned the police was a box of condoms they'd found in the glove box. One of the searching officers asked Quincy if they were gay because he thought it very odd to have condoms in a car full of men. Quincy was forced to defend his and the other boys' heterosexuality and then left to pack up the entire contents of the van on his own. They found nothing, as there was nothing to find.

Shortly after Quincy's return two large men in suits entered the cell to remove him and Wegs for questioning. They allowed Hugo to speak through the peephole to inform us that we were being held under suspicion of espionage or terrorism. I could see only half his face as he stooped to talk through the small opening. He promised to do his best for us before the hatch slammed shut.

It was reassuring to know that Hugo was still present and negotiating on our behalf, although the knowledge that we were being held under suspicion of being spies or terrorists was less comforting. Given that the alternatives didn't bear thinking about, we launched into some games to kill time.

The cell was approximately three metres by three metres and encased in solid concrete. It was furnished with three uncomfortable wooden chairs and a small table. Because of the distinct lack of subject matter, and the nature of the game, I quashed Neddy's innocent suggestion to play a game of 'I Spy'.

Conversations and games could keep us entertained for only so long, and when Wegs and Quincy had been gone for over four hours a disillusioned silence fell upon the room. I sat pensively in the corner of the cell, looking at each of my fellow inmates and analysing their viability as spies.

JB sat in the chair in front of me playing with his braided hair. He was born in Samoa, raised in New Zealand and is a carpenter by trade. He is short and muscular, and heavily tattooed with a large ring through his eyebrow. I noted that his features would be too conspicuous to make a successful spy, although, like Bond, he is good with the women. Spy rating: 2/10.

Neddy, slouching in the chair next to JB, is a tall and slender bloke with a shock of untidy blond hair. His facial features are best described as unique, and he also sported an eyebrow ring. He is also too conspicuous to make a good spy but, unlike JB, is not good with the women. Spy rating: 1/10.

Ryan was in the remaining chair opposite JB and Neddy. He sat there in silence biting his nails. He's a short bloke with badly dyed blond hair and a cheeky grin. He's a butcher by trade and therefore handy with a knife. His small stature would enable him to blend into crowds. Spy rating: 4/10.

Rosy sat on the floor to my left. He had a similarly bad blond-dye job and like JB and Neddy he had an eyebrow ring. He's a fitter and turner by trade with a short concentration span. I couldn't see Rosy spying with competence. Plus he was too nice a bloke. Spy rating: 0/10.

How anyone could suspect we were capable of gathering intelligence of any description was beyond me.

I knocked on the door to request a toilet break. This action was primarily designed to break the monotony rather than through any great need to relieve myself. All toilet visits were done with an armed guard as escort. The guard on this occasion stood right next to me and was well and truly invading the private space of a gentleman about to go to the toilet. I indicated by rolling my eyes that he might like to take a step backwards to give me a little privacy. He gruffly acknowledged my request and moved away, the end of his gun brushing my thigh as he turned. I turned my attention back to my little weapon that I'd hesitantly retrieved from my pants. I must've had the safety catch switched on because it took some time before I was able to fire. Finally I relaxed and sighed audibly as things began to flow freely. I must've been more relaxed than I realised as I accidentally broke wind, also audibly.

'Oops. Sorry about that, mate,' I apologised to the impassive guard and giggled. I'm sure he was laughing on the inside.

Things were still quiet when I returned to the cell until a turn of the key saw us all look up expectantly. Quincy and Wegs re-entered and the door shut behind them. We bombarded them with questions to which they could supply no definitive answers. They felt that things had progressed well at the end of their interrogation, and Hugo had given them a hopeful thumbs-up as they were led back to the cell. As we waited the returned team members gave us a detailed account of their ordeal.

After leaving us they'd been led away, with Hugo, to another detention cell. It was larger than our current one and had a table with five chairs and a small lamp. They took their seats facing the impeccably groomed detectives. The detectives said nothing for twenty minutes. They simply turned on the lamp, lit cigarettes and blew smoke across the table at the boys and Hugo. It was like a scene from a Hollywood film. Finally one inspector reached behind him and picked up a large artillery shell and smashed it down on the table in front of them. He demanded they tell him what it was.

The boys looked at one another. It was obvious what the object was.

'Macedonian paperweight?' Quincy suggested as he and Wegs suppressed laughter. His attempt to lighten the situation failed miserably.

'You know there is still a war going on in the Matka area?' roared the enraged detective in surprisingly good English.

The boys were then subjected to skillful and manipulative questioning for another four hours. Occasionally the inspectors would revert to extended silences before asking rapid-fire questions in an attempt to catch them off guard and trick them into revealing important information. It was a good thing they didn't have any. These detectives were experienced and educated men.

They were asked about their age, occupation, bank accounts and money. They demanded to know details of who we were and what we were doing in Macedonia. You fight for money? You going to Matka to fight for Albanians? Why so many eyebrow rings? You extremists? Is JB Aboriginal? On repeated occasions they asked Quincy if he would like a smoke. He accepted the tenth offer as he felt it was the polite thing to do, and at the very least it might stop them from continually asking. The second he accepted the cigarette they started firing questions at him about drugs.

'You smoke marijuana? Cocaine? Ecstasy? Heroin? You buy? You sell?'

They were relentlessly trying to expose any crack in their armour. It was three hours into the interrogation before the questioning became more conversational in its tone and the boys sensed that the detectives knew they had absolutely nothing to hide. The interrogators now began *asking* them what we were doing in Macedonia, instead of *telling* them. Hugo stepped forward at this point and personally vouched for our character, and told them of our holiday plans and our broken-down car. Thankfully he didn't mention it was a hearse. I would hate to think what direction that would have taken the questioning. The more senior detective immediately got on the phone to Akim and ordered him in no uncertain terms to make sure our car was ready by morning. It was now 7 p.m. Wegs and

Quincy were taken back to the cell as the detectives wanted a word with Hugo in private.

They must've had a few words to say as it was at least an hour before the cell door opened to reveal a tired-looking Hugo and the detectives.

'OK. We can go!' he said triumphantly. Despite his enthusiasm there was no mistaking how exhausted he was after eight hours of negotiating.

We jumped to our feet and exchanged man-hugs and high fives with each other. We'd been officially released into Hugo's personal custody and we couldn't wait to adjourn to the pub and put this whole unsettling incident behind us. It had been a long day.

Back at the pub Hugo sat us down to outline the gravity of the situation from which we had just escaped. We'd been told a lot of this information during previous sessions at the pub but we had only paid polite attention. This time around we were genuinely interested, and sober. We listened attentively.

Hugo explained that Albanians are the largest ethnic minority in the country but are still outnumbered by Macedonians three to one. Since the break-up of the former Yugoslavia ten years ago the Albanians believe they have been discriminated against, particularly in government representation and education. The Macedonian government, on the other hand, believes that suitable concessions have already been made to the Albanian community, so tensions between the ethnic groups run high.

The NLA (National Liberation Army), the ethnic-Albanian

extremist organisation, has committed acts of terror against Macedonian inhabitants in the north-west of the country, forcing them to leave their villages. Hugo told us of an incident that had occurred recently where NLA soldiers had kidnapped and tortured five Macedonian road workers on the outskirts of Skopje. This happened on the perimeter of a cell of NLA-controlled territory, similar to the Lake Matka district. He made a point of saying that this attack was an exception to other recent incidents because these men had been released. We're not the brightest bunch of blokes in the world, but he didn't need to tell us how lucky the boys were to have been intercepted by Macedonian forces and not the NLA.

The NLA had been active in recruiting foreign mercenaries to fight, and initially the police had thought this was our motivation for heading towards Lake Matka. The drug questioning was to identify if we had links to the large organised crime syndicates that operate the multibillion-dollar Balkan drug trade, the proceeds of which are alleged to provide support to guerrilla armies.

The police officers had planned to place us in custody, and impound our gear while organising our deportation. This would have forced an end to our journey; although, in light of Hugo's speech, the journey could have ended in a much less palatable manner. We were extremely fortunate to have had Hugo there to vouch for our character and mediate tirelessly on our behalf.

We had been placed into Hugo's custody and he was responsible for making sure we left the country the following day.

It was a house arrest but in a pub, which was fitting. We were to leave at lunchtime, once the police returned our passports that were being issued with visa extensions. If we didn't leave the country the following day the police would arrest us. We got the message loud and clear. Tomorrow night we would be gone, no worries about that.

When Wegs and I arrived in Macedonia we had figured we would learn about the current political climate as we went along. We now knew more than we needed – or wanted – to know.

'And now we drink a toast to Macedonia!' Hugo bellowed as he raised a shot of rakia to his lips. We quickly refilled the glasses so I could propose a toast on our collective behalf.

'To Hugo!'

'To Hugo!' echoed the now upstanding boys.

❋ ❋ ❋

The next morning we packed up our belongings and headed back to the pub for the last time. We walked in to be greeted by Vlad, Hugo, Dean and the two police detectives. They'd come to return our passports and to wish us all the best for the remainder of our journey. We didn't know it but these two men were the highest ranking officers in Macedonia, and had been called out of important meetings to deal with the security threat we'd inadvertently created. We chatted amicably over lemonades and they were soon laughing at our travel stories. They even mapped out a safe route for us to follow through the unpredictable territories of Kosovo and Montenegro to Croatia, and repeatedly warned us to drive only through the control towns and to avoid driving at night because of the risk of extremist forces and bandits. The extremists they spoke of were the KLA (Kosovo Liberation Army), who had similar motives and methods of operation as the NLA.

'Do not drive at night!' they implored.

Lastly they asked me to make sure I mentioned how friendly the Macedonian police were in my next *TNT* article. Consider it done, gentlemen.

The time had come for us to depart. We posed out the front of the Penguin Pub with our extended Macedonian family for a smiling team photograph. What a difference a day can make. The most notable smile belonged to Dean. He made his way over to Wegs and me.

'Notice anything different?' he said, proudly tapping his new front tooth. He was beaming with pride and thanked us for the tips that had paid for the expensive dental work. His smile was now complete.

'Now I can talk to the girls,' he said excitedly.

We headed off in Hugo's car to Akim's workshop. Akim appeared to have lost several years of his life after working through the night to fix the Big Girl, as instructed by the police. The bill certainly reflected his additional input, but we were not in any position to argue. We were just thankful that our Big Girl was up and running again. It seemed a lifetime since she'd broken down. Akim explained that the problem with the electronic ignition was caused by its saturation during the thunderstorm. It was a common problem in Fords of this vintage, so to avoid the problem recurring he told us not to drive in wet conditions.

'Do not drive in the wet,' he instructed.

We scratched up enough cash between the seven of us to pay his inflated bill and headed off to do one final errand of great importance: we had to pick up our washing.

Vlad's mum lived on the tenth storey of a typically drab Macedonian block of flats. Life in suburban Skopje isn't glamorous and Wegs and I were keen to brighten things up by thanking Vlad's mum with a large bunch of flowers and a box of chocolates. The other boys waited in their van as Wegs and I entered the building. Vlad greeted us warmly and we sat down on the neat couch as his mum presented us with our impeccably clean and pressed laundry. Vlad then interpreted on his mother's behalf.

'Mum would like to thank you very much for the laundry. You are most kind and you are welcome to leave your clothes here any time'.

We couldn't believe our ears. She was actually thanking *us* for giving her our dirty stinking laundry. We were the ones supposed to be doing the thanking. We gave Vlad's mum the flowers and chocolates and passed on our most sincere thanks via Vlad. She gave us both a warm hug.

'Thank you. Thank you,' she said in heavily accented English.

We could have happily stayed longer in Macedonia had it not been for our imminent deportation. Which reminded us, it was time we got going. The Big Girl was waiting.

We presented Hugo with our Australian flag and he promised to make room for it on the wall behind our table at the Penguin Pub. Shaking hands for the final time we climbed into our vehicles for the short drive to the border. In the rear-view mirror I watched Vlad and Hugo waving enthusiastically until they became dots on the horizon. We would never forget this place or these wonderful people.

We pulled up behind Quincy and the boys at the Macedonia–Kosovo border. Quincy jumped out and walked over to the Big Girl, signalling for me to wind the window down.

'You might need these!' he said with a broad grin and handed over our insurance and ownership papers he'd brought all the way from Whitey in Athens.

'Shit. Thanks, mate.' With the sensational events of the previous few days I'd completely forgotten about these crucial papers. Minutes later I was handing them over to the border officials who'd been expecting us. They stamped our passports and wished us all the best as they pointed us in the direction of the Kosovo entry gates.

Driving through the eerie no-man's-land between Macedonia and Kosovo I was confident the recent experiences had steeled us for whatever challenges lay ahead, but as we entered the former war-torn territory with dusk approaching and storm clouds gathering overhead, the warnings repeated in my head: *Do not drive in the wet . . . do not drive through Kosovo at night!*

12: CANNONBALL RUN

'Check one, two ... Check one, two ... Check ... Check ... Check one, two.'

'Roger that. Coming through loud and clear, Big Girl.'

'Roger that Helga. Over and out.'

The radio check took place on Kosovo's doorstep. I was behind the wheel of the Big Girl, Quincy was alongside behind the wheel of Helga, their Kombi van, as we tested the portable two-way radios we'd bought in Skopje. We would have no phone reception in Kosovo and maintaining contact between the vehicles was going to be crucial for safety and team morale.

Wegs and I had JB with us in the back of the Big Girl. Helga was like a tin of sardines with five adults on board, so it made sense for us to spread the passenger load between the vehicles.

'We need some tunes, Bro!' JB suggested from the rear of the Big Girl.

'Can do, Bro,' Wegs replied.

Wegs inserted the *A-Team* CD into the stereo and cranked up the iconic theme song to full volume. I looked over to the crew aboard Helga who were all pumping their fists in time to the inspiring tune. Quincy waved his upturned palm, indicating for me to head off and take the lead for our journey into the unknown. Despite the up-vibe music and bravado, the atmosphere in both cars was tense. We were nervous, excited and scared all in one.

'Kick her in the guts, Dav!' yelled Wegs.

With an experienced touch of the throttle I eased the Big Girl forward purposefully onto the main road. Our cannonball run through Kosovo was under way.

The plan was to follow the route that our friendly Macedonian inspectors had mapped out for us. It followed the main roads between the control towns and while it wasn't the most direct route to the city of Podgorica, it was the safest. They instructed us to stop for fuel only. Under no circumstances were we to stop and film our crossing or take photos. This was not a sightseeing trip.

We appreciated all too well that to avoid risking further brushes with the law, or with rogue bandits, we needed to play the percentages. The cameras were buried away safely in the bowels of the Big Girl and they wouldn't be seeing any action until we had made it to safe ground in Croatia. One ill-considered move or idea could have the most serious of implications. The plan was simple in theory; we hoped it would be as simple in practice. Kosovo was no place to take risks.

The inspectors had implored us not to drive at night in Kosovo; however, we'd been delayed by the late return of our passports and by our errands, and it was now 3 p.m. With six hours of driving ahead of us we could not complete the journey within daylight hours. We would have to make an important team decision in a few hours. Either that, or drive really bloody fast.

My other concern was the thunderstorm hovering over the distant mountains we needed to traverse in order to reach Podgorica tonight. Avoiding the storm was not going to be an option. At some stage today the big man upstairs was going to rain on our parade. I could only hope that Akim and his team had properly fixed the Big Girl's waterlogged electrics. Only time would tell.

Our first destination was Pristina, the largest town in Kosovo. It was roughly one hundred kilometres from the Macedonian border and we estimated it would take us just over an hour to reach. The drive began well enough as we set out along the E65. The road was quite wide by European standards but poorly maintained, and the regular potholes were bone-jarring. From the border it passed through lush fields and cereal crops that were as healthy and abundant as any we had seen on our travels. However, it wasn't long before our reasonable progress was slowed significantly by heavy traffic. The Sunday drive lasted around ten kilometres, after which we found ourselves constantly fighting for road position with large trucks and buses. We approached Pristina and our progress slowed even further as the huge amount of traffic from the E65 merged with the day-to-day traffic of small outlying villages. At times we came to a complete standstill. We hadn't envisaged encountering such a large volume of traffic and I was concerned about our schedule.

On the outskirts of Pristina we passed several heavily barricaded compounds guarded by armed soldiers in sentry towers. It seemed every second vehicle was affiliated with the army, UN, UNICEF or the Red Cross, and large supply trucks choked the undeveloped road system. The high concentration of military and international peacekeeping forces was a constant reminder that this territory was still highly volatile.

Pristina was one of the control towns on our route to Podgorica. A control town, we had worked out, was one under the control of KFOR, the international peace force responsible for overseeing the safe return and introduction of structured society in the region. We were entering a control town by day and as such I wasn't worried about ethnic extremists or bandits, but I was concerned about how the locals would react to the hearse. Would they misinterpret our presence as a tasteless and insensitive gesture? Would they respond violently? I had no idea what would transpire. We could pass through unnoticed or we could pass through and set back diplomatic relations between our respective nations for years to come. If the latter were to happen, it was fortunate that the Big Girl was registered in the United Kingdom.

We would find out soon enough. Ahead a soldier directing traffic had commanded me to stop, at the busiest pedestrian intersection in Pristina. My palms were clammy as I surveyed the crowds of dourly clad civilians to gauge their response. It was similar to our test drive of the Big Girl in downtown Cork, except this time I was completely shitting myself.

I slowed the Big Girl to a graceful stop and the pedestrians began to make their way across the street. As they passed in front of the Big Girl, every pedestrian stared at us through the windscreen. Their expressions were largely impassive, giving little insight as to their thoughts. A few men had stopped in their tracks to survey us more closely, and a couple of men had walked over from the footpath and now stood at the rear, staring inside. This made me very uneasy. The soldier blew on his whistle and instructed me to move on, which I had no hesitation in doing. I turned right at the next intersection and we moved slowly in the traffic along another street packed with pedestrians.

'Got your ears on, Big Girl?' It was Quincy. I could hear that he was laughing and I looked in the rear-view mirror to see him and Rosy riding up front in Helga, grinning like Cheshire cats.

'Roger that Helga.'

'They're lovin' it, man!'

'Hey?'

'The Big Girl, they love her. You should see the reactions from back here, mate. It's a pisser!'

I looked in the mirrors and over my shoulder and saw that Quincy was right. People were smiling and pointing, and laughing away merrily. We couldn't see this from within the Big Girl but Helga passed by just as the odd scene the locals had witnessed sunk in. Now it really was like the test drive in Cork: the locals were loving us and I was no longer shitting myself.

I wound down my window and waved to the crowds of people lining the road. I could smell the air and hear the noise of the city as we crawled along. I no longer felt like we were trespassing on these people's land. It was a surreal experience. People were waving back and smiling at us, and some even gave us the thumbs up. One man came over and shook my hand. I wondered what they thought we were doing, or who we were? It didn't seem to matter. The Big Girl had certainly brought some life to this small town.

'Mate. This rocks!' I laughed back to Quincy.

'I'll stop when I see a petrol station, mate.'

'Roger that.'

At the petrol station we got out and stretched our legs after the longer-than-anticipated journey. It had taken us over two hours to get to Pristina. Even though we'd received a rousing reception through town, we were under no illusions about where we were. We only had time for a short stop to refuel and go to the toilet, as it was imperative that we keep moving. We still had a large distance to cover between Pristina and Podgorica, and the less we had to cover in the darkness the better. There was a lot of 'non-control' territory between here and safety, and a lot of black clouds. After a quick team briefing over the map to get our bearings we headed off towards Pec, the next control town on our route.

We decided that Helga would lead the convoy for this leg of the journey. This would speed up our progress because she was a left-hand-drive van and the driver was in a better position to judge overtaking manoeuvres on the busy roads. En route to Pristina I'd been relying on Wegs to lean out his window and relay traffic information to me. It wasn't the safest mode of operation.

It was roughly the same distance from Pristina to Pec as it was from the Macedonian border to Pristina, and we guessed it would take approximately the same time. We were working on the assumption that the road and its traffic load would be the same as the E65. This would deliver us to Pec before sunset, when we would reassess our situation.

Unfortunately for us, the road to Pec made the E65 look like a German autobahn. At best it was fairly smooth and nearly wide enough for two cars; at worst it was as rough as guts and just wide enough for one car. The traffic was the usual smattering of small boxy cars, supply trucks, armoured vehicles and tractors. The tractors were the main problem affecting the flow of traffic on this small road. There were a huge number of them lugging heavily laden trailers of firewood, household furniture, young children or fresh produce. The narrowness of the road meant that finding an opportunity to overtake the slow vehicles was rare, especially as the traffic in the other direction was just as heavy, with just as many tractors. It was a real test of patience and character.

Helga would occasionally find her way past a large truck or slow tractor and then call us through on the two-way when they could see enough free road for the Big Girl to work up a head of steam to get past. I was getting used to the unnerving sensation of pulling out into traffic that I couldn't see. It was a team effort and the Big Girl was really putting in for us. I would regularly have to stoke her up to get past as many cars as possible before quickly ducking back into line. Such erratic driving was most out of character for a hearse, but the Big Girl realised the importance of our forward momentum and willingly complied with my instructions.

An hour or two into the journey we passed a large field full of floral wreaths. At the gate stood two armed guards, regulating the flow of civilians into the field. They stood beside a large stone monument adorned with cards and hand-painted messages.

'That's not one of those mass grave sites is it?' Rosy asked innocently over the two-way.

I felt sick to the stomach, as that was exactly what it was. We'd heard about the mass grave sites found in Kosovo; it was one thing to see them on the news but it was another thing to see them in person. This was definitely no place to be driving a hearse.

It was the rain, of all things, that helped hide us as we passed by this tragic site. The dark clouds that had been threatening for so long decided to open at that very point. The sudden deluge sent people scurrying for shelter, which allowed us to pass by without being noticed. The onset of the storm had saved us from one unpleasant predicament but it had opened up a whole new can of worms for us to deal with. We were now driving in the rain, against the advice of our experienced Macedonian mechanic. In fifteen minutes we would be driving in the darkness, against the advice of the experienced Macedonian detectives. Kosovo was keeping us on our toes.

It was 9 p.m. when we finally regrouped at a petrol station in Pec. It had taken us six hours to travel halfway to Podgorica. Should we wait in Pec overnight in the cars or continue to push on to Podgorica tonight? We had to decide which was the less risky of the two options. It would not be an easy decision. Was staying in town overnight an unnecessary stop, and a large risk? Was it a larger risk than driving at night? It wasn't as though we could just pull up to a motel and book in for the night; in fact, I doubt there was any accommodation available at all. Normal rules do not apply in Kosovo.

After refuelling we parked the Big Girl and Helga outside a small store to stock up on food and drink. We would need to eat and drink no matter which decision we made. Outside the store we took shelter under a canvas awning and had a team chat, while munching on potato chips and chunks of salami. There were lots of theories and questions flying around, but very few answers.

What was the weather forecast? How far was Podgorica? What was the time? Were there mountains all the way? Would the Montenegro border be open when we got there? Should we buy beer? What would the traffic be like? Would we make it without needing to refuel? Do bandits and kidnappers work in the rain?

In the end it was a simple decision. We would stick to the only thing that we knew for sure: we were most comfortable when we were on the move.

We were confident that as a team of seven grown men we could continue this journey safely overnight. We also had the benefit and flexibility of travelling in two cars, so, we finished our snacks and returned to our chariots. It was still teeming with rain and it looked as though we'd parked the Big Girl and Helga in the middle of a stream. Water was flowing along the road at a rapid rate and at axle depth. The heavy rain and blocked drains triggered flashbacks of the conditions that had stalled the Big Girl in Macedonia. As we scurried out to the car I hoped we could make it through the night incident-free. It was a risk we had to take.

The next few hours were the most intense and draining of my life. I had a lot on my mind; not to mention the warped wipers that only cleared the water at the ends of the blades, leaving a band of water right in front of my eyes. I had to crane my head down and to the right in order to look through clear glass. The rain was relentless as we headed deeper into the pitch-black hills, with the wipers going flat out.

Our headlights were also ineffective, and when on low beam they were barely strong enough for me to see one car length ahead. Each time a vehicle approached I'd be blinded by their lights on the smeared windscreen and unable to see the road. This was particularly dangerous in the steep mountain sections that had no lines on the road and no markers beside it. Helga, who had superior wipers, superior headlights, less weight and a manual transmission, often had to slow to a crawl to allow us to catch up.

The Big Girl's automatic transmission whined under the pressure of pulling three tonnes up the relentless mountain range, often struggling between gears. We weren't breaking any records but she was still pulling her weight – despite the endless climb, the rough roads and the pouring rain. In these conditions every minute she was running and every kilometre she gained for the team was a bonus. These remote, bandit-ridden hills were no place for a breakdown.

'Come on, Big Girl. You can do it,' I would say to her as I rubbed her dash, and touched the wood trim for good luck. I think Wegs and JB thought I'd developed a personality disorder because I wouldn't let anyone else drive, and for long periods of time I would speak only to the Big Girl. We had bonded strongly as she and I negotiated this tough challenge together.

I completely lost track of time that night. I was focused entirely on completing our safe passage. The first break in the tense monotony of our travels came at a KFOR checkpoint deep in the mountains. It was a tiny outpost that consisted of a small hand-operated boom gate and a tiny mobile office, and was positioned on this main road to stop the black-market traffic of weapons and drugs into Kosovo.

We waited behind Helga as an armed KFOR officer came outside and spoke through the window with Quincy. The rain was still driving hard and the guard must've been keen to get back into his warm office because he waved Helga through quickly. I pulled the Big Girl up next to him and he stooped down to look in the passenger window. Wegs had our passports ready and handed them over. He had a quick glance at each and looked at us in turn to confirm our appearance matched our photo. He looked at mine a while longer than the others, obviously wondering where the boy with the big hair and pimples had gone.

'Where you go? You follow with them?' he asked with a heavy German accent.

'Yes. Podgorica,' Wegs replied.

'Why you come here?' he asked in a surprised tone. He was asking out of curiosity and not as a formality.

'Holiday,' we replied.

'Holiday!' He looked back at us, smiled a cautious smile and shook his head despairingly. It was clear he thought we were completely mad to even consider such a risky journey, let alone refer to it as a *holiday* – but for us, as international hearse adventurers, it was all in a day's work.

'OK. You go . . . good luck,' he said in a bemused tone before walking over and raising the boom gate for us.

'Thanks, mate,' we replied in unison.

Despite the wild conditions he stood by the gate and watched us pass through. In the rear-view mirror I could see him watching us until we disappeared into the thick blanket of rain. He obviously didn't get too many holiday-makers through his lonely post – let alone in the middle of the night, in the middle of a fierce storm, in a hearse.

Shortly after the KFOR checkpoint we made our final stop at the Montenegro border. We got out of the vehicles and went inside the small building nestled within a thick pine forest. It proved to be the easiest border crossing of our lives – our passports were duly stamped and returned to us immediately by the dispirited employee. No further paperwork was required. It was all too easy. Technically we'd made it through Kosovo, but the journey wasn't over yet. We were still in the dangerous mountains, it was still dark and it was still raining. We wasted no time and jumped back in the cars for the final leg.

The poor weather continued but there was a general improvement in the outlook of the team. We cruised down the mountains towards safety, singing songs to each other over the two-way at full volume. It was the same regrettable eighties music that Wegs and I had sung on our departure from Athens after we'd said goodbye to Whitey. It was our comfort music. Anyway, it was less about the music and more about the release of built-up tension. Just as Wegs, JB and I launched into the chorus of Bon Jovi's 'Livin' on a Prayer' we came down out of the dark mountains and arrived at a reasonably large town. It was the first civilisation we'd seen since Pec and, although it was hard to tell through the heavy rain, the town appeared to be pretty well developed. Unlike the Kosovo towns, this one looked reassuringly normal. We turned the music down as Wegs reached for the walkie-talkie.

'Big Girl to Helga. Big Girl to Helga. Come in Helga.'

'Helga receiving,' Rosy responded.

'Is this Podgorica?' The boys in Helga had the only map of this area.

'That's a ten-four big buddy. Ten-four.'

We punched the air and tooted the horn excitedly as we rolled into town. We had made it through Kosovo and officially arrived on safe ground. I was proud of our team effort; this had been a tough assignment, one that had taken twelve long hours to complete. We'd negotiated the heavy traffic, the bad roads, the darkness, the heavy storm and the unknown factor. The irony was that the rain, which at first appeared as a threat to the completion of the journey, probably helped us to slip through under the radar of bandits and ethnic extremists. I was conscious that a healthy dose of good luck had also played its part. We'd learnt a lot of lessons from these recent tests of character, not the least of which was that fortune favours the ignorant, as well as the brave.

❀ ❀ ❀

We decided to rest by the side of the road until daybreak. I was exhausted after the drive, and a few uncomfortable hours rest in the Big Girl was, for once, an enchanting prospect. It seemed to be no time at all before the sun was beaming warmly through the large hearse windows, prompting us to start the day. We wasted no time in getting back on the road; this time Wegs was behind the wheel and we had Neddy and Ryan with us for the day. We drove beside the inviting blue waters of the Adriatic on a stunning September day, and it wasn't long before the coastal road delivered us in high spirits to the Croatian border. With the sun shining and the stereo pumping, the damp and dark world of Kosovo felt like a lifetime ago.

A border guard came flying out of his post with a startled expression on his face, motioning for us to turn the music down. Which wasn't surprising, it was pretty loud. As he came closer to the car we could hear him yelling as the music was turned down.

'No. No. Up. Up!' He wanted the music turned up, not down. We had misread his sign language. I duly obliged by turning the stereo up full blast and he beamed his approval as he approached me on the passenger's side. The music was so loud that we couldn't hear each other speak. He reached in and plucked the passports out of my hand and began inspecting them with his head thrashing and toes tapping.

'AC/DC?' he yelled.

'Yep. AC/DC!' I yelled with a huge smile.

He handed the passports back and yelled over the top of the car to his colleague inside the post. Another guard suddenly emerged and instantly began an air-guitar solo next to Wegs in the driver's seat.

'OK. You go!' yelled the first officer, who was now also playing his air guitar and thrashing his head around wildly. Angus Young would have been damn proud.

With police guards playing air guitar on either side of us, we were all laughing and singing as Wegs began to drive off. Except there was one problem, we didn't go anywhere. For some reason the Big Girl would not move. We'd parked on a slight incline, and each time Wegs planted his foot on the accelerator we just rolled back slightly, forcing Quincy behind us to roll back as well. I looked over at Wegs who looked completely mystified.

'What's the matter, mate?' I was worried that the electronic ignition gadget had failed again as a result of all of the rain the previous night.

'Dunno.' The guards had stopped their air guitar now and were looking in each window.

'OK?'

'Not sure,' I said. I turned the music down so that we could think straight. The Big Girl has pretty good acoustics with its rear speakers embedded in the timber coffin platform and we'd been partially deafened and disorientated by the noise. With the stereo turned off we quickly identified the source of the Big Girl's problems. It was another ignition problem, and the car wasn't even running. The ignition problem was that Wegs had not *started* the car!

'Whoops,' acknowledged an embarrassed Wegs as he kicked the Big Girl into life. The guards applauded and I cranked up the stereo once more, prompting them back into rock-star mode.

'Are you ready for a good time . . .' roared AC/DC as the Big Girl left the animated guards behind and sped off into Croatia with four thrashing occupants. Yep, you bet we were. Oktoberfest, here we come.

13: FORK IN THE ROAD

The Thalkirkin camping ground in Munich was a welcome sight for both Helga and the Big Girl. We would be camping here for the next five days, which meant that our faithful vehicles could enjoy a well-earned break. Since leaving Macedonia both vehicles had been worked mercilessly through the bad roads of Kosovo, along the winding Croatian coast, and through the steep mountain roads of Slovenia and Austria, and there had been very little opportunity for them to stop and smell the roses as we continued our push towards Oktoberfest. Fortunately, despite a temporary health scare in Croatia for Helga and a lost muffler for the Big Girl in Austria, the girls had made it safely through.

Thalkirkin was a large camping ground in central Munich. It was very similar in size and function to the El Molino camp site we'd stayed at on the outskirts of Pamplona, and was where all the large tour groups from London would be staying throughout Oktoberfest. We'd arrived a day early in order to secure ourselves a good camp site before the masses turned up. Wegs and Quincy had both heard that Thalkirkin authorities frowned upon travellers in campervans because members of the Van Tour had caused trouble here in the past. Our early arrival was also designed to show the camping ground operators that we didn't belong to the Van Tour, and therefore allow us to camp at Thalkirkin and soak up the party atmosphere. Staying elsewhere was not a desirable option – we would be missing out on fun, and none of us liked the sound of that.

Wegs and I completed the booking formalities at the camping ground office just as Helga and the boys arrived at the entry gate. We'd staggered our arrivals so it didn't appear we were in a convoy, or on a tour of any sort. A burly and officious security guard made his way over to Helga, but before arriving at Quincy's window he stopped and looked under the car.

'Sorry, mate. She's leaking oil. You can't camp here,' the guard said in a thick South African accent.

'Hey, mate?' replied Quincy.

'She's leaking oil. We don't allow vehicles in that leak oil.'

'Mate. Helga does a lot of things, but she doesn't leak oil,' Quincy said as he jumped out and began to look under the car. He knew the intricacies of his car like we knew the intricacies of our Big Girl. There was no oil visible under Helga.

'She's not leaking oil, mate. Look,' Quincy said, pointing.

'I have. You can't camp here if she leaks oil,' repeated the stubborn guard, without looking.

'You've got to be joking, mate. Is it because we're in a van that apparently leaks oil, or is it just because we're in a van?' Quincy asked.

'The oil.'

'What if I go and get a mechanic to look at her and write a letter saying she doesn't leak, even though it's obvious she doesn't. Or we could just put a tray under her to make sure,' reasoned Quincy.

'No.'

The irony was that the guard hadn't even looked under the Big Girl when we'd arrived; he'd merely raised the boom gate and waved us through with a friendly smile. If he had looked under the Big Girl he would've seen her dripping oil at an impressive rate. Actually, if the guard had cared to look at the road after we'd passed by he probably would've noticed a nice consistent trail of oil that he could have followed all the way back to CAB Motors in Cork. However, it was clear there was another agenda at play here.

The situation was starting to deteriorate as the manager of the park came over to see what the cause of the disturbance was. He was a small angry man with a strong New Zealand accent and clearly the one who'd instructed the South African security guard to refuse entry to anyone travelling in a van. For the next ten minutes an animated and at times heated discussion ensued between Quincy, the guard and the manager. Wegs and I were watching from a few metres away and could see that the stand-off was now causing a lot of traffic congestion. The backlog of traffic and waiting campers finally influenced the angry manager to allow the boys to enter. Quincy and the others had only partially convinced the manager that they weren't troublemakers as he had confiscated their passports and made them pay a bond as security. He was taking no chances with the apparent riff-raff.

An hour later we had set up an impressive camp site at the rear of the Big Girl and Helga. We had one swag, five tents, two card tables and a handful of camp chairs arranged at the back of the open cars. There were a few soft tunes playing and things were surprisingly orderly as our favourite camping ground manager arrived on the scene, flanked by two security guards. He wasted no time on cordial greetings before he read us the riot act.

'There will be no loud music, no unruly or drunken behaviour, no noise after midnight, no littering, no damage to any property, no . . .' and so the list went on. 'If there is any trouble from one of you guys you'll be out on your arse before you know what's fuckin' hit you!' he said, pointing his finger at all of us before storming off with his stone-faced cronies. It was hard not to return his verbal hostilities but we managed to bite our tongues. We were finally camped together and we didn't want to risk being evicted. It wasn't so much what he had to say, but how he said it that made us all angry. My mum wouldn't have liked this bloke: he didn't mind his p's and q's.

It was difficult to understand his unfriendly approach. Just because the boys drove a van didn't make them, or us, troublemakers. We just wanted to camp and use the facilities, enjoy the atmosphere and then pay our money and go. As long as he didn't put up any little dome tents nearby for me to trip over while drunk, and his canteen didn't serve Guandong-style chicken with cashew nuts, there would be no damage to any of his property. Besides, we'd paid a bond and the boys had surrendered their passports as security. This bloke needed to relax.

'I don't like that fella, eh,' said JB. It was a hilarious understatement, typical of JB. He had a simple approach to life, yet he was strong enough to pick up the little manager and snap him in half. We roared with laughter and put the incident behind us. After all, we weren't here to argue and cause trouble: we were here to drink beer.

● ● ●

And drink beer we did, for four long days. The four days became something of a blur as we literally soaked up the atmosphere of Oktoberfest. Each day seemed to merge into the next, and my recollections are vague at best. I remember catching a morning train; seeing big beer horses; entering big beer halls; drinking big beer steins; singing lots of beer songs (repeatedly); dancing badly on tables; talking rubbish to anyone who would listen; eating pork; admiring Bavarian beauties; queuing for the toilets; thinking my mates were great; vomiting once; constant rain; sleeping in a wet swag; and having a bloody great time.

However, my fondest memory came on our very last evening, after the Oktoberfest showgrounds had closed for the day. We'd arrived back at the camping ground en masse (Wegs, Quincy, Ryan, JB, Neddy, Rosy, myself; and a few new mates: Dowks, Rossco and Luke) and merged into the throng of travellers partying at the Thalkirkin bar. It wasn't long before the team dissipated as girls were met and the search for a possible mate began. I was pissed and tired and before long I realised that my work here was done. I finished my bottle of beer and was secretly retreating in the direction of bed when an attractive girl approached me.

'Are you one of the guys from *TNT*?' she asked. 'With the hearse?'

'Yeah,' I replied, surprised. I'd only written three articles to date but it seemed that this *TNT* gig might have some fringe benefits I hadn't envisaged.

'Really? My friends and I love your articles, we read them every week back in London!' she said excitedly.

'How did you know it was me?' I asked, given that the Big Girl wasn't nearby.

'I recognised you from the photos. Are you the writer?'

'I am,' I said proudly, hoping to impress her. I was also trying to sober up as best I could, but it wasn't easy.

'Really? That's so exciting, I look forward to them every week. They are really fun to read,' she said, and looked me up and down. She's checking me out, I thought to myself. Things were looking good. Maybe my night didn't have to end just yet.

'Do you really write them?' she added, after further thought.

'Yes. Really.'

'Are you sure?' She looked me up and down again with a doubting eye, and paused for some time before commenting as she walked off. 'Bullshit. You look like a bricklayer!'

❀ ❀ ❀

On the fifth morning we woke and packed up camp instead of heading into town to drink and celebrate. After four days we'd done more than enough of that. We did a very rough job of packing up our tents; it was still raining hard and we had little desire to be out in the miserable conditions any longer than was absolutely necessary. We would have to deal with it later. It took us very little time to have everything stored away in the cars and our rubbish cleaned up.

Wegs paid for our accommodation and secured our passports while I finished the last of the clean-up, ready for a quick getaway. The Helga team had done likewise. We tried to start the cars only to find both Helga and the Big Girl had flat batteries from lack of use over the past week. The biggest problem with this was that we had to ask the manager for his assistance in jump-starting both vehicles.

It was an hour later before the manager arrived on his small tractor with some jumper leads. It was raining and, not surprisingly, he wasn't happy. Not one little bit.

'It's not my job to start your bloody cars. If you can't even organise yourselves it's your own fault. You should be more careful. I've got a camping ground to run. This will cost you . . .' and so he went on, and on. I chose not to listen to his endless rantings and ravings. Once again I found it difficult to bite my tongue, but arguing with this objectionable man at this late stage of the game would get us nowhere. I just wanted to get the car started and get out of there.

Both cars roared into life once jump-started and we paid our little friend the large sum of money he demanded for his great inconvenience. Goodwill was in short supply around this place, and it was a pleasure to leave a few minutes later. We waved and smiled to the manager as the Big Girl followed Helga out the gateway, leaking oil the whole way.

We met up at a service station further along the road to say our final farewells to our travelling companions and great mates. We filled up with fuel and stocked up on lemonade and potato chips to help ease the hangovers. Everyone milled around between the two vehicles saying very little, although many strong handshakes and man-hugs were exchanged. We promised to stay in touch and then returned to our respective chariots. Wegs pulled the Big Girl up at the kerb and waited for Quincy to bring Helga up alongside. Our vehicles had also formed a great bond over the past weeks. The Big Girl and Helga tooted their horns as they bade farewell to one another.

'Good luck, boys!' roared Rosy out of Helga's passenger window.

'Thanks, mate. You too!' I responded out of the Big Girl's passenger window.

With that Helga turned left towards England and the Big Girl turned right towards Australia. As we set off in different directions Wegs and I held a raised finger out both windows, in our team salute. In the rear and side mirrors we could see five hands sticking out from Helga, doing the same.

'Berlin?' Wegs asked, turning to me.

'Berlin.'

'Madonna?'

'Umm . . . can't find it,' I said as I flicked through the CD wallet, laughing on the inside. 'Groove Armada?'

'Yep, OK.'

We took up our position in the slow lane of the A9 travelling from Munich to Berlin. Wegs and I listened to the tunes without speaking, just staring straight ahead. We needed some quiet time to contemplate the time spent with our mates, and what now lay ahead, on our own. There was no doubting we'd miss the fun, the camaraderie and the synergy of our teams.

Oktoberfest had been a significant milestone and destination for the team. Now it had passed we had to recalibrate our thinking towards the ultimate destination: home. As we cruised along in the thick snow towards Berlin, Australia could not have felt further away. The holiday component of the journey had been completed, and completed well. The adventure component was about to commence. We knew that on arrival in Berlin we would have to confront our worst fear: organisation. We had no idea where to start, but we had procrastinated for long enough. Tomorrow had arrived.

14: TOMORROW

Since leaving Munich, our plans for the remainder of the journey had again changed. Between Munich and Berlin we had spoken about driving through Poland and the Ukraine on our way to Moscow, and from Moscow we had thought it best to send the Big Girl on a freight train to Beijing. My early idea to run the Big Girl twenty-four/seven across 10 000 km of Siberia in the middle of winter had been revised on the grounds of commonsense. The new plan was to freight the Big Girl while we took the Trans-Siberian Railway through to Beijing, and to rendezvous with her there. It was the only practical option, but it wasn't necessarily the easiest one to organise. Numerous language, logistical and cultural barriers stood between us and the actualisation of this grand plan.

❂ ❂ ❂

We found the Jetpak hostel tucked away in a suburban 'forest', on the edge of a large inner-city park. A winding driveway led up to the hostel, a long weatherboard bungalow that had formerly housed the Luftwaffe and anti-aircraft guns during the war. After checking into our rooms we returned to the Big Girl and began to spread out our sodden tents, clothes and sleeping bags on the lawn to dry. The German owner of the hostel, Neil, and his Ukranian assistant, Walter, soon joined us.

'Oktoberfest?' enquired Neil, sighting a few of our souvenired steins.

'Yeah. It was just a little bit wet,' Wegs responded, as he stretched out his dripping tent.

'We're hoping to dry out our clothes and bodies,' I added.

'Yes, I understand,' Neil smiled knowingly. 'Nice car! You have driven all the way from England?' He and Walter walked over and admired the Big Girl. Thankfully there were no 'dead' jokes forthcoming.

'Ireland actually,' Wegs answered, 'and we're hoping to get all the way back to Australia – one way or another.'

'Really? Where you going next?'

'Umm, we thought we might drive through Poland to Moscow,' I replied.

'Ukraine? You will go through Ukraine, yes?' Walter chipped in. 'My family in Kiev . . . you can stay . . . I will fix for you.'

'Not really sure which way we will go, but thank you, Walter. Thank you,' I answered, slowly.

'I wouldn't recommend it, though. Driving through the Ukraine that is. It can be very dangerous. There is a lot of corruption,' Neil said.

'Yes. Maybe if you don't know way of life in Ukraine it is hard. And roads . . . very bad,' Walter added.

'From Russia you will go to China?' Neil asked.

'Yes, that's the plan. We hope to send the car by train from Moscow to Beijing. We know it's not realistic to drive all the way through Siberia,' I answered, not bothering to air my twenty-four/seven theory. I had accepted its futility.

'Ha ha. Yes, in your car it might be very difficult I think,' Neil was laughing. 'I think you best to send it on train from Germany, or maybe Finland. Driving through Ukraine and also in Russia is not good ... lots of corruption ... lots of police ... and in foreign car you will have problems. I think train is best.'

'Can you take cars on the Trans-Siberian Railway?' I asked Neil.

'That I do not know. You will need to speak to Russian travel agent in the city. I will get the address for you.' Neil, followed by Walter, disappeared back inside.

❂   ❂   ❂

We woke early the next morning and skipped breakfast at the hostel in favour of getting into the city and, more specifically, Sputnik Travel, to commence logistics. We would grab a coffee later. Wegs was navigating from a map Neil had given us; this together with his excellent directions had us on the city's doorstep much sooner than we had anticipated. It was only 8 a.m.

'It's still early. Let's drive around for a bit,' suggested Wegs.

'OK. The traffic's not too bad.'

En route to the city that morning we'd driven through leafy suburbs where the traffic flowed freely; the streets were wide, well maintained and well signposted, and grid-like in their orientation. It reminded me of Melbourne's eastern suburbs. However, now that we found ourselves on the boundaries of the inner city, the domestic suburban scene had been replaced by the diverse urban cultures of Berlin. I was not sure whether we were north, south, east or west of the city but, wherever we were, distinct changes in neighbourhood characteristics confronted us every few blocks.

As we skirted the city, to the north I think, we could see hardcore punks milling around the streets or queuing up to enter seedy back-alley clubs that probably never closed. Deep, thumping bass beats could be heard emanating from these clubs. Berlin was the home of techno, and the hard-house clubbing scene. Heading east, using the imposing Fernsehturm TV tower as our landmark, the feel of the city changed again. Old buildings lined the streets, with cafes, galleries, restaurants and pawnshops giving it an alternative and artistic aura. For some reason it reminded me of San Francisco.

'Seems it's cool to be a geek in these parts,' I said to Wegs.

The dress code had changed significantly from the studded leather outfits of a few blocks ago; here it seemed cool to wear cardigans, vests and berets. Even glasses seemed 'in', and obviously the narrower the cooler.

'I would've been cool if I'd grown up here,' I commented.

'Huh?'

'Mum and Dad always dressed me in vests and cardigans when I was a kid. I think it was because normal jumpers wouldn't fit over my big head.' I had a huge head as a child, and I'm still growing into it.

'Shut up, dickhead,' Wegs laughed. 'We'd better cruise into town now. It's after nine.'

'Roger that,' I confirmed.

We took the Karl-Liebknecht-Strasse and followed the smooth-flowing traffic into central Berlin without incident. Navigation in Berlin really was a breeze compared to other European centres. It was exactly as I had imagined a large German city would be: clean, ordered and efficient; and yet, as someone from my parents' generation would describe it, still *trendy*. I liked Berlin, it had a nice vibe.

As we had come to expect, we found Charlottenstrasse easily and pulled the Big Girl into a large all-day car park. According to Neil's directions, Sputnik Travel was only a couple of blocks away. The name sounded as Russian as beetroot, and I felt confident we would find out all we needed to know to get our team to China.

We entered an unassuming-looking building and took the lift to the third floor. Along the corridor was a door with a small sign: Sputnik Travel. Wegs pushed open the heavy door, revealing a spacious room lined with brown timber panels, and walls covered in maps of the former Soviet Union. In the far corner a large man, best described as Boris Yeltsin with a beard, rose from behind a large desk and waved us to take a seat in front of him. Sputnik Travel had no secretary. It also had no computer.

'Yes?' grunted the Russian, addressing us in English. Our bright clothes obviously identified us as Westerners.

'Ahh, we would like to make some enquiries about the Trans-Siberian Railway,' I stated politely.

'Yes, OK. What you want to know?' he answered pleasantly enough, his formidable presence relaxing slightly.

I stated the nature of our proposed Trans-Siberian journey, outlining the fact that we needed to transport not only ourselves to China, but our vehicle also. He listened intently, jotting down notes as we spoke.

'Trans-Siberian train is passenger only. I can organise ticket for you but you will need to have visa for China and Mongolia before we can do ticket,' he informed succinctly. 'The visa will take, maybe ... three week,' he estimated, confusingly holding up four fingers. Perhaps he'd had a couple of Smirnoffs for breakfast.

'OK.' I said slowly, buying time to think over what this meant to our plans. I looked over at Wegs, who shrugged his shoulders.

'For the car I do not know but I have a friend. One moment.' He excused himself to make a phone call. He used one of the old sliding dial phones that we had at home when I was young. You know the ones, where you have to stick your finger into the hole on the round dial, and turn it around to the end to dial the number. This drab office sure was old, and Russian.

I wondered if perhaps it was all just a front, and this was not a travel agency at all. I've seen enough James Bond films to know that Boris more closely resembled a KGB agent than a travel agent. I amused myself by sticking my gum under the desk in front of me, as if it were a bug.

Before my imagination ran too wild our 'agent' completed his vociferous call and slammed down the phone. He told us there were many companies in Moscow who could organise the freight to China. Our problem would be getting the Big Girl to Moscow. He also warned us against driving. He finished by saying that he didn't know of anyone who could assist us with the freight from Germany.

'You get China visa, then return,' he told us in a stern manner, indicating that the meeting was over. We thanked him, shook hands and departed. I controlled my desire to salute.

Wegs and I left the large building and immediately adjourned to a *trendy* inner-city cafe around the corner. We had a lot to think about in light of the recent information. There were lots of questions and very few answers. The only way to progress was to deal with what we knew for sure, and at this stage all we knew was that we needed a Chinese visa. It was time to be proactive. We finished our coffees and headed off in the direction of the Chinese embassy.

'Oh you have got to be kidding!' Wegs shouted as we stood at the locked gates of the Chinese embassy. It was 12.05 p.m. and the embassy had closed for the day, just five minutes before our arrival. In typical embassy fashion they were only open for a few hours each day.

'You're going to love this then, mate,' I said to Wegs. While he was complaining about our misfortune I'd moved a few metres away to read a paper sign stuck to a door. Although I couldn't read either German or Chinese I clearly understood, from the dates on the notice, that the embassy was to be closed for the next four days.

'Great, that's just great. Lazy bastards,' added Wegs. Sadly, there was no intercom for Wegs to shout into to release his anger.

It was a Monday and that meant it would be an entire week before we could start the organisation of our first visa. Suddenly, our visas were going to take at least a month to obtain and we hadn't even started to coordinate the Big Girl's travel. We seemed to be banging our heads against a brick wall. Even though we had no real time limits, our financial budget meant we couldn't wait an entire month before moving on with the next leg of the journey. It would also eliminate our momentum and possibly our enthusiasm.

After letting off some steam outside the embassy we regrouped in the Big Girl. We could do nothing about our visa situation for a week, so we decided to head towards an Internet cafe to do some research on hearse freight between Germany and China. Surely we could work something out.

We made our way back along Friedrichstrasse, passing through Checkpoint Charlie, before finding a car park near an Internet cafe we'd seen earlier in the day. We ordered a couple of Cokes and then set about our research. Wegs wasn't overly experienced in Internet research so I was yelling instructions across to him at his terminal around the corner of the desk. I instructed him to do as I was doing: open Google and type in some keywords that I hoped would send me in the right direction. I entered:

International-Rail-Freight-Germany.

For the next hour or so I cast my eye over numerous web sites relating to rail freight in this part of the world, and had begun to gain a basic appreciation for the industry. I couldn't find a company that took freight, by rail, to Russia or beyond, but I had discovered that the rail gauge varied between Germany and its eastern neighbours. This had been for national security reasons during World War II, and the different size gauge was still in existence today. This meant that all rail freight departing Germany had to change trains at each border and, as a result, it was a very costly exercise. This information did little to cheer me up. It was looking less and less likely that it would be possible to freight the Big Girl from Germany to China, especially given our lack of experience and resources. In the course of browsing these sites I'd discovered that Finland was the only country with a rail gauge compatible to Russia.

International-Rail-Freight-Finland.

'How are you going, mate?' I enquired, while I waited for my computer to search. I couldn't see Wegs' face but I knew he was agitated; I'd heard him swearing and grumbling to himself for the past hour.

'Nah. No good. I type in keywords but keep ending up in web sites on the other side of the fuckin' world. I hate this shit. I can never find what I want.'

'Keep going, mate.' I wasn't really listening; I was in a bit of a zone, with my mind racing as it threw around different ideas, questions and scenarios.

My computer flashed up another long list of unlikely web sites for me to peruse. I clicked on the first one which sounded unexpectedly promising. As I scanned their homepage I could see that this Helsinki-based company had been sending heavy machinery from Finland to the Far East for twenty-five years. It wasn't much to go on but it was something, and something was more than we had so far. I clicked on their generic contact form and entered my details and an information query. I held little faith in my short note to the faceless entity, but sent it anyway.

SENT ITEMS

Dear Sir or Madam

I request information as soon as is convenient for you about transporting our car from Finland to Beijing along the Trans Siberian Freight Route. We are Australians filming a documentary based upon our overland travels to Australia. We are in Germany at present and wish to travel to Beijing as soon as possible.

We will be taking the trans siberian route and would like to meet our vehicle in Beijing. Your company is the most professional we have encountered and we will happily make the trip to Finland to use your service.

We would like to move quickly on this and would appreciate your thoughts so that we can make plans as soon as possible.

Thank you for your time.

Regards,

Dav Ardlie

I had taken a couple of liberties in the note but didn't think it would hurt to mention we were filming a travel story, which technically we were, although not professionally. Never mind, if drawing a slightly long bow was going to assist us in our planning then I thought it was worth mentioning. I doubted I would hear back from them anyway. After sending this quick note I decided to have a break from the tiring research for a few minutes to check my emails. I logged on to my account and saw that I had a reply from a mate of mine, John Delbridge (JD), who was in Australia.

I'd emailed him, after consulting with Wegs, to see if he'd like to join us for the remaining legs of our journey. I knew he was at a loose end back in Australia and that he wasn't ready to face the workforce just yet. Life on the road was easier with three; it allowed the emotional, physical and financial burden of travelling as a team to be shared. However, it was imperative that all three had similar interests and outlooks on life, as otherwise the new structure would be deemed to fail – something I was not prepared to risk. Wegs was in favour of the idea; he'd met JD back in Ireland and they'd got along well.

JD's email said he'd decided to come along, which was great news. His skills and companionship would be welcomed in the challenging times ahead. He was proposing to fly from the warmth of Brisbane to the cold of Moscow, to rendezvous with us. I emailed him to say we were delighted he was coming on board and suggested he organise his visas but to refrain from booking flights until Wegs and I had finalised a couple of little logistical concerns. I signed off by saying we'd be in touch shortly.

I returned to my inbox and noticed that I'd received an email while I was writing to JD. It was from the Finnish freight company I'd emailed a few minutes ago.

INBOX

Dear Sir,
Thank you for your interest. The very first question:
What kind of vehicle do you have? We will contact you next week,
but this question is very important.

With best regards
Timo Mäntylä
Product Group Manager
VR Ltd
VR Cargo
Helsinki, Finland

I could have been knocked down with a feather. I have never received a reply from a generic web site contact form, let alone a reply sent through within minutes. Timo hadn't given enough information in his brief reply for me to know if they could organise the car freight, but it sounded promising.

I quickly replied as I wanted to continue this relationship with the friendly Finn.

SENT ITEMS

Dear Timo
Thank you for your hasty reply. We have a Ford Granada Estate.
6 m long
1.7 m high
1.7 m wide
I can be contacted on my mobile phone and look forward to hearing from you soon and obtaining a quote.
Thanks mate
Dav Ardlie

I had guessed at the dimensions of the Big Girl and also glossed over the fact she was a hearse. I didn't want to get too excited and tell Wegs about the reply because I still needed to know for sure if they could send a car to China. I sent the quick reply hoping to strike while the iron was hot. I had my fingers crossed in the hope that Timo was still at his computer and had not popped out for a quick sauna.

I received an immediate reply.

INBOX

Hello.
The transport it self is quite easy to arrange. The big question will be, how the Chinese custom authorities will treat your car. It is possible, that it is treated like an ordinary 'luggage' and that can cause a big delay at the Chinese border. Therefore I suggest, that you contact nearest Chinese embassy and try to get sufficient papers with permission to take it to Peking. Otherwise the risk can be high. Easiest solution if possible could be, that you send your car home or to the next destination and hire a car in Peking.
With regards
Timo Mäntylä

The first line told me all we needed to know.

'Wegs. We're going to Finland.'

'Hey?' he replied, sounding happier than he'd been earlier.

'I've found some blokes in Finland who can take the car for us.'

'Really?'

'Yep.' I went on to explain all that I had learnt about VR Cargo in the last twenty-five minutes. I didn't know much but I reckoned I knew enough and, besides, it meant we could keep on the move.

'Righto. Finland it is,' said a surprised but supportive Wegs.

It had been a dynamic twenty-four hours and now, after

a day of deliberation, it seemed that driving through the former Soviet Union had been dropped in favour of rail freight from Scandinavia. It just felt right, and that's all the justification we have ever needed. Tomorrow we would head to Finland.

I wanted to record the moment as I sensed this was a significant decision, and one that might ultimately determine the success or failure of the journey. I set the camera up in front of Wegs and turned it on before racing around to my seat in the background of the shot. I asked Wegs to tell the camera of the decision that had just been made.

'Well, apparently we're going to Finland tomorrow to find a company up there who can send headers, harvesters, houses and hopefully hearses all the way to China.'

'Couldn't have said it better myself, mate. Well done.'

As I stood up and moved over to turn the camera off, I caught sight of Wegs' computer screen. The cheeky bastard's monitor was proudly displaying the official web site of the Collingwood Football Club.

'Got the hang of those Internet searches then, mate!' I said pointing at his computer.

Australian-Rules-Football-Collingwood.

15: A GIRL DOWN

Helsinki, like Berlin, was easy to navigate. The roads were wide, well signposted and well planned, enabling an easy passage for the sizeable Big Girl. She'd been running better than ever since arriving in Finland, obviously relishing the cool Scandinavian climate. After losing the last two feet of her exhaust pipe on a speed hump back in Austria, the Big Girl now sported a throaty exhaust note while idling, and increased power when accelerating. We now owned a tough-sounding, high-performance hearse.

The new and improved Big Girl certainly turned a few heads as Wegs turned into the Helsinki train station car park – completely sideways.

'Whooaaa . . . Big Girl,' Wegs screamed as the Big Girl's substantial rear end drifted out around the corner. It took Wegs completely by surprise, as she'd never done this before. Only his skilled hearsemanship stopped the pendulum-like effect of the weighty rear end spinning us around completely.

'Nice move, mate!' I complimented Wegs as he powered off in the fishtailing Big Girl.

'Shit, it's bloody icy! I can see why they have those noisy tyres now!' said a pale Wegs. All the other cars in Finland were fitted with steel studs in their tyres, making them roll noisily along the normal bitumen but providing extra grip in ice and snow. We would have to be careful driving in Finland because the black ice was hard to see on the road.

We parked and made our way into the central train station. In our time on the road this had become our modus operandi for negotiating large and unfamiliar cities. Once at or near the main train station one could always rely on finding accommodation, Internet cafes, important tourist information and parking. It was the best place for us to start our quest to find Timo and his freight company.

Sure enough we found an Internet cafe in the station just minutes after leaving the Big Girl. I logged on to my email and took down a copy of Timo's contact details before heading over to the phone booth to make the call. While I was doing this Wegs was organising a street map of the inner city from the cafe attendant.

I dialled the strange sequence of numbers. 'VR Cargo,' answered a male voice, in heavily accented English.

'Timo Mäntylä?' I queried.

'Yes, this is Timo.'

'It's Davin Ardlie ringing, Timo. I emailed you about sending a car to China,' I added, hoping this would jog his memory.

'Ah yes,' he said, 'you are the Australians with the car in Germany.'

'Yes, except that we are now in Finland.'

'Already Helsinki, very fast.' It was only two days since I'd contacted him from Berlin.

'Yes, we got the ferry yesterday.'

'You have pen?'

'Yes.'

'I have number for you to call a friend of mine. He will help you,' Timo said, before giving me the long phone number. 'His name is Jarmo Stjerna. He is . . . *the man*.'

For the past couple of days I had imagined Timo as our logistical saviour, so I felt a touch uneasy about him forwarding us on to another company, concerned he may be passing us off as a liability for someone else to deal with. I had a knot in my stomach when I said my goodbyes to Timo and began dialling Jarmo Stjerna at Railtrans. Coming to Finland suddenly felt a bit rash.

The number was engaged on each of the three times I tried. After a fourth unsuccessful try I consulted Wegs and we decided to go and meet Jarmo in person. A brief glance at the city map showed us that Railtrans' head office wasn't far from the train station, so we took off on foot. We were off to see *the man*.

We crossed the busy road out the front of the train station and headed for the small central business district of Helsinki. I knew Helsinki wasn't a big city, around 500 000 people, so we hadn't paid much attention to the map, assuming the Railtrans' office would be located near the small gathering of high-rise buildings in the centre of the city. We wandered along Mikonkatu and into the CBD. Outside a big department store a large digital screen announced that the time was 12.15 p.m., and that it was minus three degrees Celsius. This was definitely the coldest Wegs and I had ever been and we were badly underdressed for the conditions. Even the locals were well rugged up, exposing only their faces to the elements.

As we walked it occurred to me that the weather reflected how far our journey had come. When we left London in early summer we'd packed no warm clothing because we'd only planned to be travelling in the warmer months around Europe. Never did we think we'd end up confronting a Scandinavian winter. Our breath billowed out like smoke, and we noted that we'd definitely have to do something about our light wardrobe. This journey wasn't going to get any warmer.

'Where to now, mate?' I asked Wegs. I hadn't been paying attention to where we were going, preferring to wander along admiring the new city, and the beautiful Finnish women.

'Fucked if I know.' Wegs had obviously been enjoying the new surroundings as much as I had.

'You got the map?' I asked.

'Yep.' Wegs retrieved it from his pocket.

'Where are we?' We looked around to find a landmark or a street sign. A hundred metres to our left was a busy waterfront market. Helsinki certainly was a compact city. We'd been walking for only ten minutes and had already crossed the business district and now found ourselves down by the port.

'That's the Kauppatori – the market,' read Wegs, pointing. We strolled over, taking cautious strides on the icy footpaths, having nearly gone arse up a number of times already.

The Kauppatori was thriving. Fishermen were noisily

trading fresh fish; stallholders supplied locals and tourists alike with preserves by the jar, vegetables, fruit, flowers, fur hats and gloves, scarves, woollen jackets and all sorts of other local arts and crafts. Boats backed up to the wharf bobbed up and down peacefully, all proudly displaying the Finnish flag and providing a beautiful backdrop to this colourful snapshot of Helsinki. We found a large bench and sat down with some fish and chips while we familiarised ourselves with the map.

'Aaagh fuck!' I yelled, jumping up from my seat in shock. While I was looking over Wegs' shoulder at the map, a seagull the size of a pelican had landed on the table next to me and snatched a piece of fish from my hand.

'Ha ha ha ha. You bloody whimp. It's only a seagull!' laughed Wegs with his mouth full.

'Look at the fuckin' size of it!' I squealed, pointing to the massive feathered thief now perched on a rope high above the market, eating my fish.

Wegs wasn't to know but I'd been scarred by a similar incident in my childhood. On a year-seven school camp I'd been sitting with some mates eating fish and chips, happily dangling my legs over the edge of St Kilda pier in Melbourne, when a seagull swooped from behind and plucked my fish straight out of my hands. It had scared the shit out of me, as it had done today, and my mates had laughed at me, just as Wegs was doing now.

At the time I was upset to have lost my lunch, and angered by my friends laughing at me. I was too young to laugh at myself back then. My teacher, Mrs Findlay, must have sensed this as she came over to console me.

'Don't worry, Davin, it could have happened to anyone. That was just *bad* luck.' As she uttered these reassuring words there was a quick flash of white and a loud squawk followed by an even louder scream. The squawk was the seagull's, the scream was mine. I dropped to my knees, clutching my neck. I'd been hit. Laughter erupted as my misfortune once again humoured my so-called mates. The same bird had attacked again, striking me on the neck with a precision turd. Obviously the fish hadn't been cooked to his liking. This threw Mrs Findlay into compassion overdrive, and she bent over and wiped me down frantically with her handkerchief.

'Don't worry, Davin, it could have happened to anyone. That was . . . *good* luck.'

Despite being let out of writing a report on our school camp and getting a free ice-cream, I'm still not sure that being crapped on by a bird, especially in front of your schoolmates, is actually good luck. Perhaps if I had been convinced from that schoolday experience I may have wandered over and stood temptingly below the nefarious Finnish seagull. If Mrs Findlay was right, then being anointed by this gargantuan seagull should deliver more than its fair share of good luck – and if we were going to get the Big Girl to China we were going to need our fair share of it. However, I decided against it for now; I would keep it as plan B.

❂ ❂ ❂

Despite our rapid walking rate we were decidedly blue in colour when we arrived at the head office of Railtrans. Standing in the foyer we asked to speak to Jarmo Stjerna and took a seat. It was beautifully warm inside the plush office and we relished the opportunity to thaw out.

After making a quick call, the polite receptionist said, 'Mr Stjerna will see you now. Please follow me.'

We walked along a narrow corridor and were ushered into an expansive office. Behind the desk stood a large man with receding grey hair; he wore slimline glasses, a smart suit and a bloody great big smile. He came around the front of his desk and shook our hands strongly.

'Hello, Mr Stjerna. Dav,' I said, introducing myself.

'Paul,' Wegs did likewise.

'Jarmo,' he said, still smiling broadly.

'Come. Sit. Sit.' He motioned towards two chairs opposite his large leather chair, and asked the receptionist to bring some coffee. The office was adorned with numerous photos of trains and detailed rail maps of Finland, Russia, China and Mongolia. I nodded to Wegs, indicating this was a positive sign. It felt right.

'We Finns are not much good at small talk, so let's get down to business,' opened Jarmo.

This was fine by me as I was keen to know if it was possible to do as we proposed. I outlined our plan to Jarmo, omitting the fact that the Big Girl was a funeral car. I didn't want the man who held the key to the success of our journey to think we were freaks.

'There may be some problems, but it is possible . . . yes,' he said, after I explained our situation. These were the most comforting words I'd heard in a long time. It was great to know that the infrastructure existed to freight the Big Girl to the Far East, and that Jarmo was on our side. It justified the risk we'd taken in coming to Finland.

Jarmo took down from his bookcase photo albums that documented his many hunting, fishing and camping holidays in Mongolia. In twenty-five years of dealing with freight to the Far East he'd been on many trips to remote regions of Mongolia, and he strongly recommended we take the time to visit these places while we had the opportunity. He was turning out to be a Mongolian ambassador as well.

Jarmo showed us his holiday snaps for well over an hour. He'd made a remarkably good fist of small talk, considering it doesn't come easily to the Finns. By this time we felt so comfortable that we even told Jarmo we were travelling in a funeral car, which was met with thunderous laughter. He thought that was fantastic, not freaky. Prior to our request the strangest cargo he'd dealt with was the freight of 120 live sheep over twenty years ago. He'd had to organise the passage of one hundred female and twenty male sheep and two Mongolian shepherds. The Mongols had brought no clothing with them so Jarmo had provided extra clothes, and organised for their container to be fitted with a stove, food, beds and a crate of vodka. The journey ended up taking three weeks in the middle of a winter blizzard; only one sheep died, which was duly eaten by the shepherds. Jarmo's intervention had meant that 119 sheep and two very pissed shepherds had made it safely to Mongolia through a dangerous winter. This was an inspiring story; we now knew that the Big Girl would be in safe hands.

Outside the Penguin Pub with Vlad and Hugo prior to the boys' extradition from Macedonia

Serious logistics – Dav and Wegs
consider their options, Berlin

The gorgeous Tehri, Helsinki

Relaxed times – Jarmo 'the man' shows us some holiday snaps, Helsinki

Tense times – Jarmo makes the call that could determine the fate of our journey

Packing the Big Girl away for her Trans-Siberian adventure – Laapeenranta, Finland

Staple Russian diet of vodka and potatoes, Moscow

Trans-Mongolian drinking games

Noodle transaction somewhere in Russia

Driving through the nothingness of the Gobi

Team Gobi, Mongolia

Introducing the friendly Mongolians (that's a toy gun!) to technology, in a Gobi ger

JD and the old man moments before the knuckle presentation

Inca, Wegs and Dav ask directions in the middle of the Gobi

Team photo, Bangkok

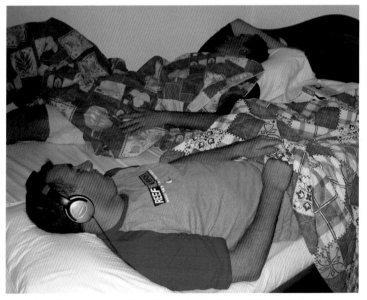

Travelling 'companions' not travelling 'partners' – Wegs and JD top and tail, China

Wegs with his favourite read, Thailand

Nice and cheesy, Bangkok

Wegs' novel approach to border security,
China/Vietnam border

Appeasing the concerned official

Sunrise on the last morning of our international misadventures, Ko Pha Ngan

JD at the Bangkok Hilton business suite

Our first glimpse of the Big Girl, Fremantle

Reunited at last, Fremantle

Final farewell, Albany

Dav heads off to cross the Nullarbor – solo

Once story time had finished Jarmo got straight down to business and made a couple of calls to freight contacts in China and Korea. He wanted to establish the likelihood of any customs' problems, and also placed a call through to a friend on the Russian border who he knew could help facilitate the quick passage of the car. He worked diligently and efficiently on the phone, instructing his secretary when on hold and also studying the large rail maps on the wall before him. At the end of each phone call Jarmo kept us informed of developments, while Wegs and I sat back drinking coffee and eating chocolate biscuits. Jarmo asked his highly efficient secretary to fax our details to the Russian border and to create a pro-forma invoice to assist with the border crossings. To make it look official he told her to stamp it with a round rubber stamp.

'I do this because you won't have any rubber stamps. Yes?'

'Yes. Good idea,' we offered, each with a mouthful of biscuit. He was right, we didn't have any round rubber stamps with us.

It took a further hour for Jarmo to complete his phone calls and preliminary paperwork. His enquiries had been very productive and he now thought it would be best to send the Big Girl all the way across Russia to Vladivostok by train, then by boat to Pusan in Korea and then by boat to Tianjin in China. We stood beside him as he pointed to the proposed route on his large wall maps. It was an impressive journey. It involved traversing 15 000 km through Siberia by train and then a visit to both Korea and China by boat, before the hopeful reunion with us in Beijing.

Things were looking promising although there was one very

important factor still to be determined. The factor that would ultimately determine whether the passage, which we had now identified as being possible, could go ahead.

'Jarmo, roughly how much do you think this will cost?' Wegs asked.

We had no idea what sort of cost was involved in such a procedure. It was an anxious moment as we waited to hear what the future held for our journey, or if there was going to be a future at all.

'I am not sure. One minute.' He reached for his calculator and began furiously pressing buttons.

'Shit,' I whispered under my breath to Wegs, who raised his eyebrows in response. It took five minutes and fourteen separate calculations before he reached a figure. It was a sphincter-clenching moment for Wegs and me as we prepared ourselves for the answer.

'Approximately twelve hundred US dollars, but I can't say for sure at this stage.'

It took us a moment to work out what this was in Australian dollars. It was a lot of money, but considering the distance and handling involved it seemed like a pretty reasonable deal.

'Is this OK?' Jarmo asked. Wegs had gone slightly pale and Jarmo looked concerned.

'Yes, I think so,' I said, nodding my head, still ruminating over the figure. I needed a beer, and I sensed that Wegs needed a toilet.

'OK. I will need maybe one week to organise,' said Jarmo. 'I will call you when we need to meet next. Here, I also give you this name. It is travel agent near here. Mention my name . . . they will help you. Maybe only one week to get all of the visa you need.'

We left our meeting with Jarmo confident the passage of the Big Girl was possible, and confident we could also organise our own passage without too many headaches.

Jarmo had indeed proven to be *the man*.

❀   ❀   ❀

We followed Jarmo's directions to the travel agency. We'd turned blue again by the time we arrived, as it was late in the afternoon and the temperature had dropped even further. Wegs and I were greeted by Tehri, a friendly and absolutely drop-dead-gorgeous Finnish woman. As she walked back to her desk Wegs and I turned to each other and raised our eyebrows excitely. We followed behind and I pointed to myself, indicating that she would like me best. Wegs brushed my hand aside and shook his head before pointing at himself. We were all smiles as we sat down before the Finnish goddess.

Wegs and I spent the next half-hour interrupting and talking over the top of one another as we told Tehri of our plans to travel to China. It was an immature point-scoring exercise as we battled for the lion's share of her affections. We were even kicking each other under the table in a bid to distract the other as they chatted away. It was bloody hard not to laugh. I doubt that either of us particularly impressed Tehri that afternoon but we had a great time; not only was she very attractive, she was also very friendly and very good at her job.

Wegs and I handed over our passports at the end of our consultation and Tehri predicted that we would have all of the necessary visas in a few days. Given our recent experiences with embassies, we liked the sound of that. We shook hands and thanked her profusely before stepping back out into the icy cold. As we made our way out the door I poked Wegs in the ribs.

'Did you see the way she looked at me, mate?' I said, grinning.

'Ha. You've got nothing, mate. It was all me,' Wegs retorted as he pushed me into the path of a light post. 'Especially once she looks at your passport photo!'

❀   ❀   ❀

Five days later, I was surprised when my phone rang while Wegs and I were having breakfast at the hostel cafe. My mobile phone had only been used for text messaging on the trip and this was the first time it had rung in over four months.

'Hello, Davin speaking.'

'Hello, Dave. Jarmo Stjerna here, please come to my office in one hour. We are ready to go.'

'OK, Jarmo. See you soon.' It was a brief conversation because, although Jarmo spoke pretty good English, it was much easier to converse in person, with the occasional assistance of sign and body language, than over the phone. Wegs and I returned to the hostel and packed up our belongings into the Big Girl. The wheels were in motion.

Back at Jarmo's office he informed us that all the paperwork was in order and that once we'd finalised the payment he would personally escort us to the loading yard to pack up the Big Girl. This escort was well and truly above the call of duty because the yard was located 200 kilometres away in Laapeenranta, near the Russian border. There was no doubt Jarmo was giving us silver service. He handed over the invoice for US$1200 as quoted. We excused ourselves to go to the bank to arrange payment and also to visit the gorgeous Tehri, to get our passports.

The transfer of funds went smoothly and it wasn't long before we were again sitting in front of Tehri. I noticed she hadn't got any less attractive since our last meeting. She was wearing a tight black top and had her long blonde hair tied in perfect pigtails. Wegs and I were smitten once again. She handed back our visa-laden passports and everything was now in order for our immediate departure.

'I tried to call you guys the other day. My friend was having her birthday and I was wondering if you wanted to come to her party at the disco, but I could not get through to your phone.'

Did we hear that correctly? We could have cried. As we killed time over the past few days we'd been dreaming of such an enchanting prospect. Little did we know that we actually could have attended a birthday party full of gorgeous Finnish women. Wegs and I began kicking each other under the table.

'It is a shame because it was a very good party. You would have liked it very much I think.' Tehri was rubbing salt into the wounds now.

'Yes, it is a shame. Thank you anyway,' I squeaked, trying not to show my disappointment. I was crying on the inside.

Back at Railtrans Wegs and I sat before Jarmo for the final

time. We'd set the camera up in the back corner of the office to record our last official meeting. As I finished mounting the camera to the tripod and returned to my seat his secretary entered the room with a large cardboard box.

'Here. A gift for you.' Jarmo pointed to the box and smiled.

Wegs and I delved inside to find two identical Railtrans' uniforms. They were winter outfits made out of high-quality Gore-Tex fabric. Wegs and I tried the jacket and pants on over the top of our clothes as Jarmo looked on proudly.

'You will need this for Mongolia. It will be much colder than here.' I shuddered at the thought of how cold Mongolia must be, as the temperatures here hadn't risen above freezing since we arrived.

'Thanks, Jarmo. Thank you very much.' We shook his hand strongly. This was a wonderful gesture because Wegs and I hadn't been able to afford any winter clothing of this quality. We'd purchased gloves and a thick jacket each but they had been of the cheap-and-nasty variety. We now had the wardrobe to survive the cold days ahead. The only problem was that our matching outfits made us look like brothers, or worse still a couple, but it was better than the cold alternative.

'OK. Now we go,' stated Jarmo.

❂　❂　❂

We headed off to Laapeenranta in convoy, carefully following Jarmo in his Volvo. It was a very relaxed trip as we cruised along the freeway, stopping only to pick up a spare windscreen for Jarmo's cousin's Volvo and for a quick hamburger and fries.

Halfway to Laapeenranta I was shocked to hear my phone ring again. It was JD, calling for an itinerary update. With all that had gone on in the last week, and our hasty departure today, I'd forgotten to send him an email outlining our new plans.

'G'day, mate,' JD said in his familiar deep voice.

'G'day, mate. How things?'

'Good. I'll be brief, mate, because this call is costing an arm and a leg.'

'Yep, no worries.'

'I can't get a Russian visa for another three weeks, which is a pain in the arse, but I have my Mongolian and Chinese visas organised. I reckon I'll have to skip Russia unfortunately. I can't see it working in time,' said JD.

'Yep, that might be a bit too long to wait,' I said, thinking out aloud. 'What about meeting us in Mongolia?' On the strength of Jarmo's recommendation Wegs and I had decided to stop off in Mongolia en route from Moscow to Beijing.

'Well, funny you should mention that. I have a flight tentatively booked to Ulaan Baatar. I just need three days' notice to confirm.' JD had thought ahead nicely.

'That sounds like a plan, mate. I'll email you from Moscow once we have our Trans-Siberian ticket and timetable and let you know . . . the three days will work well.'

'Done deal.'

'OK, that's sorted, good work. How's the golf form?'

'Terrible. See you in a week or so. Say g'day to Wegs.'

❊ ❊ ❊

Two hours later we parked behind Jarmo at the container yard and followed him into the office. It was dark and everyone had left the office for the day, except for a bubbly blond character called Markko. Jarmo introduced us to the man who would assist us with loading the Big Girl the following morning. It was a quick hello and a quick goodbye to Markko, who had stayed behind for two hours just to greet us. We would see him again in the morning.

We hopped back in the cars for the short drive to a hotel that Jarmo had organised. He came into reception with us to confirm the booking and began speaking in rapid-fire Finnish to the man behind the counter before they both broke out into laughter.

'He wants to know if you want a twin room or a double room,' said Jarmo, grinning broadly. Wegs and I were obviously going to have to do something about our matching uniforms. This was not a good start.

'I tell him a double!' Jarmo said, roaring with laughter.

'Hey? No. No. No,' Wegs and I said in chorus, playing along with him.

'Ha. No. No. I have the twin room booked for you!' Jarmo admitted, and we all chuckled.

'It is now that I must say goodbye.' Jarmo was serious again as he thrust out his hand. 'Markko will deal with everything for you tomorrow. Just remember to call Mr Bruce Chu when you get to Beijing. He speaks very good English and he will help you with your car. Any problem, then please call me. Good luck.'

Wegs and I thanked Jarmo for all that he had done. It was difficult to find the words to convey the depth of our appreciation. We shook hands firmly and promised him that we would stay in touch. We walked Jarmo out to his car and as he backed out of his park he wound down his window.

'I hope you enjoyed your time in Finland and that you think kindly of we Finns. I wish you the best of luck and please, keep in contact. I would like to know that you make it home safely one day.'

⚉   ⚉   ⚉

After a refreshing early morning sauna Wegs and I checked out of the hotel. We'd left early because Wegs wanted to do some shopping before we packed the Big Girl away for her solo trip to China. We found a large supermarket near the freight depot and Wegs ran inside to do his errands. I remained in the car as I wanted to spend as much time as possible with the Big Girl before we parted ways. I was surprised at how emotional I was at the thought of the team separating for the next month. I sat in the car for forty-five minutes waiting for Wegs, enjoying my time in the Big Girl, playing air guitar and belting out some comfort tunes at full volume.

From the supermarket we made the short trip to the depot. The reliable Markko directed us to the rear of the yard where we could see a container and two workers waiting for us. I pulled the Big Girl up to the open container and turned off the ignition. Wegs and I got out and introduced ourselves to Markko and his two workers – no one spoke English. There was a lot of head nodding and smiling as Wegs and I removed our bags and camera equipment.

We stood back and handed over the keys. 'Be careful with her, mate,' I said, knowing full well he had no idea what I was saying. She was in their hands now.

It was bitterly cold and Markko offered to take us to the warmth of his office, but we opted to stay and film the departure of our integral team member. It wasn't long before the Big Girl was safely lashed down and entombed inside the container, her home for about a month. Wegs stepped forward at this point and, as a former wharfie, requested to close the doors on the Big Girl. He locked the Big Girl away and tapped the outside of the container, indicating to the forklift driver that all was in order.

'Good luck, Big Girl.'

The huge forklift made its way to the Big Girl's container and blew a plume of black diesel smoke as it lifted up our weighty lady. It backed up a short way, then proceeded forward to the huge pile of packed containers behind us and lifted the Big Girl up high and stacked her on top of two other large blue containers.

'There she goes,' said Wegs, waving.

It had taken less than an hour to complete the last step in a complex logistical process that had started over two weeks ago in an Internet cafe in downtown Berlin. I was excited that we'd organised the Big Girl's journey but also sad that we couldn't be with her for this leg of the adventure. Wegs and I walked back to Markko's office in silence.

We thanked Markko as he dropped us at the train station. Sitting down on our bulging backpacks inside the concourse, we began our long and boring wait for the evening train to Moscow, in silence. This was different from other turning points on the trip because, for the first time on the journey, Wegs and I were now truly alone: we were a girl down.

The loss of our key team member was obviously weighing heavily on both of us. I chose to digest our new situation by leaning back against the cold wall, absently watching the other commuters go about their daily business. Wegs, in his restless fashion, began to vigorously unwrap and play with the items he'd bought from the supermarket. After a minute or two of paper scrunching his loud voice distracted me from my daydream.

'That'd be right, instructions in every bloody language except for English!' he said, bemoaning an apparently useless purchase.

As he angrily screwed up the instructions and tossed them towards the bin, I saw the cause of his angry outburst and looked at him disparagingly. 'Mate, it's a bloody thermos.'

DAV WEGS

16: THE WOOL CURTAIN

The cabin door slid open abruptly and a male and female customs official entered, each with a loosely tethered Alsatian. The officers were heavily built and intimidating, and both were sporting thick moustaches.

'Passports!' barked the officials (not the Alsatians).

Wegs and I jumped to and promptly handed over our passports that we had at the ready. Tehri had warned us to have our official documentation with us at all times when in Russia because we could be stopped anywhere for a random inspection. In this instance it was at a border control where the customs officials board the train to conduct their checks, instead of when the passengers alight. The officials motioned for us to leave the cabin and wait in the hallway while they searched our luggage. The unfriendly dogs were soon jumping all over the cabin's dated decor and sniffing away at our belongings that the officers had removed from our bags. It was strangely nerve-racking to witness this vigorous search, even though we had nothing to hide. Once the dogs had finished we were permitted to return to the cabin to repack our bags and fill out a lengthy and confusing customs declaration. It was a complex form that required us to declare all goods, valuable or not, that we were carrying into the country. We took care to declare our camera equipment and to fill out the remainder of the form, making doubly sure we ticked the NO box when asked if we were carrying:

- or imparting any radioactive substances
- weapons, ammunition or explosive materials
- drugs or psychotropic substances.

We returned the paperwork to the gruff and officious guards who proceeded to analyse the forms thoroughly, before eventually signing and stamping them in an animated manner.

'Day – vin?' said the female officer, obviously confused by my ugly passport photo. I raised my hand to acknowledge that I was Dayvin and she thrust my passport back under my nose.

'Pow – ell?' She passed Wegs his passport without waiting for him to respond. Wegs and I were the only ones in the four-berth cabin.

The green-uniformed officers pulled their salivating dogs back into the corridor and shut the door as abruptly as they had opened it fifteen minutes ago.

'Welcome to Russia, Dayvin,' said Wegs.

'Thanks, Powell.'

We entered Russia under the cover of darkness and as we stared out the window of the stationary train I felt a tension similar to what I'd experienced in Kosovo. It was pitch black outside and all we could see was a lone officer with his Alsatian standing beneath a solitary platform lamp, the only movement provided by their warm breath in the cold night air and the occasional snowflake. Russia was conforming to just about every stereotype I had formed over the years. It felt like we were on the set of a World War II movie, or a KGB thriller. It was an exciting yet daunting introduction to an unfamiliar country. It wasn't even twelve hours since we'd left Finland, but there could be no doubting that we'd left the familiarity of the Western world behind.

❊   ❊   ❊

Wegs and I spent our first two days in Moscow taking in the main sights. It was unusual for us to dedicate time solely to sightseeing, but we felt that we may never return to Russia. There was also the thrill of being behind the Iron Curtain, as I still thought of it, that I found intriguing after digesting countless espionage novels. However, once we'd wandered the stony expanse of Red Square, admired the bizarre beauty of St Basil's Cathedral, toured the imposing Kremlin and rode the Gorky Park amusements in pouring rain, we'd pretty much *done* Moscow and its landmarks. Our interest soon turned to observing the Russian people and their way of life.

During our days scouring the city and the surrounding suburbs we'd seen little of Russian life that had inspired us. Beyond the impressive architecture of the central city, nearly all of the buildings, residential or commercial, were drab and lifeless concrete blocks. At the feet of these constructions swarmed equally drab boxy cars, spreading pollution around these poorly kept areas. Most of the men dressed in a manner reflecting their utilitarian surroundings, and many wore hollow and dispirited expressions. One taxi driver, Uri, was a lawyer by profession, but couldn't find work due to record high levels of unemployment. He, like many Russian men, drove their family cars around town offering cheap taxi fares to make some money. He told us that Russian men, in general, had low self-esteem and that many turned to alcohol as a result. Day-to-day life for the average Muscovite seemed a fairly bleak affair. I guess that was one of the reasons why we found ourselves at the Hungry Duck nightclub on our second night in Moscow.

Back at the hostel Wegs and I had made a couple of new mates in Matt, an Aussie, and Steve, a Pom. Between the four of us we'd polished off a bottle of vodka as we sat in the common room chatting about our experiences. We all held a grim view of everyday life in Russia but decided that, before making a final judgement we should investigate the local nightlife – to round off our social analysis. For Wegs and me, a dodgy nightclub was the true barometer of a society.

From the outside, the Hungry Duck was like any other lifeless Russian concrete building and I held little hope it would offer the type of entertainment we were seeking. There was a long, cold queue to negotiate, and we couldn't hear any noise from within. Finally we reached the front of the queue and followed the security guard through a maze of doors and thick curtains. On entering the bar my perceptions of Russian life changed forever. From the inside, the Hungry Duck was a heaving and raucous nightclub, oozing with life. We shot each other wicked smiles. This was more like it.

For the next few hours we mixed it up with the partying Russians, downing more than our fair share of the local drop. The bar was as lively and lawless as any I'd ever witnessed. It seemed that you could do anything here. The bar staff even invited us to pour our own drinks as they focused their energies on helping patrons, two at a time, onto a huge podium behind the island bar, to dance or strip, depending on what took their fancy. The bar also had a very healthy ratio of women to men, which we weren't used to. We were also not used to the striking beauty of these Russian women, with their thick full lips and deep probing eyes. There was not a hollow and dispirited expression in the place. Wegs and I were in heaven.

Soon everyone was dancing on tables, bars and podiums. At an opportune moment the large podium behind the bar cleared and Wegs and I sensed this was our cue to show off our wares. We excused ourselves from the two Russian girls we were trying to talk to and jumped up onto the vacant podium, immediately launching into our trademark break-dancing routine. We did a quick performance of lame knee and head spins, before finishing off with a congratulatory high-five. Normally this is guaranteed to make any girls that we may have met run for their lives, but not Nelja and Lina. They actually thought we were serious and, what's more, they thought we were good at it. We were getting along famously with these lively girls and soon found ourselves sharing a taxi back to their place. It was important to conduct a thorough social appraisal.

The taxi ride took over an hour before it delivered us, not surprisingly, to a large concrete apartment block. We entered the cold building and climbed the concrete staircase to the fourth floor.

'Please be careful. George does not like men very much,' Nelja informed us as she opened the door. George, we soon discovered, was her Alsatian. George greeted Nelja and Lina with a wagging tail and licking tongue, a display of affection that ended as soon as Wegs and I walked through the door. George immediately raised his hackles, bared his front teeth and growled menacingly. Nelja held George firmly by the collar as we slid with our backs along the wall to get past. She was correct: George didn't seem to like men very much.

'It is OK,' Nelja assured me, before instructing George in Russian. Lina led Wegs into her small bedroom and Nelja took me, and George, into her equally tiny room. It was a basic flat with two bedrooms, a tiny kitchen and an even smaller bathroom. From Nelja's room I could see Wegs in the adjacent room.

'G'day, mate,' I said and waved.

'G'day,' he replied, returning my stupid gesture. Between the rooms there was a large window that had no glass. We could have reached out and touched each other. Lina erected a woollen blanket over the gaping hole for some privacy.

'Seeya later,' I said, with a stupid grin.

'Seeya, mate.'

Nelja turned her little television on full blast, presumably to give some aural privacy and not for me to watch the blaring Russian news bulletin that was on.

'Come, now we must walk George,' she told me.

Was she serious? It was three o'clock in the morning and

she wanted to walk her dog! I was starting to dislike George, who growled as I shot him an angry glance behind Nelja's back. We walked back down the four flights of stairs and out into the thick snow. It took George ten minutes to mark his territory and clear his bowels, in what was, without doubt, the longest ten minutes of my life.

Back at the flat Nelja and I returned to her room and quickly took off a few layers of clothing before jumping into bed. As we started to get comfortable with one another I heard the pitter-patter of feet behind me. I turned around to see George sitting next to the bed, watching my every move; his shiny white teeth were well lit by the light from the roaring television. He made no noise, but it was clear he didn't approve.

'Don't worry about George. He is just a big teddy bear,' soothed Nelja. But I did worry about George. He was a big teddy bear with big sharp teeth.

I can't speak for what Wegs may have been doing on the other side of the wool curtain, but I certainly wasn't going to risk initiating any intimate actions with Nelja that may be mis-interpreted by the watchful George. I spent the remainder of that surreal night lying next to the sleeping Nelja, adjacent to a protective, insomniac Alsatian, watching Russian soap operas.

In the morning the girls prepared a breakfast of dry bis-cuits, cured meat and black tea. The food was uninspiring but the gesture was genuine and appreciated. After breakfast Nelja and Lina walked us to the nearest train station and told us what line to take and what stop we needed to get off at in order to return to our hostel. They were lovely and fine ambassadors for their country, and had certainly given us an interesting insight into Russian life.

Once on the underground system Wegs and I congratulated one another on the dedication we'd shown in appreciating the local culture. After last night Russia had taken on a whole new perspective for us. It was refreshing to know that beneath the cold and regulated exterior there was a warm and carefree underbelly. We'd learnt that life in Russia need not be dull and boring – as long as you're a good drinker, a dog lover and an acceptable break-dancer.

❀ ❀ ❀

I awoke on the morning of our third full day aboard the Trans-Mongolian Railway in the same manner that I'd woken the previous two days: with a dry mouth and a sore head. Except this morning Wegs was punching me to wake me up so I could see the last of Lake Baikal as it flicked past the window. Lake Baikal is the largest and deepest freshwater lake in the world and the vast blue expanse was a truly amazing sight in its mid-morning splendour. Sadly, its beauty was lost on me as I lay there with my dry mouth pondering whether, if given a large straw, I could drain this lake and deny it of its two impressive credentials. I reckoned I could give it a good nudge.

We took the Trans-Mongolian train service because it passed through Mongolia en route to Beijing. We'd organised to meet JD in Ulaan Baatar, the capital of Mongolia, in a week or so, and planned to spend a bit of time in this remote country. The rail journey from Moscow to Ulaan Baatar takes five days, and even for seasoned travellers, five consecutive days on a cramped train is a strong test of one's travelling resolve. Wegs and I had joined forces with other backpackers in a bid to combat the monotony; unfortunately for our weary livers, this involved drinking copious amounts of vodka.

It wasn't that the train journey was without beautiful scenery or colourful characters to help pass the time, it was just there was so much time to pass. None of us had ever been on a train for longer than three hours, let alone three days with two more days still to travel, but we had finally settled into a daily routine.

The third day was a perfect example of our daily Trans-Mongolian routine. After torturously watching the cool and unattainable waters of Lake Baikal rattle past I went in search of some relief for my dry mouth, wanting to get rid of the stale vodka aftertaste and freshen myself up for the day. I climbed down from my top bunk, apologising to Victor and Maria, our Ukrainian cabin mates, for stepping on the edge of their bed. As usual, they looked up from their soup and smiled and waved to me as I disappeared in the direction of the bathroom.

Once again my day started with the unpleasant task of cleaning footprints off the toilet seat. There is a Chinese service and a Russian service that operate between Moscow and Beijing, and we had booked ourselves on the Chinese service because the timetable suited our departure from Moscow. The only difference between the services was that on our train we had Chinese conductors and predominantly Chinese passengers who chose to stand, as opposed to sit, on the toilet seats. I watched my morning movements drop straight down onto the snowy tracks below, and then turned to splash some water on my face and hands before brushing my teeth. After my Trans-Mongolian 'shower' I returned to join Wegs on the narrow corridor seats outside our small cabin.

It was around midday and Wegs had kindly prepared some two-minute noodles for me. We sat in the corridor and slurped away at the boiling hot noodles, which had become our staple diet on the train. Stupidly, we'd left Moscow with little money for the journey. We'd rushed to make the train and after paying for our tickets had decided against withdrawing more roubles. We hadn't taken into account the fact that we'd need to eat and drink for the next five days and now found ourselves existing on a shoestring. It was touch and go if we could make it stretch the remaining two days to Ulaan Baatar. We couldn't afford to eat in the dining carriage and instead we bought noodles from local vendors when the train stopped briefly at stations along the way. We had nothing else left, not even a bottle of lemon-ade or a sweet biscuit, until the next stop. And having a roaring hangover made poverty all the more intolerable.

After lunch we settled into our afternoon routine. It was a book-a-day journey. Wegs was reading one of the novels that had been doing the rounds between the backpackers on board the train. I sat in my small corridor chair and began writing some notes for my next *TNT* article, which was due just hours after our scheduled arrival in Mongolia. This was my favourite time of the day; the hypnotic effect of the train's relentless move-ment encouraged writing and reflection. Not to mention taking in the impressive scenery. We were travelling through the last section of Siberia before crossing into Mongolia later that day. I sat and stared out the window, like every other day, amazed that anyone could live in such a cold and desolate region. In fact, I felt like I was watching a movie, because although this barren scenery was only metres away it seemed a world apart as we rattled along in our warm cocoon through Siberia.

Occasionally we'd pass small villages with shanty-like wooden dwellings pumping smoke out narrow chimneys nestled in shingled roofs. There were few signs of life: a man bashing a hole into a frozen lake to fish, an elderly woman chopping wood and the odd cow freezing its udder off in a fenceless white expanse. My Australian upbringing was no preparation for understanding what life was like in Siberia. It hurt my brain trying to imagine it.

The afternoon was punctuated by frequent encounters with the friendly passengers in our neighbouring cabins. Each time they walked by us or we walked by their cabin we'd be pulled in to drink a shot or two of vodka with them. Wegs had made good friends with a Mongolian police officer and postman in the cabin next to us; they'd call him in every half-hour or so for a shot of vodka and, in the absence of any intelligible conversation, an arm wrestle. I'd formed a similar relationship with some Russian miners two cabins down, who were returning to work in the remote Mongolian mines. Their command of English was very limited so my conversations with them were also restricted to smiling, pointing, nodding, laughing, arm wrestling and, of course, drinking. Vodka, it seemed, was the key to surviving this incredibly long journey.

As a result of our fraternising Wegs and I were slightly tipsy when the train pulled up at a small station for a refuelling stop later that afternoon. The day had gotten away from us and it was now early evening. Soon it would be time to locate our other partners in crime. Firstly though, we had to buy some provisions for the following day.

We rugged up in our Railtrans outfits and walked out onto the platform, where vendors screamed and begged for our business from behind a wire fence. Normally they'd be allowed onto the platform but that wasn't the case at this station. The touting vendors had lit fires next to their card-table stalls and were banging on the fence to get our attention. The trains were an important source of income for these poor locals and I felt bad that we couldn't buy more than the bare essentials. Our budget was so restricted we decided to forego the sweet biscuits, our daytime snack, so that we could afford the essentials: four packets of two-minute noodles and a large bottle of vodka.

As we completed the transaction a sharp female voice began yelling instructions in Russian over a screechy public-address system. The fires, the darkness, the pleading peasants and the barking PA created an eerie, totalitarian atmosphere that was spooking some of the female backpackers. Anna, our Danish neighbour from the train, was scared by the 'Big Sister' announcement and she made her way briskly back on board the train. I could understand her concern: the environment was cold and unfriendly and the Russian language has a way of making even a timetable announcement sound like an air-raid warning. I was pretty glad to get back onto the train myself.

Once the train was in motion Wegs and I made our way to the dining carriage, vodka in hand, for our daily rendezvous with our Trans-Mongolian buddies: Lars, Magnus, Tobias and Ida from Sweden; Anna from Denmark; Julia from Germany; Gana from Mongolia; and Matt, our Australian mate from Moscow. It was a long and challenging walk through ten carriages to the other end of the train where the dining car was located. Passing from one carriage to the next involved opening and closing four doors, and negotiating the freezing cold air trapped in between the carriages. We spread ourselves out over two tables in the quiet dining car, which wouldn't remain quiet for long as we launched into drinking game after drinking game. When drinking games are played with straight vodka it doesn't take much time for things to get out of hand, and every night someone ended up running the length of the deserted dining carriage stark naked.

These frivolous nights of song, dance, tall stories and drinking continued well into the early hours of the morning. The night of the third day was no different and at 2 a.m. Wegs and I set off on the difficult journey back to our cabin. Negotiating forty doors on a moving train when fully loaded with vodka was nigh impossible. After bashing and crashing our way through ten carriages, probably waking everyone despite our efforts to be quiet, we found it necessary to make a quick snack prior to bed. Our bodies were conditioned to eating in the small hours of the morning when drunk and, given the lack of available kebabs and hot dogs, we pulled out our two-minute noodles and set about their preparation.

Walking on the train when drunk had been difficult but it was nothing compared to making two-minute noodles on a moving train when drunk. By the time we'd unwrapped the containers and covered them, at great personal risk, with boiling water from the urns at the end of the carriage, they'd become ten-minute noodles. We sat on our narrow corridor chairs to eat them quietly, so as not to wake Victor and Maria. Unfortunately I spilt the noodles all over the floor and boiling water all over my foot.

'Ssshhhit, that'sh bloody hot,' I said, as I rubbed my burnt foot and pushed the errant noodles under the heater with my non-burnt foot. Deep in concentration, Wegs said nothing.

'Ssshhhit, they're bloody sshhlippery little basshtardsh!' I cursed as I dropped more noodles on the ground. This second spillage was louder than the first and attracted the attention of our Chinese conductor. He came skipping down the corridor with his ever-present dustpan and broom, and knelt down in front of me and began sweeping up the noodles from around my feet and between my toes.

'Ssshhorry, mate. It wassh an accsshident. Ssshhorry.' I felt terrible as he fussed around in his pyjamas, cleaning up my mess.

'Thank you! Thank you!' he said to me, nodding his head to reinforce his sincerity. Although, in hindsight, it did rather sound like, 'Fuck you! Fuck you!'

17: SOMETHING UNEXPECTED

'Dave. Dave. Wake up, Dave,' whispered a voice. I tried to focus on the person leaning over me by placing a hand over my left eye and squinting through my right.

'Huh?' I grunted, as Inca, our Mongolian hostel operator, materialised before my eyes.

'Dave. Your friend. Mr John Del – bridge. I get your friend now,' he whispered.

'Uh huh,' I squeaked. Inca stood up and tiptoed out of our dorm room, being careful not to wake Wegs, or Anna and Adrian, our dorm buddies.

'What did Inca want?' Wegs croaked, without opening his eyes. Despite Inca's best intentions he'd managed to wake the stirring Wegs.

'I think he's going to get JD from the airport,' I said. Yawning sleepily, I rolled back over onto my side.

'Oh, yeah. Let's hope he drives around the block a few times before he gets back,' Wegs sighed.

'Uh huh,' I said and drifted back to sleep.

JD was due to fly into Ulaan Baatar that morning after his flight had been delayed the previous day due to inclement weather. JD's arrival was significant, and had we not celebrated Wegs' twenty-fifth birthday last night we would've been as excited by his impending arrival as we'd been the day before, when he was expected to arrive. Unfortunately, after excessive vodka consumption at a dodgy Mongolian karaoke bar that we'd hired for Wegs' celebrations nothing could excite us, other than more time in bed. It was a sad indictment of both Wegs and myself that we couldn't get off our arses for our long-awaited rendezvous with JD. But we needed more sleep before we would be capable of anything and, knowing JD as we did, we were sure he'd understand.

❀ ❀ ❀

'Happy birthday, mate!' yelled JD, scaring the shit out of both Wegs and me.

'Aaagghh!' screamed Wegs, and sat up abruptly in bed. I was performing similar actions in my bed on the far side of the dorm; fortunately Adrian and Anna were already up and about. We must've fallen back to sleep for a good couple of hours.

'Here you go, mate.' JD offered Wegs a present wrapped in a familiar Australian duty-free bag. Wegs took a peek inside and screwed up his face as JD roared with laughter.

'Thanks, mate,' Wegs said wryly as he pulled the 1.5-litre bottle of Smirnoff out of the bag for me to see. 'Thanks a lot.'

'No worries, mate,' JD chortled. He made his way over to my bed and thrust out his hand.

'G'day, mate.'

'G'day, mate.'

The team was back to three.

●   ●   ●

Inca pulled the jeep up alongside a large cairn and told us to leave the car and follow him. As we trudged through the thin layer of snow behind him he explained that these were sacred sites and it was a Buddhist ritual to stop and acknowledge them. We weren't exactly sure what these large rock piles symbolised but we obediently picked up a handful of rocks and walked around the cairn three times, throwing the rocks onto the pile as we circled. The locals observe this ritual in the belief that good luck will befall them, and they often make a symbolic gesture to specify their chosen fortune. In and around this particular cairn we could see about a dozen crutches scattered haphazardly. Apparently people who have recovered from a broken leg come here and sacrifice their crutches, believing this will prevent them from suffering broken legs in the future. I liked the philosophy and cursed myself for not bringing an empty vodka bottle with me. After four days in Moscow, five days on the Trans-Mongolian and one huge night in Ulaan Baatar, I would have gladly foregone any future vodka consumption and accompanying hangovers.

We bundled eagerly back into the jeep, keen to thaw out our achingly cold extremities. The cairn was on an exposed hill on the outskirts of Ulaan Baatar and Inca guessed that the temperature, inclusive of wind chill, was around minus twenty degrees Celsius. This place made Finland and Russia feel almost tropical in comparison. Thank goodness for Jarmo, as otherwise we wouldn't have been able to withstand these numbingly cold temperatures. It was so cold we could only stay outside the car for less than five minutes before our toes and fingers, even when protected by gloves and thick socks, began to ache painfully. In the short time outside our wet noses had iced over and even our hair had frozen. In Mongolia you didn't feel the cold in your flesh – because it was numb – you felt it in your bones. It was so cold it hurt. But it wasn't long before the efficient heater in our jeep had us removing layers of clothing and breathing through runny noses.

We left the sprawling Mongolian capital behind as Inca piloted our bouncing jeep towards the wide-open spaces of the Gobi Desert, on our way to the Chinese border. Instead of jumping back on the Trans-Mongolian service at Ulaan Baatar we'd decided to make our way overland to China by jeep and visit some of the places Jarmo had recommended. When we'd asked Inca how to go about this he immediately offered his services as a tour guide. He was, in fact, a retired tour guide, but because he'd had so much fun at Wegs' karaoke party he wanted to personally show us the desert where he grew up. All we had to do was pay for the hire of the jeep, the fuel and the supplies, and Inca would show us the rest. He'd checked the train timetable and in one week's time he'd drop us at Sainshand, over 1200 kilometres away, where we could intercept the Trans-Mongolian service to complete our transit to Beijing.

It was a last-minute decision, just the way we liked it. Bring on the Gobi.

❃ ❃ ❃

Six hours later our bone-jarring drive rolled to a stop. Since leaving Ulaan Baatar we'd stopped only to visit the Buddhist cairn and to change a flat tyre. It had been a long and rough day in the saddle as Inca sped across the bumpy tracks leading to the Gobi Desert. The last four hours of the day's journey had been along a narrow track carved through deep snow. In places the snow was over bonnet height and the track was often washed away by watercourses hidden under the thick white carpet of snow. Generally Inca 'found' these by driving into them at breakneck speed, forcing the relocation of occupants and luggage throughout the cabin. As Inca gathered the jeep back onto the track he would astutely observe, 'Ha ha, river', laughing like a maniac as he continued to drive like one.

We were lucky to be in a strong and functional Russian-built jeep, as I doubt many of the 4WDs we drive at home would have survived such abuse. It was astonishing we'd only suffered a flat tyre as a result of this reckless driving; there were still six days to go, however, which should give Inca plenty of time to fulfil his apparent desire to snap the jeep in half. Only time would tell if the jeep, Wegs, JD and I would survive the journey in one piece. Despite the spine-compressing bumps we were all, Inca included, having a lot of fun.

As darkness set in we pulled up outside five round canvas tents known as gers. These gers are the traditional homes of the nomadic people of the Gobi. They are made of canvas, lined with thick wool and supported by a wooden frame that's raised in the centre. It's a simple construction that can be packed up within a day if the family is forced, through a bad season, to relocate. Inca jumped out of the jeep and ran inside one of the gers to ask the local family if we could stay the night. That was how things worked out here; there are no reservations in the Gobi. Within a minute he came rushing back to say it was OK, and that we should gather a few of our essentials and come inside. There wasn't enough room for us to take in our large backpacks. We grabbed some gifts for the family, a couple of books and our toilet bags from the back of the jeep. I doubt we would've lasted long enough to unpack all of our bags anyway, for now that the sun had fallen and the wind had picked up it was unbearably cold. Inca had told us that during the night the temperature would fall to around minus forty degrees Celsius, and it must have been every bit of that as we grabbed the closest items from the back of the jeep.

It was dark and cold, and in our haste to get inside JD and I both struck our heads painfully on the low door, shaking the entire ger. The poor Mongolian family had no idea what had hit them when two grimacing and one laughing guest burst into their small and orderly home environment. We were like giants inside the colourful ger, stooping as we walked over to make our introductions, via Inca, to the family. Wegs wasn't laughing for long as he donged his head loudly on a kerosene lamp hanging from the ceiling. The ringing and hollow sound (of the lamp) proved to be a great icebreaker and the family were soon all smiles as we shook their hands, before moving back to sit down on one of the two beds in the ger.

Prior to our departure from Ulaan Baatar we'd purchased enough gifts for each of the six families we'd be staying with. For the man we had vodka and cigarettes; for the children, if any, we had an assortment of chocolates and sweets; and for the wife we had some money to cover the cost of our food. At Inca's recommendation we'd purchased the cheapest possible vodka, as he said that Mongolian men drink it irrespective of quality. He told us we should immediately present the man of the ger with a gift, so I stood up and handed over the rocket fuel and a packet of equally cheap cigarettes to the father, who accepted the offering with outstretched hands. Wegs delved into our box of goodies and extracted two Snickers bars that were frozen solid and handed them to the eagerly awaiting children, who accepted them in the same polite fashion as their father.

'Might be a trip to the dentist coming up,' JD observed as the young boy and girl tried to crack the frozen bars with their teeth. It was a scary sight. I could only imagine that Mum was the dentist in these parts, and ice, a length of string and the front door were the tools of her trade. So we were glad to see the enterprising young kids place their chocolates on top of the small stove, which their mother was busily stoking with fuel.

While the children were waiting for their rare treat to thaw they came bounding back over to play with us and our gadgets. The boy and girl were around eight and six years old respectively, and both had lively intellects and a thirst for knowledge. It was rare for them to meet foreigners so they wanted us to teach them words in English and to play with our assortment of cameras and musical equipment. JD pressed play on his portable CD player and inserted the earplugs into the young boy's ears. His face lit up as the strange music played. He then placed one of the earplugs into his sister's ear so she could also enjoy the Bon Jovi experience. I was impressed to see him sharing, knowing full well that I'd never have shared the earplugs with my sister when I was that young. In our household it would have definitely ended in tears (most likely my sister's) and me being sent to my room, leaving neither of us to enjoy the music. The teamwork of these siblings was no doubt essential to family life in the Gobi.

While we were playing with the kids, the father began on the vodka. After ceremoniously downing the first shot he stood up and brought the next shot over to us in a small silver cup and offered it to Wegs. Inca instructed Wegs to firstly receive it in two hands, then to dip the third finger of his right hand into the vodka and flick it towards the ceiling of the ger for Buddha, then repeat the action for blue skies and finally for nature. Once Wegs had completed all three flicks Inca instructed him to drink the vodka, which he did with a grimace. It seemed that our thrifty vodka purchasing had come back to bite us on the bum. We'd come to the Gobi to escape vodka for a week, not to immerse ourselves in it. Especially not in vodka that was most likely re-labelled paint stripper.

After polishing off the bottle of horrific vodka as politely as we could, our attention turned towards the mother. Our evening meal was nearly ready. We'd only grazed on snacks in the car so far that day, and a wholesome home-cooked meal was an enchanting prospect. Inca had forewarned us that meals in the Gobi were simple, consisting only of meat, predominantly mutton, and pasta, as no vegetables could be grown. I would have loved such a meal as a child, as in our household my mum would never serve dessert unless we'd eaten all of our veggies. It was torture, and I began to think that perhaps growing up in the remote Gobi wasn't so bad. These lucky Mongolian kids would never have to experience the pain of stuffing down unpalatable brussels sprouts before tucking into their mutton pudding.

The ger was warming up as the small stove began pumping out some much-needed heat. The stove was only lit at night in order to preserve their precious fuel source for the duration of the long winter. Now that the fire was burning well we were able to remove a few layers, stripping back to a comfortable t-shirt and pants ensemble. While we sat in the warm ger awaiting our vegetable-free meal I asked Inca what the mother was using for firewood – we hadn't seen a single tree since we'd arrived in Mongolia.

'From the camel,' he smiled.

'From the camel? You mean camel shit?' I asked, using supporting gestures.

'Yes, shit,' Inca said, nodding his head and also pointing to his bum.

'Really?'

'Yes, shit.'

That would explain the dubious odour the fire was producing, but I wasn't convinced. Inca had proven to be quite the practical joker over the previous couple of days. I stood up and walked over to check if Inca was talking a load of bullshit – or a pile of camel shit. I looked beside the mother and could see that it was the latter. Then, as if to reinforce the point, she picked up a nicely dried camel turd from her neatly stacked pile of poo and placed it in the roaring furnace. It burnt surprisingly well, did camel poo.

Minutes later our steaming hot mutton dumplings were served to us, three at a time, on a small plate carried over by the children. We took the meal in both hands and waited for the dumplings to cool down. The mother passed over a bottle of tomato sauce for us to add to the dumplings. I noticed this was the lone condiment in her small pantry cupboard that contained only flour, tea and sugar. These Mongolians existed on the meat of whatever animal had been killed most recently, normally lamb but also goat, camel, cow and horse, plus plain pasta made from flour and milk. In the average Mongolian ger there were no prizes for guessing what was for dinner.

Once the dumplings had cooled, we picked them up, dipped them in some sauce and got stuck in. Immediately the three of us looked at one another with large mouthfuls of dumpling to see if we were thinking the same thought. Our wide eyes and bulging jaws said it all – the sheep in question had obviously led a long life wandering the Gobi in search of grass, and the little nuggets of mutton took some chewing. However, despite the high level of mastication required they were pleasant enough to eat – the tomato sauce was quite tasty. We made all of the right noises so the mother knew that we appreciated her cooking, but we politely declined her offer of seconds. I was still slightly hungry but my jaw was too tired to negotiate another chewing marathon. We rubbed our stomachs as we passed back our empty plates to indicate that we couldn't possibly fit in another cannonball dumpling. A week of mutton was looking like a tough prospect.

After dinner Inca and the father set about noisily repairing our flat tyre, with the assistance of the young son. The mother and the daughter were doing the dishes and tending the poo fire, while Wegs, JD and I read books and listened to music. The small ger was a mix of noisy activity and leisurely relaxation. It was now so hot that we were sitting around in our boxer shorts and t-shirts. It was impossible to think that it was minus forty degrees Celsius outside.

Once the chores had been attended to we began our preparations for bed. Wegs, JD and I dressed for the cold again because we needed to go out for a loo stop prior to bed. It would be a very brief stop. After our noses had frozen earlier in the day we were worried about what might happen if we spent too long peeing in the cold night air.

We raced back inside to the sauna, having refrozen in the short time we'd spent outside. As we made our way back in Inca began to get animated and called us over.

'Sorry. I forgot to tell you about Mongolian customs,' he said. He motioned for us to sit next to him. 'There are some rules.' We sat down and Inca outlined the main rules we needed to follow so we didn't contravene family customs.

- Guests are only allowed on the left side of the ger. The right side is family-only. Under no circumstances should we cross to the right side.
- Walking between the two support poles of the ger is forbidden. These two poles symbolise the man and the woman supporting the family. Walking between these poles will weaken the structure of the family and cause the breakdown of the marriage.
- Receive everything with two hands and never the left hand alone; pass with the right hand.
- The ger is orientated from south to north. Everyone must sleep with head facing the north – for religious reasons.
- No whistling inside.
- No hats inside.

It was unfortunate that it had taken Wegs to come in from the toilet break with his hat on, me to come in whistling 'Patience' by Guns N' Roses and JD to come in through the family side of the ger for Inca's memory to be jogged. It would've been useful information four hours ago, as I knew we'd all walked between the poles on several occasions already. This poor family was in for some rough days ahead. I looked apologetically over to the kids who are always the real losers from divorce. Our actions meant they were likely to grow up without a father figure as I guessed that, in this case, Mum would be the one granted custody. I felt terrible. Who would show that little boy how to drink vodka properly?

Fortunately there were no hard feelings and soon we were all tucked away in our makeshift bedding, neatly aligned with our heads to the north. The father turned off the kerosene lamp and made his way to the right-hand side of the ger.

'Night, Weggsie. Night, JD,' I said, like a little boy on a sleepover.

'Night, Dav. Night, JD.'

'Ni-night, Weggsie. Ni-night, Dav,' JD replied. We chuckled and drifted off to sleep, occasionally coughing to mask the passing of wind.

❂ ❂ ❂

It was an early and chilly start to the day. The banging of the door woke us and we popped our heads up from our tin-of-sardines formation. Inca and the father were manhandling the cumbersome spare tyre, and through the open door I could see the sun rising over the distant horizon. The boys and I packed up our bedding and belongings but when we arrived at the jeep Inca was trying in vain to get it started. The engine had frozen overnight and didn't sound at all interested in firing into life. I poked my head under the bonnet for a token inspection.

'Should have left it running twenty-four/seven,' I said sarcastically within earshot of Wegs, hoping to elicit a response.

'Shut up, Ardlie,' Wegs responded predictably. I laughed heartily, but not for long as Inca was calling us to give him a push start.

We pushed the heavy jeep back and forth with no success. Inca popped the hood again and asked me to fetch the crank handle; I shouldn't have been surprised that these square Russian jeeps actually have a crank mechanism for such instances. I ran off in the direction of the ger and burst inside, being mindful to lower my head, only to find I'd entered the wrong ger. My arrival caused the unsuspecting family to shriek with fear and leap up from their warm beds.

'Whoops. Sorry.' I didn't wait for an answer but retreated backwards, bumping my head solidly for good measure.

'Wrong one!' I called over to the boys in an embarrassed fashion, but they were too busy play-wrestling with the kids to hear. These gers all looked alike from the outside.

I arrived back at the jeep with the crank handle just as the father was placing a bucket full of burning camel poo under the front of the car. The crank handle had little effect beyond tiring us all out, so we adjourned inside for a few hours to wait for the multi-purpose camel droppings to do their stuff.

After two bowls of mutton porridge and a mug of camel's milk tea, the team, and finally the jeep, were ready to hit the road. We thanked the family via Inca and with handshakes, and bundled into the cramped jeep, strapping ourselves in for the rough ride ahead. We waved a long goodbye to the friendly family who had stayed outside to see us safely off. We watched them until they were out of sight before turning our attention to the endless white expanse that lay before us.

The path ahead was amazingly featureless and glaringly white in the sunshine. It felt like we were driving off the edge of the world as we sped towards a horizon that boldly separated the bright white of the flat plain from the brilliant blue of the clear sky. The cloudless sky that overlooked us that day was proof that toasting Buddha brings about good fortune. It was also the first time I'd ever been thankful for drinking vodka the night before. The Gobi Desert was defying the norm.

❂   ❂   ❂

JD had brought with him a variety of books for the journey, on subjects ranging from Ancient Eastern philosophy to contemporary personal development, as well as some literature classics. Over the course of our week in the desert, Wegs and I flicked through these books, and learnt how to play chess. It felt like we'd come a long way since Ireland, and reading these books while travelling through the vast expanses of a country we'd only ever heard of from Chinese takeaway menus was stimulating and empowering. So stimulating that our discussions no longer centred on women and alcohol, but digressed to the subject of the future and what paths we might follow on completion of this journey. Wegs spoke passionately about fulfilling his childhood desire to become a fireman, and I decided that I should actually learn to surf – instead of just telling girls I could. The ambitious quest to get a hearse across the world, one way or the other, was starting to bear unexpected fruit.

It was our last night in a Gobi ger and I put my book down for a moment to take in the surroundings. Our days in the desert had been as similar as they were distinct from each other. Every day saw us speeding through the ever-changing geography of the Gobi, and each night saw us staying with local families.

The families were as diverse as the landscape, but there was an intriguing familiarity between life in all of the different regions of the Gobi we'd visited. Over the past days we'd left the snowy expanses behind and moved on through cavernous valleys, rocky plains, grassy knolls, expansive sand dunes and, on many occasions, a whole lot of nothing. It was the alluring nothingness of the Gobi that we'd immersed ourselves in that gave it everything.

At first glance one thinks that the desert is an oppressive environment: battered by the extremes of temperatures and devoid of life. However, if you take a closer look, you will *know* that it's an oppressive environment battered by extreme temperatures, but it's only devoid of life as *we* know it. Life in the Gobi is as simple and pure as it is complex and challenging, but for all the challenges that nature can throw at these hardy souls, they survive: through persistence, subsistence and resilience. When I was rattling through Siberia in my warm Trans-Mongolian cocoon I'd been unable to imagine what life was like in such a harsh, remote and desolate region. Our time in the Gobi had shifted my paradigm into one of comprehension. By coming to the desert and living with the locals, albeit on a temporary basis, we'd been able to focus on what the Mongolians *gain* by living this way, and not what they *lose*.

I could never live here myself, I knew that, but at least now I could appreciate why people do.

❂   ❂   ❂

Our last day in the Gobi was a leisurely one. We slept in, sat around the small stove drinking filtered coffee from JD's personal percolator, and played knuckles with the family's two young boys.

'One hour we leave,' Inca said.

'No worries, mate,' Wegs replied. Wegs turned to JD. 'Reckon you'll be ready, mate?'

'Yeah, mate. You better start packing up all your little bags now,' I chipped in.

'Piss off, ya cheeky pricks,' JD laughed into his coffee, drawing heavily on his cigarette.

JD had been with us for nearly a week now and hadn't once managed to be packed up and ready to leave on time. After indiscriminately stuffing our belongings into our backpacks, Wegs and I always seemed to be waiting for JD to pack his socks into his sock bag; his underwear in his undies bag; fold his jumpers together, pants together and shirts together; before turning his attentions to his protracted grooming procedure. It would be nothing for Inca, Wegs and me to be in the loaded-up jeep with the engine running, while JD sat inside in his pyjamas, with bags unpacked, sewing on a button. It was infuriating to say the least.

JD and I hadn't worked together as project managers for over three years, and I'd forgotten how anal he could be. He is a highly intelligent man, smarter than Wegs and me put together, but for as long as I'd known him he'd never grasped the concept of time.

Despite his poor sense of time JD, at thirty-two, was proving to be the father figure on this journey. He was always making sure we'd eaten enough, that we were warm enough, that we had brushed our teeth before bed and that we'd gone to the toilet before getting into the car for the day. And like every father, he also had more than a passing interest in making sure the car was packed properly. It was little wonder that Wegs and I often referred to him as Dad.

Our stay with this final family had been particularly enjoyable. We'd arrived before dark the previous evening, which gave us more time to spend in the family environment. During the afternoon we'd ridden tiny Mongolian horses, much to the amusement of the family, and much to the detriment of our genitals – Mongolians make their tiny saddles from solid timber.

We'd also spent a lot of time with the kids, playing cards and helping the brothers build toy trucks with blocks of wood and flat AA batteries for wheels. The father taught his young kids woodwork by encouraging them to drive the only nail they had into a block of wood and then retrieve it with pliers. They worked tenaciously and thought laterally as they struggled to remove and then straighten their only nail. We saw repeated instances between these siblings that would have ended up in jealous fights in most Australian families, but instead ended up in beautiful examples of teamwork and sharing. The simplicity of life and the strength of the family unit in Mongolia never ceased to amaze me.

After sharing coffee with the family, Inca asked if the old man present, who was the kids' grandfather, could get a lift with us back to his home in Sainshand. That wasn't a problem for us and we were soon on the way in the crowded jeep, with the old man riding shotgun with Inca up front. The trip into town was the usual teeth-rattling ride we had come to expect, and we were keen to return to the smooth passage of the Trans-Mongolian. The old man, who looked every bit of seventy-five years old, didn't seem to mind being thrown around like a rag doll. Even in old age, the Mongolians are as tough as nails.

Sainshand is a large town by Mongolian standards. It has a train station, two shops, a hotel, a school, a smattering of apartment buildings, and is surrounded by suburbs of gers nestled behind tin fences. We parked outside a gate in a tin fence that led to the old man's ger. As we prepared to say goodbye Inca informed us that the old man had invited us to join him for lunch, and that we should accept the invitation.

We stopped and removed our hats before carefully stooping through the door. It was much the same as the other colourfully painted gers we'd entered in the Gobi. It had small beds on either side, two support poles in the middle, a small stove, a couple of cupboards, a large pile of blankets and a shrine to Buddha at the northern end. We said hello to his elderly wife and made our way towards the left-hand bed, making sure we walked around the support poles. We'd finally become cognisant of Mongolian customs and it had been several days since we'd last worn our hats inside or broken up a marriage.

The elderly wife dipped a ladle into a large pot on the stove and deftly poured us each a bowl of mutton soup, being careful not to knock the sheep's head simmering in the broth. We accepted the unattractive offering in the same polite manner we'd accepted all of the unattractive offerings of the past week. This mutton soup would be easier to consume than the mutton porridge, mutton dumplings and mutton pasta that we'd been living off to date for one very significant reason: it was going to be our last mutton dish for the journey, and hopefully forever. We'd learnt the hard way that the Mongolians have a greater reliance upon the humble sheep than even your average Kiwi – albeit at a much less intimate level. But despite the various presentations of the meat over the week, the Mongolians had proved, unequivocally, that you just can't dress mutton up as lamb.

During the soup consumption we sat and looked through the old man's photo collection as he proudly showed off his fourteen grandchildren and two great-grandchildren. At the end of the photo session the old man stood up and went to one of his two cupboards. He removed three small woollen pouches and made his way over to us. He placed one pouch in each of our outstretched hands and murmured something to us.

'He says thank you for your kindness,' Inca translated. 'You have given him a lift through the desert for no personal gain, and you were kind to his family. You are good people and he wishes you the best.'

The old man removed a pouch of his own from his pocket and withdrew three lamb's knuckles. He rattled them in his closed hands and then threw them on the floor like dice.

'He can read from the knuckles by how they land,' Inca said. The old man inspected the strewn knuckles and murmured something to us again. We turned to Inca.

'He says the knuckles say you will have safe travels. No problem,' Inca added. 'You should use these knuckles that he gives you to know about any situation.'

It was humbling to be presented with a personal gift that would assist us to negotiate the path ahead. Even though we couldn't read the signs of the knuckles ourselves, it was the sentiment that counted. We shook the old man's hand and stood up to leave. He murmured again and waved us to follow him.

'He asks you to leave through the family side ... this is a great honour.'

This final gesture highlighted just how far we'd come in our week in the Gobi. We'd arrived as ignorant home wreckers, and departed as extended family members. Our time in the desert had taught us a lot about the Mongolians, and a little bit about ourselves as well.

❂   ❂   ❂

I looked at myself in the train's shaking bathroom mirror and saw the same expression I'd seen on Wegs' face in Nice, on Whitey's face in Pompeii and JD's face in the desert after Inca had hit a large bump in the jeep. I knew instantly that I was about to shit my pants. I turned and hurriedly wiped the footprints off the Trans-Mongolian toilet seat. My time had come and, unlike poor JD in the jeep, I had sufficient time and warning to get to a toilet. I sat down quickly and waited, and waited, and waited.

Despite the horrendous stomach pains my bowels refused to move. Unlike the other guys, my upset stomach was a result of an overly solid stool. It had been more than seven days since my last movement as I'd chosen, while in the cold and inhospitable desert, to take two Immodium tablets each day to avoid going to the toilet. Setting my stomach like concrete appeared to be a good idea at the time, but, much like my Siberian driving theory, commonsense would ultimately prevail. Commonsense which in this case tells you that eating twenty-four mutton dumplings, twelve horse dumplings, five camel dumplings, seven bowls of mutton porridge, five serves of mutton pasta and one bowl of mutton soup without going to the toilet is actually a really *stupid* idea.

I was left to ponder the errors of my ways for the next two hours as I negotiated the excruciating passing of a faecal fence post. Hindsight has never been more painful.

18: LOST IN TRANSLATION

It was a motley crew that arrived on the doorstep of the Far East Hostel in Beijing on a cold Monday evening. It had been ten days since our last shower, although anyone who saw us arrive that night would have assumed it was a lot longer. Everything about us was filthy; our clothes were filthy, our skin was filthy and our hair was filthy. However, there was nothing filthier, in terms of general appearance, than our assorted facial hair.

As a fair-haired bloke I had a pathetic and sporadic gathering of wispy ginger hairs around my chin. This embarrassing lack of facial hair made me look like a teenager who had yet to shave, but who was growing what hair he had in order to prove to the world that he'd finally struck puberty. On the other hand, Wegs had grown heavy stubble, with only the whites of his eyes providing any contrast to the dark shade of his hairy face. This facial hair mask made him look like a caveman. And finally there was JD, who, rather unfortunately, had grown the bulk of his facial hair on his upper lip. The concentration of hair in this area made him look forty-five years old. It was a classic seventies porno mo, and it made him look as though he'd just stepped off the set of *Delbridge does Dallas*.

It goes without saying that our first course of action was to go straight to the bathroom for a long overdue shower and shave. We had to remove the lingering dirt of the Gobi Desert and rid ourselves of the socially unpleasant 'eau-de-ger'.

❀ ❀ ❀

The Big Girl wasn't scheduled to arrive until later in the week, so we found ourselves with a few days to kill. We spent our first day washing and resting in the basic yet functional surrounds of the Far East Hostel. We had to restore our clothing to an acceptable level of cleanliness and catch up on some sleep before we dared to venture beyond the sanctuary of the hostel. The tranquillity of the Gobi had not prepared us for the cacophony and hustle and bustle of Beijing. It was a rendezvous with our mate Matt, from Moscow and the Trans-Mongolian, that would draw us out from the quiet of the hostel and introduce us to the wonders of this vibrant and diverse urban environment.

The hostel was located deep within a crowded network of small alleys near Tiananmen Square. Matt, who had been at the hostel for a week already, capably led us from the hostel and through the disorienting maze of backstreets. I was glad that we had Matt with us, as navigating our way around these manic and unfamiliar streets alone would have been nigh on impossible. To our foreign eyes every street looked the same. I wandered along behind Wegs, JD and Matt, being careful not to lose them.

The tiny streets were alive with rowdy vendors hocking

everything from pigs' trotters and stillborn chickens to burnt DVDs and 'real-fake' leather luggage. Tucked away between the stalls were numerous little restaurants and what appeared to be an inordinate number of hairdressing salons. Although, I guess in a city of twelve million people there are a lot of mouths to feed and a lot of hair to cut.

Other than the pushy traders one had to be careful to avoid the bell-ringing bikes and horn-tooting cars making their way through the thick pedestrian traffic. It overloaded the senses and kept you on your toes. However, even if you managed to avoid eye contact with traders and colliding with bike riders, there was one thing you couldn't avoid: the odours. For the most part these streets were full of the agreeable and exotic aromas of fresh or fried produce, but, from time to time, one would unknowingly walk into what we soon named a 'pocket'. These pockets of bad air would whack you in the face as you wandered innocently along. Normally they were attributable to a communal toilet block, a sewer grate in the road, or mothers holding their babies above the flowing gutter to poo. The stench was foul enough to bring up your breakfast, but every time we encountered one we could only laugh and speed up to reach cleaner air on the other side of the pocket. It was an occupational hazard in these parts.

Matt halted at a small intersection.

'We turn left here, next to the bloke with the bad teeth selling the glazed duck, guaranteed to be "flesh this week",' Matt quipped with his best Chinese accent, before heading off down another street lined with stalls, restaurants and hairdressers.

'Why are there so many hairdressers around here?' My curiosity was aroused.

'Mate, all is not as it seems with these hairdressers. They are a front for a bit of "jiggy-jig", if you get what I mean,' Matt told me. 'The two Dutch guys at the hostel can vouch for that personally.'

Come to think of it, all of the 'hairdressers' we'd seen had been attractive young girls in suggestive outfits.

'Really?'

'Yep. Diversification,' smiled Matt.

'Ha ha. Blow dry or blow job.'

A couple of minutes later Matt stopped again, at the next intersection.

'We turn right here, next to the old lady selling the fake binoculars. Be careful, she can see you coming from a mile off!'

'*Ni hao*,' he said to the tiny old lady.

'*Ni hao*,' she replied through her brown teeth as she stuck her crappy plastic binoculars under Matt's nose, thinking she may have a sale. She thrust them at all of us, in turn, as we continued walking.

'No, thank you.'

'No, thank you.'

'No, thank you.'

We walked to the end of this street, which delivered us to a busy intersection opposite Tiananmen Square. Matt showed us the leather shop that was the final landmark for us to commit to memory. He assured us that if we followed these in reverse order we would make it back to the hostel.

'There's the post office and next door is a great Internet

cafe. The computers are much faster than the ones in the hostel,' said Matt, pointing to buildings on the other side of the road.

We crossed the intersection and stood at a bus stop on the corner of the infamous Tiananmen Square, looking across its expanse towards the walls of the Forbidden City. Guards lined the perimeter of the square, casting a watchful eye over the swarming public and tooting traffic. Around the square the deep red colours of large Chinese flags dominated the skyline, against the hazy brown light of a Beijing day. I was instantly enamoured with Beijing. Ireland could not have felt further away: we'd completed the transition from West to East.

❀ ❀ ❀

For the remainder of the week we hired bikes and rode around aimlessly, observing at a leisurely pace the customs of the Chinese. In these relaxed days I posted our tapes home and even managed to find a Sony service centre in the city and arranged a long overdue service of both cameras. The Internet had again proven invaluable in making a difficult task achievable. It also provided more positive news that week: my editor at *TNT* in London had emailed to say that my 'Only Fools and Hearses' column was to be extended until we made it all the way safely home to Australia. I was prompted by this good news to make the phone call I had been dreading all week. The Big Girl was due today, Friday 13 November: it was time to call Mr Bruce Chu.

I retreated to our hostel room and pulled out my phone.

I buggered up the complex international and local codes before finally getting through on my fifth attempt.

'*Ni hao,*' answered a Chinese woman.

'Um. *Ni hao.* Could I speak to Mr Bruce Chu, please,' I said, nodding my head even though I was on the phone.

Thankfully she replied in English. 'Yes. Please wait.' I hummed along to the Chinese on-hold music for a couple of minutes.

'Harro. Mr Bwooce!' Mr Bruce boomed into the phone.

'Um. Hello Mr Bruce, this is Mr Davin. I ring to ask about our car that we send from Finland?'

My request was met with silence, then I heard the receiver clunk down on a table and a discussion in Chinese in the background. The female voice returned onto the line.

'Mr Bwooce welly scared to speak English, welly scared. He tell me to say we have no information of what you ask. OK?' She didn't give me a chance to say that this was actually not OK, before the line went dead.

I sat back on my bed and laughed hysterically. I recovered my faculties quickly and decided to call Jarmo; he was the only one I could turn to.

Initially I thought Jarmo was drunk because he was slurring his words and not making any sense.

'Monday, Dave. Monday,' was all he could say.

In my haste to resolve this farcical situation I'd forgotten that we'd progressed through several time zones since leaving Finland. I had called Jarmo at two-thirty in the morning.

* * *

Thirty-six hours later I found myself standing on the corner of Tiananmen Square, preparing to smash my phone into a thousand pieces after yet another fruitless phone conversation. This time the call was not about locating a missing hearse; it was about locating a Russian goddess.

The night before, Matt, JD, Wegs and I had gone out on the town to relax and forget about our logistical concerns with the Big Girl. At Vic's nightclub we had all managed to meet some nice girls, in what was predominantly an expatriate crowd. Matt had met Rachel from England, JD had met Anastacia from Russia, and Wegs had met Anna from Australia. Through Matt's relentless coercion I'd been fortunate to make the acquaintance of Tania, a blonde and busty Russian goddess.

Matt and I had been propping up the bar and admiring the blonde Russian beauty from afar for the majority of the evening. She was the sort of girl you see at a bar and never talk to because her beauty is intimidating. She appeared to be without male company so Matt suggested I get the barman to send her a drink. I wasn't comfortable with the idea. I'd never used that type of approach before; it was too James Bond for my liking. Matt was persistent though and eventually I gave in, safe in the knowledge that I would be a whole bar length away when she rejected my cheesy offering. I instructed the barman and watched nervously as he delivered her vodka and tonic, shaken not stirred. She raised the glass, looked over and met my eyes and smiled. With my heart in my mouth I kept my cool and returned the smile, accompanied by my raised glass and dipped head.

'Did you see that, mate?' I said to Matt. 'It worked!'

'That was the easy bit. Now you have to go and talk to her,' beamed Matt.

'No fuckin' way!' I couldn't possibly go over to talk to her and embarrass myself at close quarters.

'Look at her. You won't be able to live with yourself if you don't try. What's the worst thing that can happen?'

I paused for a few moments, thinking. I knew he was right. It wasn't going to be easy for me, but if I'd learnt anything from this journey so far, it was that sometimes you have to move out of your comfort zone in order to realise what you're truly capable of. Without saying a word I slammed down a tequila shot, slapped myself in the face and walked off to sacrifice my self-esteem.

The Russian beauty was alone at the bar. She raised her deep-set eyes from her vodka and tonic as I stood before her with false bravado, trying hard not to talk to her bulging breasts.

'Ardlie. Dav Ardlie,' I said as we clashed our glasses by way of introduction.

'Tania.'

And that was that. Four hours later, after a frisky taxi ride home through suburban Beijing, the lovely Tania and I exchanged details outside her apartment. We shared a long goodnight kiss and arranged to meet up the following evening for a romantic night out. As the taxi pulled away I patted myself on the back for a job well done.

❀ ❀ ❀

I made my way to a taxi rank at Tiananmen Square and called Tania as we'd arranged the previous night. She answered the phone after two short rings.

'Hello, Tania?'

'Yes.'

'It's Dav calling. I am at taxi rank to come to meet you for a drink.'

'Dave. Do you not want drink?' she said confusingly.

'No. No. I *do* want drink!' I said, dispensing with superfluous words.

'No? Why no?'

'No. I mean, yes. I do want drink. I am at taxi rank to meet you somewhere. What about Vic's?'

'You don't want see me? Why you no want see me? You change mind?' I was at a complete loss as to why Tania thought I didn't want to see her. I noticed that Tania's command of English wasn't as good as I had recalled, although admittedly I couldn't hear a single word she said the night before. I had spent the night just nodding my head and smiling. She had obviously done the same.

'I DO!'

'My English is not so good. I do not know what you speak. Here, my friend, she will tell me.' I could hear some fumbling in the background as she passed the phone to her friend. I crossed my fingers in the hope she spoke better English than Tania.

'*Ni hao! Ning nong chu wing bang ching ding . . .*' Her friend had started talking to me in Chinese! I couldn't believe my ears. I was living a nightmare.

'Hello. *Ni hao*. I don't speak Chinese!' I yelled into the phone.

The friend kept on yelling in her native tongue, sounding like a mosquito dying in my ear. It was a hopeless situation that ended abruptly when the line went dead.

'You've got to be joking,' I said, laughing deliriously, like I'd done after my fateful call to Mr Bruce.

After a couple of minutes my phone rang with Tania back on the line. Sadly, the situation only became more confusing, as we went through the same painful exercise in misunderstanding before my battery went dead, and with it any chance of a reunion with the girl of my dreams. I threw my head back in despair: I had brushed my hair for nothing.

And so I found myself alone in Tiananmen Square, a frustrated and confused man. I sat down on a bench and placed my lifeless phone beside me, so I wouldn't throw it away. Despite its comic aspect, the disappointment of my failed date with Tania seemed to bring to a head all of my growing concerns. I leant forward and placed my head in my hands, fighting the rising demons of self-doubt.

What the hell was I doing here? Why was I sitting here in Beijing, chasing Russian women by night and liasing with agents in Finland and Korea by day to organise the passage of a hearse, which was probably lost in Siberia en route to China? Who the fuck was I trying to kid? I hoped Wegs and JD didn't think I'd dragged them on a wild goose chase in pursuit of my selfish and stupid desires. Although, that would've been the furthest thing from their mind at that point in time; they were out on a double date somewhere with the girls they'd met last night, assuming they could find them.

I picked up my phone, sucked in a few deep breaths and ambled off in the direction of the hostel. A slow evening walk would help ease the frustration, doubt and guilt that weighed heavily on my mind. If not, I could always stop off for a quick haircut.

*   *   *

The friendly waiter pulled aside a thick curtain and ushered us into our small private dining room. Wegs stepped in first and, reminiscent of our time in Mongolia, struck his head painfully on the low door.

'Aaagghh fuck,' Wegs said, rubbing his forehead.

'Ha ha ha. Mate, next time duck!' JD roared with laughter. At his request we were holding a team meeting, at an exclusive Peking duck restaurant. JD loves his food and the excitement of dining at this restaurant had seen him cracking every lame 'duck' joke imaginable.

'I hereby call this meeting to order,' I announced as we were served our first course of duck and three chilled beers. Our first, and only, order of business was to make a team decision about how to approach the remainder of this journey. It was Monday evening and I'd received an email from Jarmo earlier that afternoon informing me that the Big Girl was stuck in a Siberian snowstorm, and her arrival date was unsure. It could be anything from one week to one month, or longer. He apologised for the inconvenience and asked us to consider our preferred course of action, which he would do his best to organise.

The team engaged in a surprisingly logical discussion of

our options as we dissected the consequences of the Big Girl's delayed arrival over four courses of crispy-skinned Peking duck and several beers.

'Excuse me, fellas. Just got to duck off to the loo,' interjected JD with a broad grin.

Wegs and I shook our heads and laughed half-heartedly.

The meeting continued on his return and by our fifth beer we had made a team decision. We couldn't afford to wait for an indefinite period for the Big Girl's arrival. We would request Jarmo to forward the car onto Bangkok, and in the meantime we would travel overland through China, Vietnam and Laos to Thailand. We had genuine concerns about being allowed to drive in China, so this option was a more efficient use of our time and kept up our momentum.

The shared decision-making process had relieved me of a lot of the doubts and guilt I'd been harbouring, but I still carried a sense of failure for not delivering the Big Girl to the team, in China. I didn't mention anything, preferring to keep my concerns to myself.

'Excuse me!' JD called out to our busy waiter. 'Could we have the duck bill?'

❂ ❂ ❂

On Tuesday afternoon I stared out the train window, watching the outer suburbs of Beijing disappearing from view as patchwork fields of rice and maize slowly replaced them. It was hypnotic to watch field after field of Chinese workers engaged in back-breaking manual labour. In between these fields there were people furiously sweeping streets, flogging stubborn water buffalo, carrying their own weight in firewood – working, without the assistance of technology, for survival. Their uncompromising approach to life resembled that of their Mongolian neighbours, but unlike Mongolia, there were people everywhere in China, with no areas wholly untouched. My eyes were watching these repetitive scenes but my mind was elsewhere.

'Your go, mate,' JD said, after finally moving a pawn. I stared back blankly, forgetting that I was playing chess.

'What's on your mind, mate? You're away with the pixies.'

'Don't really know, mate. Just thinking about the Big Girl and the logistics not working out, and what we're doing – the whole thing really.'

'Well, mate, if you're worrying about the Big Girl and things not going to plan, then don't. It's a redundant emotion.' We knew each other well and JD could tell I was a bit weighed down. 'You told me yourself that this journey was all about fun, first and foremost. I joined this trip with you blokes for one reason, and one reason only – to have fun every day. I've had fun every day since arriving and I haven't seen the hearse once! Don't break your own rules and focus on the negatives, especially when they're out of your control. Focus on the fun.'

'Yeah, I guess I'm just struggling to comprehend what it all means, mate. You know, why are we here, doing what we're doing?'

'Well, mate. Who really knows. Let's just keep doing what you guys have been doing from the start and see what happens. The trip's progressed beyond just the story of three mates and a hearse. There's a greater journey that we're all undertaking, and whether the Big Girl is with us or not for the physical journey, no longer matters. She's the reason we're all here and, because of that, she is always with us.' JD proffered, with a healthy dose of Zen. JD was the only bloke I knew who not only read philosophy, but was smart enough to apply it.

'Yeah, Dav, "a good traveller has no plans, and is not intent upon arriving"', a voice murmured from the bunk bed above. It was Wegs, quoting a Taoist phrase he'd just read from *Tao Te Ching: The Book of The Way*. I guess I now had two mates smart enough to apply philosophy!

'Thanks, mate,' I laughed.

'A pleasure, my son.' Wegs bowed his head in his best Zen-master impersonation.

I moved my Queen and smiled wickedly.

'Checkmate!' I said smugly, as I closed in on my first ever chess victory.

'Um, Dav. That's the bishop, not the Queen.'

'Shit. Sorry, mate. I was wondering why she had a beard.'

DAV WEGS JD

19: TIME GENTLEMEN, PLEASE

'No thankssh,' I said pleasantly, and picked up my walking pace.

'Come. You want me? You want to play with me? I play with you!'

'No thankssh,' I repeated, more sternly this time.

'Come. You play with my body, I play with yours.'

'No! Pisshh off!' I yelled, looking the persistent little Thai prostitute in the eye to convey my lack of interest.

'Come on, big boy. You want massage?' She was fondling me now as I tried to walk briskly along Khao San Road. The Swedish girl I was returning to the hostel with was laughing heartily, and making no attempt to save me from this tactile hooker.

'I think she likes you!' Ottilia observed with a huge smile on her face.

'Well, I sshhure as hell don't like her,' I responded. 'Look. Jusshht pleasshe pisshh off,' I added angrily, brushing the small Thai woman away. Finally she took no for an answer, and walked off with a sad expression on her face. The young prostitute didn't know her game very well if she thought a man walking home with a blonde Swedish girl on his arm was a potential punter. She would definitely have to refine her approach if she wanted to pursue a career in Bangkok's competitive sex market.

'Sshhe wassh pretty full on,' I said to the giggling Ottilia. I tucked my shirt back in after the unsolicited molestation and tapped my back pocket – out of habit. It was empty. I stopped in my tracks and frantically patted all of my pockets to locate my missing wallet. Nothing. It was gone and I knew exactly where it was. The young Thai hooker obviously played a more sophisticated game than I had given her credit for. I turned around to see the light-fingered lady of the night showing me a clean pair of heels, and I took off in hot pursuit.

'Ssshtop. Ssshtop!'

I could feel the beer sloshing around in my stomach as I worked up a wayward pace. It was an ungainly spectacle: me wobbling along the footpath as fast as I could go chasing the little prostitute who was shuffling along awkwardly in her high heels. With my tongue hanging out and my heavy breathing I felt like a lumbering rapist as I closed in on the squealing girl. The chase ended when she lost traction rounding a corner at high speed and ended up in a bushy hedge. I grabbed her by the arms as she struggled to her feet, hysterical.

'Where ... issshh ... my ... wallet?' I screamed in between deep breaths. My fitness wasn't what it used to be. I didn't wait for an answer but ripped the handbag from the wailing woman. I tore it open and rummaged through all of the useless things women carry in their handbags in an effort to locate my wallet. It wasn't there. I began to panic. Had I just mugged an innocent and defenceless woman? I was too tired, and far too drunk, to think clearly. I threw her bag down in anger next to the hedge – and right next to my wallet. The cheeky little thief had dropped my wallet in the hedge to hide it when she'd fallen over.

'Ah ha!' I exclaimed. As I bent over to pick it up the hysterical prostitute drove her pointed high heel into my midriff with a powerful kick, knocking my unsuspecting body to its knees. Enraged, I quickly rose to my feet, amongst a furious flurry of wild slapping and high-volume abuse. I flapped my arms around protectively before grabbing and restraining her firmly by the elbows. It was at this point that the psychotic prostitute began yelling at me in the most masculine voice I'd ever heard – from a woman.

'Aaagghh!' I yelled, realising *she* was a *he*. Instinctively I pushed the man-talking woman away, causing him/her to go sprawling along the pavement beside the scattered contents of his/her handbag. He/she hurled abuse at me in a scarily deep voice as I retreated hastily back towards the waiting, and still highly amused, Ottilia.

'That is no way to treat . . . a woman,' Ottilia said, trying hard not to split her sides.

'She ish a bloody bloke!' I said excitedly, still coming to terms with my shock encounter with one of Thailand's famed lady boys.

'I know. Don't worry, it could have been worse.' Ottilia could hardly speak she was laughing so hard. 'You could have found out the hard way!'

❀ ❀ ❀

We were not a pretty sight as we made our way into the neatly appointed offices of Interfreight Pty Ltd. The poor receptionist didn't know what to make of the three severely hungover blokes standing before her.

'Hello?' she said cautiously, obviously hoping we had come to the wrong place.

'We're here to see Mr Sinthu,' I said cautiously, hoping we had come to the right place.

'Um, OK. One moment,' she replied before picking up the phone and speaking in rapid Thai. Presumably she was informing Mr Sinthu that there were three weird-looking blokes dressed in shorts and singlets, dripping with sweat and smelling of booze, here to see him.

A few minutes later a short man with a light beard emerged from an adjacent office.

'I am Sinthu,' Mr Sinthu said as he approached us wearily.

'Mr Sinthu, I am Mr Davin,' I said and thrust out my hand.

'Ah, Mr Dawin. I get your email. Please come.' I had emailed Mr Sinthu earlier that morning after receiving news from Jarmo that the Big Girl had arrived in Bangkok, like he'd promised. Mr Sinthu was our contact for delivery, as Mr Bruce had been in Beijing; fortunately Mr Sinthu, unlike Mr Bruce, wasn't afraid to speak English. I had opted to come in person this time, not wishing to risk the disappointment and inconvenience of another fruitless phone call. We followed Mr Sinthu over to his desk and sat down.

We spent the next hour taking it in turns to explain our position to the helpful and unflappable Mr Sinthu. He believed that our desire to drive the car through to Malaysia and ultimately Singapore would be extremely difficult to organise because of stringent Thai laws concerning the importation of foreign vehicles, but he would do his very best to help us. This was the first time he had dealt with such an odd request, and he needed to call Thai customs to make some preliminary enquiries. While on hold he cupped a hand over the mouthpiece and pointed out the window of his tenth-floor office to the dockyards below.

'Your car . . . in there,' he smiled. 'Welly close.'

We turned together and stared out the window. After being separated from her for nearly two months it was surreal to know that the Big Girl was now so close. When we had left her in Finland we had no idea if we would ever see her again. I felt a tingle of excitement and pride to know that she'd made it safely through her own challenging and parallel journey, to be here in Bangkok to reunite the team. Despite fierce Siberian weather and numerous logistical amendments to her passage across Finland, Russia, China and Korea en route to Thailand, she had made it. The reunion was so close I could taste it.

Mr Sinthu rounded off his long phone call and looked over to us with a concerned expression.

'OK. Mr Dawin, this will be welly difficult. We must go to wisit customs.'

* * *

I followed the fleet-footed Mr Sinthu into the oppressively brown main hall of the Thai Customs House. Large and ineffective fans hung from the high ceilings of the open hall, serving only to recirculate the stifling heat and humidity among the swarming mix of uninterested public servants and impatient clientele. Mr Sinthu made his way through the lines of waiting people, occasionally pausing to ask a passing employee for directions to the vehicle-import department. Once at the correct department Mr Sinthu and I were instructed to take a seat at the end of the long queue, and wait. After two long and sweaty hours we had progressed only marginally towards the front of the queue. I began to wish I'd chosen to go back to the hostel to recuperate as JD and Wegs had done. Mr Sinthu returned with another plastic cup of lukewarm water and sat back down beside me.

'A few more hours, I think,' he said, as if it would be no problem.

I sighed and leant back on the uncomfortable bench, staring up blankly at the high ceiling, resigned to the long wait. The negative and obstructionist aura of this institution was starting to get to me. Things did not feel right and, before negotiations had even started, I could sense I was losing the abundant confidence I held just a few hours ago. My hangover was now the least of my concerns: I was more concerned about what lay behind the plain brown facade of Thai bureaucracy.

❧ ❧ ❧

Over dinner the boys listened attentively as I used the last of my mental energy to explain the key points that Mr Sinthu and I had unearthed in our long day at Thai Customs.

- To drive in Thailand we must provide Customs with security: a bank guarantee for 308 per cent of the Big Girl's value (approx A$16 000, 400 000 Thai baht). This bank guarantee is only exercised if we do not leave the country within thirty days. It is enforced by Customs to ensure we do not import the car to sell for financial gain – a big problem in Thailand.
- To drive in Malaysia and Singapore we must provide a 200 per cent guarantee in addition to obtaining a 'carnet de passage' – an official form allowing the transit of foreign-registered vehicles.
- To avoid this and to send the car on to Australia we must obtain an import permit from Australian Customs. If the car arrived in Australia without this permit we would be fined A$10 000 and risk having the Big Girl sent back to the port of origin.

'Fuck it. Let's send her home and go to the Full Moon Party,' Wegs said. It was a predictable response from Wegs, who's partial to taking the path of least resistance. I was too tired on this occasion to recognise this was just another case of him speaking before thinking, and I got irritated. I only get angry when I'm tired.

'It's not as easy as that, mate,' I replied testily.

'How long will it take?'

'Not really sure, mate. At least a week,' I said.

'Fuck. What about the Full Moon Party?'

I felt the Big Girl deserved our best efforts, and I had hoped Wegs might have shown more desire to explore the options of an Asian reunion with our old friend. Fortunately, JD interjected with a compromise.

'Wegs, why don't you go to the Full Moon Party and Dav and I will stay on here to organise the car. We'll come and join you on the island once everything's sorted,' JD reasoned.

And so it was decided. Wegs would leave the following morning for Ko Pha Ngan and his beloved Full Moon Party, and JD and I would stay on to identify the Big Girl's best options. It wasn't desirable to separate the team – Wegs and I had done everything together since we started – but in this instance it was the only sensible option. It wasn't a job for three anyway.

❂ ❂ ❂

One week later.

'Mr Dawin, for you,' said the polite secretary as she placed a fax, and a freshly brewed pot of coffee onto my desk before leaving.

'You beauty!' I said to JD.

'Import permit?' JD looked up from his computer.

'You betcha,' I replied.

'Good shit,' JD beamed.

After six days of unsuccessfully negotiating with Thai officials the release of the Big Girl, we'd been forced to apply to send her directly home to Australia. The faxed copy of the Big Girl's approved import permit from Australian Customs was the first good news in the six days we'd spent dealing with logistics and knocking heads with bureaucracy. I jotted a number down and asked our complimentary secretary to fax a copy of the permit to Mr Sinthu.

Despite all the frustrations of the past week, we'd had a great time. Since Wegs' departure, JD and I had relocated from the hostel to the more refined Bangkok Hilton. Any self-respecting backpacker would've been horrified to see JD and me conducting our business from the fully appointed Hilton business suite by day, and stuffing our faces on room service in front of the 24-hour adult channel by night. It certainly belied our standing as budget travellers, but after a long month traversing Asia on buses, horses, bikes and boats, and staying in cheap accommodation, we considered it an early Christmas gift to ourselves.

For JD and me, working side-by-side in the business suite was a reminder of our days together as project managers, except, this time around, the resources and rules of engagement were very different. Over the course of our hectic week we'd visited the offices of the Australian embassy, Austrade, Australian Thai Chamber of Commerce, Thai Board of Trade, Thai Chamber of Commerce, Westpac Bank, Tourism Thailand and the Malaysian embassy. We scheduled these varied meetings in order to identify a way around the mountain of red tape – rather than going over or through it. These meetings had failed to deliver a magical solution, but they *had* identified what we needed to do to secure bank guarantees, arrange 'carnet de passages' and organise the import permit. Mr Sinthu had been right; releasing the Big Girl as desired was going to be 'welly difficult . . . welly difficult, indeed'.

In between meetings we retired to the plush Hilton business suite to conduct Internet research and send emails. In the end it was a reply email from the Driver and Vehicle Licensing Agency (DVLA) in the United Kingdom that decided the fate of the Big Girl's Asian adventure.

INBOX

CUSTOMER REF : V109561
Thank you for your email.
Our records indicate that B499XRN was last registered in the United Kingdom in July 2000, in the name of Mervyn Eric Kleeman.
Regards
Customer Enquiries Vehicles

Not only was the Big Girl *not* registered in our name, she wasn't even registered at all! The news sent a shiver up my spine. The cheque we'd sent to the DVLA prior to our departure had obviously been lost, or misappropriated. As a result we'd been driving an unregistered, uninsured vehicle for over five months and through fifteen countries in Europe – and driving from the right-hand side! I felt sick at the thought of the potentially disastrous outcomes if we'd struck another vehicle, or worse still, a person. Luck could not begin to describe our good fortune.

That email had been received on our fifth day and, with the information we had at hand, we knew instantly that driving the Big Girl in Asia was now impossible. I'd contacted the

DVLA to ask them to supply documentation that would prove our registration and ownership. Their email effectively undermined our plan to unleash the Big Girl on Asia, as registration was the prerequisite for obtaining the necessary paperwork. It was a sobering moment, but not the end of the world. The lack of registration confirmed beyond doubt the decision we were firming on anyway: to send the Big Girl directly home to Fremantle. The other options were looking far too difficult to organise and also far too risky. A couple of Thai businessmen we'd spoken to over a cognac at the Hilton bar had warned us against providing a bank guarantee over our passage through the country. Corruption within government, they said, made this too risky, and financial risk was the only risk that our budget outfit couldn't afford to take.

We had diligently identified all the options on behalf of our Big Girl, and in that knowledge, we could now proceed with the trip without guilt. At a micro level it was inconvenient; at a macro level it was inconsequential. As always, the journey would continue.

❂   ❂   ❂

'Well, mate, once Mr Sinthu gets that fax we're done,' I said to JD, who was sitting at a computer across from me.

'I guess we'll just have to spend Christmas and New Year on a tropical island then,' JD lamented, with tongue firmly planted in cheek.

'Yep, I'm afraid so,' I said as my computer beeped to alert me to an incoming email.

INBOX

Dear Mr. Davin,
Permit received. Will inform about freight schedule soon.
Noted with thanks and wishing you have a nice holiday.
Best regards.
Sinthu G.

'Shit, that was quick,' I said, reading Mr Sinthu's instant reply before my computer beeped once again. This time it was an email from our missing team member, Wegs.

INBOX

boys. ive got to get off this island . . . . . otherwise I may never leave . . .
. . . . beers, buckets of whisky, and no sleep for 40 hours . . . . . great full
moon party . . . . big parties planned for xmas and nye . . . . pity
about car situation . . . . . . good work though . . . . hurry up and get
your arses down here . . . . this is the island to forget about . . . .
everything . . . . see you soon . . . . wegs

With negotiations concluded, our work in Bangkok was done. It was definitely time for the one reunion that *was* within our control. It was time to reunite with Wegs, and help him share the burden of the anarchistic lifestyle on Ko Pha Ngan.

❂   ❂   ❂

I looked towards the waiting crowd as our ferry pulled into the run-down dock. In the middle of the crowd of people a large arm slowly emerged, with an index finger pointed firmly skyward in our team salute. It had only been a week since we'd last seen Wegs, but JD and I returned the symbolic gesture with big excited smiles.

Wegs did not look well. In the week since we'd seen him he'd lost his youthful looks and had taken a few years off his life. He was tanned but his skin appeared leathery, and heavy circles of baggy skin surrounded his bloodshot eyes.

'Geez, mate . . . you don't look so good,' I said as we shook hands firmly.

'You make me feel young,' said JD.

'Yeah, this place is killing me,' responded Grandpa Wegner, a smile cracking his worn face. 'You'll love it!'

Wegs had been going hard ever since he arrived on this party island. It had started with the Full Moon Party on his first night, and continued all week. We sat down at the Cactus Bar and clashed our glasses together. It seemed that tonight was going to be no different for Wegs. If anything it would be bigger because the team was back together, and it was Christmas Eve.

'Cheers, boys!'

☻   ☻   ☻

JD and I quickly embraced the Ko Pha Ngan culture under Wegs' experienced guidance, and before we knew it Christmas Eve had rapidly become New Year's Eve. We'd spent our days sipping G and Ts, and the nights gulping Mekong and Coke. It was a cycle of self-abuse that made Ios look like a health retreat, and we loved every minute of it. Each night was treated as a dress rehearsal for the main event, New Year's Eve. JD and I had obviously followed the script closely because, as we sat at the bar for the final performance, I could see in the mirror that we too had tanned leathery skin and heavy circles of baggy skin surrounding our bloodshot eyes. If the booze wasn't so ridiculously cheap we could've asked for a senior's discount.

❂ ❂ ❂

'Ten . . . nine . . . eight . . . seven . . . six . . . five . . . four . . . three . . . two . . . one . . . HAPPY NEW YEAR!'

We screamed out the countdown along with 10 000 of our closest friends enjoying New Year's Eve on the sand of Haad Rin beach. JD, Wegs and I exchanged drunken man-hugs and New Year's greetings with each other as we stood on the steps of the crowded Cactus Bar. We watched the fireworks display in silence, partly because of the significance of the moment, but mainly because our ears were ringing so loudly from the pumping music that we couldn't hear anything. The fireworks stopped after a short display and the thumping beat, which drives the lifeblood of Haad Rin, resumed to keep the bass-craving revellers satisfied. We returned to our respective podiums and danced, occasionally pausing for shots of tequila, and spent the entire evening together – not caring to chase girls or change venues. This night was special for reasons beyond welcoming in a new year; the curtain was soon to be drawn on our international misadventures and, for that reason, it was a night to savour.

The night would end, as all nights do, with the rising of the sun. The tide had come in and was lapping against the front steps of the Cactus Bar. The first light of the new year revealed that the temporary bamboo bars and elevated dance floors, which had been in the middle of the beach last night, were now out in the shallows, with waves crashing over them. The crowd had begun to thin but the hardest of the hardcore people still danced on these floating structures as if their life depended on it – and given that most of them were high on mind-altering substances, it probably did.

We left the club together and waded home through the lapping water without speaking, our thoughts literally ringing in our ears. We'd started something back in Ireland, something that now saw us wandering a beach on a remote Thai island, six months later. Calm fell on the team as we walked three abreast along the beach: it was time, time to finish *that* something.

'It's time, fellas,' I said quietly.

'Yep. Let's go home.'

20: THE END ... OR THE BEGINNING?

'Oh, good. Right on schedule,' JD said sarcastically from his couch bed.

'For fuck's sake!' I added despairingly, as the neighbour's leaf blower roared into life like it had done at the same time every morning. 'This really takes the gloss off being unemployed,' I said, jumping up from my mattress on the floor and heading to the shower.

We were staying in Perth with Chantelle, a friend of Wegs, and every day we'd been subjected to her neighbour's noisy morning routine. He started at around 9.30 with his infernal leaf blower – blowing the same leaves out onto the street that he had blown out the day before. Depending on what day of the week it was, the leaf blower would be followed by the chainsaw, lawn mower, stump grinder or whipper snipper. Anything, it seemed, as long as it was motorised. I couldn't believe that it hadn't occurred to him he could simply rake the leaves up and dispose of them once and for all. I guess raking is just not noisy enough.

The morning shower was cool and refreshing, in contrast to the heat and discomfort of a long night on the floor without airconditioning. We were lucky to have a base but Chantelle's small two-bedroom unit in Como was like an oven and sleeping through the night was not possible. The heat and the DIY neighbour increased my already strong desire to move on, so I raced out of the shower when I heard my mobile phone ringing, sensing it may be news of the Big Girl.

'Hello, Davin speaking,' I said, dripping wet.

'Hello, Bevan, it's Michelle from AustAsia Freight in Fremantle. I'm ringing to confirm the arrival of your goods from Bangkok,' Michelle said, obviously not catching my name. It wasn't the first time this had happened, so I didn't bother to correct her. It was the first time, though, that I had ever been called Bevan.

'Excellent,' I said, 'how do we get them released?'

'There's some paperwork to deal with and I'm ringing to organise a time for you to come in and see Ryan. Ryan is our freight manager and he'll be dealing with your goods' release.'

'We can be there in an hour,' I said.

'Great. Shall we make it eleven o'clock?'

'Done deal. See you then. Thanks, Michelle.'

'No worries. Thank you, Kevin,' Michelle said.

* * *

Unlike Mr Bruce Chu and, to a lesser extent, Mr Sinthu, Ryan Cook immediately instilled me with confidence. He was a like-minded lad and interested to know why we were importing a car from Thailand.

'Actually, it's no ordinary car, mate. It's a funeral car that we've driven and freighted across the world from Ireland.'

'Ha ha. I love it!' Ryan said as he laughed uproariously and double punched the air. 'Well, we better get the show back on the road then, fellas.'

'Shit, yeah,' came the team chorus.

The discussions progressed in a more business-like direction and an hour later Ryan presented us with the bill for the Big Girl's release, which included stamp duty, customs and quarantine charges, wharf charges, handling charges and 10 per cent GST.

'Oh!' Wegs and I said in unison. It was a similar sphincter-tightening moment to the one we'd experienced in Jarmo's office, except this time we didn't need to calculate exchange rates. The figure, like many expenses we'd incurred, was roughly double what we'd anticipated. Wegs and I looked at one another and, rolling our eyes in dismay, reached for our wallets.

'Got any dishes that need doing, mate?' I quipped to Ryan as our flying credit cards landed on the table before him.

'Sorry, boys. We don't see a cent of this. They're standard government charges.'

There was no point getting upset over the disappointingly large figure, as there was nothing we could do but accept it.

'On credit or savings, fellas?' Ryan asked, looking up from his papers. 'Ah ha, credit,' he said with a knowing nod of the head. Our funds were getting desperately low.

With the credit-card payment processed and approved, we left the office and headed to the unloading yard. It was time to catch up with an old friend. Ryan had called some friends in Customs and organised for us to witness the opening of the Big Girl's container. We'd been looking forward to this moment ever since we personally closed the doors on her container four months ago, in Finland.

We sauntered towards the hundreds of containers stacked in the Customs yard. Somewhere inside one of those containers was our beloved Big Girl, at the end of her own long and impressive parallel adventure. I'm sure that every time her container had been opened she had hoped it would reunite her with her long-lost boys, only to be disappointed as strange-sounding men pushed and prodded her into another dark box. We hoped that lengthy confinement had not broken her spirit. I took solace knowing that when the doors of her lonely container opened for this last time she would be greeted by some familiar and excited voices.

When we arrived at the back of a blue container, Ryan handed Wegs a large set of bolt cutters and motioned for him to cut the seal. Wegs, revelling in the wharf-like environment, cut the bolt and pulled open a squeaking steel door. It was an anxious moment. We had absolutely no idea what to expect – would the Big Girl even be in there? Would she be dusty? Dirty? Mouldy? Would anything have been stolen? We opened the doors fully and looked into the dark container.

Silence. Relief. Excitement. For so long now it had seemed that this moment may never come. It didn't feel real, but it was.

Before us was the Big Girl, exactly as we had left her, resting in peace.

With the help of Ryan and two workers we pulled and pushed the Big Girl out of her container and into the holding yard. Apart from a heavy layer of dust she appeared to be in perfect condition. We couldn't open her until Customs had completed their inspections, so we'd have to wait until tomorrow afternoon to get back in the Big Girl. But for now, just knowing she was alive and well was all the comfort we needed. We posed for a few photos beside her with Ryan before we had to leave.

'See you soon, Big Girl,' we said and departed, watching her over our shoulder the whole way. After all the trials and tribulations, the Big Girl was finally back with us.

From the Customs yard we headed straight to an Internet cafe on South Terrace, the 'cappuccino strip' of Fremantle. I had to organise the delivery of the original import permit before Ryan could release the car to us, and I had to write my final *TNT* article. In the article I thanked the magazine and the thousands of readers who'd followed our exploits through my weekly column. Writing the column had been thoroughly enjoyable and a real privilege. It had added another element to our journey, and the encouragement of our loyal followers through emails or random meetings around the globe had provided support in times of difficulty and doubt – even if I had been mistaken for a bricklayer.

※ ※ ※

'Mate. I've got some news,' JD said as he handballed the footy to me. We were on the way to have a kick at a park a couple of blocks from Chantelle's unit.

'What news?' I asked, and handballed the footy over to Wegs.

'I'm going home. I've run out of time and money.'

'When are you going to head off?' I asked, disappointed but not surprised.

'In two and a half hours.'

'Shit!' Now I was surprised. We walked along in silence for a while.

Wegs broke the silence. 'Who's going to sew our buttons back on now?'

'Ha ha ha. You're a big boy now Paul, I'm sure you'll cope,' JD replied. 'I booked a flight online this afternoon. I've stretched it out as long as I could . . . I've been stewing over telling you blokes for a while, didn't want to let the team down.'

'Mate, you're not letting the team down at all. It can't be helped,' I said.

'Well, we better go and have a beer then, mate,' said Wegs, officially cancelling footy training.

There was a certain irony about JD's arrival shortly after the *departure* of the Big Girl, on the other side of the world, and his departure shortly after the *arrival* of the Big Girl, in Australia. JD had been the Big Man, in the absence of the Big Girl.

It was with regret that, a few hours later, Wegs and I watched JD walk off towards the departure lounge of Perth airport to complete his journey by plane, and not by hearse. All that could be seen, as he disappeared into the throng of travellers, were two wobbly legs sticking out below his massive backpack and one arm sticking out above, index finger pointed firmly to the skies.

❂ ❂ ❂

The timeless riff of Lynyrd Skynyrd's classic road-tripping anthem 'Sweet Home Alabama' boomed through the Big Girl as she cruised towards Albany, the end of the road for Wegs.

The song that I had imagined was playing when we started our journey from Dover was now actually playing in the twilight of the adventure, in Australia – and it couldn't have been more apt. We were desperately hoping that the Big Girl's wheels would indeed keep on turning, to return both Wegs and myself to our long-suffering families. The Big Girl had been off the road for four months and we were unsure how her lack of condition would affect her performance. We just needed her to make it back to my home in Victoria, where she could be rested in a garage until our next journey.

Darkness was approaching as we entered Wegs' home town of Albany. Being back in the Big Girl had not only reunited the team but had reinvigorated us as well. It was empowering to be back within her familiar and homely confines. Her hypnotic motion, her familiar musty odour and her idiosyncrasies reminded us of the carefree months cruising overseas. We chatted feverishly about the 'good old days', never wanting them to end but knowing that very soon they would.

'Tell me what you're thinking, mate,' I asked Wegs, sticking the video camera in his face.

'Well . . .' Wegs thought for a moment. 'After two years away I never thought in my wildest dreams that I'd be returning to Albany in a hearse, the Big Girl. It's been an amazing two years and an even more amazing last eight . . . nine months. We've done something nobody has ever tried to do before, or at least I think so, anyway it doesn't matter because we've done it the best way we could . . . and the only way we knew how. And nobody can take that away from us.'

'Shit, mate!' I wasn't expecting Wegs to be so profound. 'Anything else?'

'Yeah, being back is exciting but also a bit scary.'

'Scary?'

'Yeah, you know. About what to do . . . where to live, all that sort of stuff.'

'What scares you the most about being back home after so long, and after having done so much?' I asked, à la Michael Parkinson.

'Umm,' Wegs thought hard again. 'I'm scared of the day I wake up and you're not in the room, mate.' It was unusual to hear Wegs speak like this and I began to choke up slightly. 'You know, the fun'll be over, and it'll be back to reality.'

'Yeah, I know.' I was also starting to come to terms with the end of an era that had seen us share a room in Dublin for six months, and every hotel and hostel room around the world for the last nine months. Like finishing high school, it was a day that was always going to come but one that you never thought would.

❀ ❀ ❀

The morning after the joyous family scenes at Wegs' overdue return found us running a variety of important errands. The first was to pick up an extension ladder for Wegs' dad Phil so he could paint the house for Wegs' mum Norma. The sight of the Big Girl rolling down the main street of Albany with a shiny new extension ladder strapped onto the flower rails had the Saturday morning shoppers aghast. I pulled up at the pedestrian crossing and waited for the gawking public to cross the road.

One man stopped in his tracks and yelled out, 'She must be a pretty deep grave, mate!'

His dry wit set the tone for what was to be a wonderful day. We carried out our assigned domestic errands in high spirits as the Big Girl continued to entertain. After a couple of hours we'd completed them all except for the most important one; one that we'd been waiting many months to do. Wegs directed me to a small street, not far from his parent's house. I drove the Big Girl along the narrow street and wound down my window as I pulled up in front of a busy building site.

'G'day!' I yelled out. One of the blokes looked up from his work, dropped his tools and walked over.

'G'day,' he replied with a broadening smile. 'Nice car!'

'Well, you better jump in, mate,' I said. The large-framed man had no hesitation in walking around to climb into the passenger's seat that Wegs had vacated.

'Thirsty?' Wegs asked from the back seat.

'Bloody oath!' Whitey replied. 'Kick her in the guts!'

❋   ❋   ❋

The remainder of the weekend was spent taking friends and family for joy rides in the Big Girl, writing newspaper articles and, of course, plenty of drinking. We had a lot to catch up on with Whitey – it had been six months since we'd last seen him in Athens. We spoke little about what had happened since his departure, preferring to reminisce about our days together on the road. The disappointment of Whitey's forced departure was long forgotten, as we told the same old war stories time and time again; ones that grew bigger and bolder each time they were told and that we never got sick of hearing. After a couple of beers it felt like Whitey had officially rejoined the team, and after a couple more it felt as though he'd never left.

However, the celebrations were always going to be curtailed by the onset of the working week, otherwise known as reality. We'd deferred my departure for long enough. It was time for the final dissolution of the team.

Wegs stood beside the Big Girl on a sunny Monday morning in Albany. Leaning in the window he shook my hand firmly, then tapped the roof as he'd done to the Big Girl's container back in Finland to indicate that all was in order.

'Look after her, mate.'

'Yep, she'll be right,' I replied. 'Catch you later, mate. I'll give you a call from the other side of the Nullarbor.'

And that was that. No superfluous small talk; we'd long since not needed to communicate verbally in order to know what the other was thinking.

'Yep. Good work, mate. Catch you later.'

I eased the Big Girl away from the kerb and down the road.

I looked in the rear-view mirror to see Wegs, as I had expected, standing in the middle of the road with arm raised and index finger pointing firmly to the heavens. Predictably, my arm was out the window, doing likewise. 'Beep Beep!' the Big Girl chipped in with her final goodbyes.

I turned down the same small street I'd turned down on Saturday, and as I approached the building site I began tooting the Big Girl's horn and again thrust my arm out the window in the team salute. Standing atop a timber-framed roof was a big bloke with a mane of unkempt hair and large man-features, reaching for the skies with his raised right arm. No words were needed, I simply glided slowly past the saluting Whitey in the beeping Big Girl and returned his beaming smile. At the end of the road I tooted the horn for the final time and set off in the direction of home.

I pulled over on the outskirts of town and reached over to the glove box to extract the little woollen satchel containing my Mongolian fortune knuckles. I placed them on the dashboard in front of me. Ever since the old man had given them to us I'd superstitiously kept them close by, hoping to benefit from their Mongolian message of 'safe travels – no problems'. It was going to take three long and sweltering days to negotiate the Nullarbor crossing, and, as I set out on the final challenge of our journey, I wanted as much mental and physical comfort as I could get.

❀　❀　❀

On the last night of my Nullarbor crossing, I lay back on the warm bonnet of the Big Girl, drinking a stubby and gazing at the night sky. Above, the silhouettes of the overhanging gum trees framed my unimpeded view of the Southern Cross. With only six hours to travel to Adelaide the following day, I finally relaxed in the knowledge that we, the entire team, had achieved what we'd set out to do.

I thought back to earlier in the day when I'd passed through a long section of roadworks. The road was reduced to one lane and I'd been instructed to wait by a well-fed man holding a 'stop' sign. He was staring in my direction while talking into his two-way radio. I reached into the glove box and pulled out one of our UHF radios that hadn't been used since our cannonball run through Kosovo. I rested it on my leg and flicked it to channel 40; from my project management days I knew this was the preferred channel for truck drivers and road crews. The radio crackled into life.

' . . . dunno what it is mate. She looks like an XD Falcon from the front,' as he stared hard in my direction, 'or one of them old Cortinas.'

'Shit, wonder what it is then? Sure it's a funeral car, mate . . . seems a bit odd?' came another voice over the radio, presumably the man at the other end of the roadworks holding the 'slow' sign.

'Hang on a minute, I'm sending them through,' the man at my end added as he turned the 'stop' sign around so that it read 'slow' and motioned for me to move off. 'Yeah, mate, she's a fuckin' funeral car all right, with curtains and stickers all over it, and some sheila behind the wheel.'

Despite the affront to my masculinity I had to laugh; this

was the first time I'd ever been mistaken for a female. I felt sorry for the bloke, because if he thinks I look like a woman then he's in for one hell of a shock if he ever visits Thailand.

'I can see it coming now, looks like a fucking funeral procession with all them cars behind her with their headlights on and all,' laughed the second voice on the radio, which belonged to the person I was now approaching.

I reached the end of the roadworks and passed by the second man, waving as I went.

'Ireland to Australia, eh?' he was reading one of the stickers on the back of the Big Girl. 'Why would you do that?'

'Yeah, dunno. Those Irish are mad fuckers!'

I doubt we ever really knew exactly what it was we were doing, but, as I lay here on the bonnet, I knew what we had done.

We had a lot to thank the Big Girl for. She was responsible for great mates becoming even greater mates, and even better blokes. With her beguiling appearance she'd inadvertently become our Trojan Hearse, providing an unexpected vehicle from which to launch a hedonistic assault on the world. Even in her absence, she'd led us to amazing people in far-off lands, transforming a whimsical flight of fancy into a serendipitous rite of passage.

A large road train rattled past noisily, forcing the branches above me to wave violently in its wake and bringing my thoughts back to the present. As I enjoyed the last warmth of the Big Girl's bonnet I saw a shooting star, but strangely didn't feel like making a wish. I no longer felt I needed to carry Mongolian knuckles to *know* what will happen in the future, to wish on falling stars to *make* things happen in the future, or to be shat on by seagulls for *good luck* in the future. From now on, as long as I ate my fish and chips with caution, I figured I could work it all out for myself.

EPILOGUE

Well, I did make it safely to Adelaide the following day, as expected. I stayed with friends for a couple of days while I waited for another mate of mine, Nathan, to fly in from Melbourne to join me for the tail end of the journey. It was a last-minute decision that saw Nathan and me redirect the journey from Adelaide to Sydney, and then back down through Canberra to Melbourne. I wanted to show the Big Girl a bit of Australia, and Nathan had been keen to come along and do a bit of filming on the camera, to round off our physical and visual journey.

Poetically though, the journey finished with the surprise addition of a former team member. For as luck or fate determined, JD happened to call me for a chat as we were passing through Melbourne, less than half a day from home. It was a conversation we were able to finish in person, as Nathan and I picked up JD in Melbourne and abducted him for the drive down the Great Ocean Road to Port Fairy, the end of the line. It was amazing to finally have JD in the Big Girl, considering he'd spent three months as a member of the team without ever laying eyes on her.

On a Monday afternoon in Port Fairy, my home town, we took up residence at the Caledonian Hotel. It was too early for me to arrive home in the Big Girl. Dad wasn't due back from work until after 5 p.m., and I wanted to time my entrance so that both Mum and Dad would be at home for the long-awaited arrival. So, it was decided we'd best spend the afternoon celebrating the completion of the adventure, and honouring the country where it all began, by drinking Guinness.

Not surprisingly, it was Mum and Dad who had to come to us for the reunion. Although we'd managed bring the Big Girl from one side of the world to the other, we couldn't manage to bring her the remaining two blocks home: we were far too pissed. It was Dad, still dressed in his dark work suit, who piloted the Big Girl the short distance home from the pub. Fittingly, the journey finished in the manner in which it was conducted – the script kept us guessing right to the end. As we pulled up at home and Dad killed the engine, signifying the end of the adventure, I knew I couldn't have asked for more – except, perhaps, to have found Tania.

Also from Penguin

OFF THE RAILS

Tim Cope

This is the story of two twenty-year-old Australians who travelled for fourteen months on recumbent bicycles from Russia, across Siberia and Mongolia, to Beijing. It is as much a story of perseverance, passion and belief as it is about the people and remarkable landscapes of Siberia and Mongolia.

Tim and Chris are not just fearless adventurers but philosophers on wheels, willing and able to open themselves up to everything from the voice of the Steppes to the Russian villagers and the nomads of the Gobi desert. From this they draw an often funny, moving and inspirational tale of living out a dream. Mixed into this journey is the story of their tumultuous relationships as two opposing wills battle it out in the midst of heat, snow and hunger.